THE ILI CRISIS

Oxford University Press, Ely House, London W.1

GLASGOW   NEW YORK   TORONTO   MELBOURNE   WELLINGTON
BOMBAY   CALCUTTA   MADRAS   KARACHI   LAHORE   DACCA
CAPE TOWN   SALISBURY   NAIROBI   IBADAN
KUALA LUMPUR   HONG KONG

THE ILI CRISIS

A STUDY OF
SINO-RUSSIAN DIPLOMACY
1871–1881

BY

IMMANUEL C. Y. HSÜ

OXFORD
AT THE CLARENDON PRESS
1965

For my beloved wife

DOLORES

Preface

THE ILI CRISIS is a subject of considerable significance in modern Chinese history. Its settlement in 1881 not only marked China's first diplomatic victory in the nineteenth century, but also made possible the establishment of a province in Sinkiang for the first time in two millennia. The resolution of the crisis also influenced the atmosphere in the Ch'ing court during its twilight years, and produced far-reaching effects on later Sino-Russian relations.

My interest in the subject was aroused in the fall of 1958 when I learnt from Professor Charles Jelavich of the University of California, Berkeley, that he had acquired the papers of Nikolas K. Giers, the Russian assistant foreign minister who was in charge of the Foreign Office at the time of the Ili crisis. Among the papers was the official correspondence between Giers and A. G. Jomini, senior counsellor in the Foreign Office, on the Ili negotiations with the Chinese. Professor Jelavich, then arranging the publication of these papers with the E. J. Brill Press in Leiden, graciously placed a set of galley proofs at my disposal. The Giers–Jomini correspondence throws new light on Russia's position during the Ili crisis, and it corroborates information contained in the Diary (*Dnevnik*) of the Russian Minister of War, D. A. Miliutin, chairman of the special committee that was appointed to formulate Russia's China policy. Further research led me to the record of conversations between Jomini and the Chinese negotiator, Marquis Tseng (*I-li ting-yüeh Chung-O t'an-hua lu*), kept by the Chinese interpreter at the conference, the complete works of Marquis Tseng himself, and innumerable Chinese memorials, edicts, diaries, and private letters of leading statesmen.

However, not only China and Russia, but several other countries were also involved in the Ili crisis. Britain, in particular, was active: Hart and Wade counselled the court in Peking, Gordon came from India to help with defences, and the British embassy in St. Petersburg offered confidential advice to Marquis Tseng. The French minister in China pursued a policy of dissuading Peking from waging war so that Russian strength could be preserved to checkmate Germany. The German minister, on the other hand, did his best to promote war in the belief that trouble in Asia afforded Germany opportunities to gain concessions. The Japanese, then severing the Liu-ch'iu islands from China, posed the possibility of collusion with Russia, while the United States exerted an influence in the cause of peace. Such an array of international activities necessitated multi-archival research in Europe, Asia, and America.

A summer grant from Harvard's East Asian Research Center in 1959 enabled me to spend several months at the Center and the Harvard-Yenching Institute library. Travel funds from the University of California made it possible for me to consult materials at the National Archives and the Library of Congress in Washington, D.C. A summer teaching appointment at Harvard in 1961 gave me further opportunities to continue work at the East Asian Research Center. When my research in this country was completed, I was fortunate to receive a John Simon Guggenheim fellowship to carry on the project in Europe and Asia during my sabbatical year in 1962–3. I visited the archives of the French and German Foreign Ministries in Paris and Bonn, and spent several months at the Public Record Office and the British Museum in London, where I found a wealth of materials, including Her Majesty's confidential prints and other secret reports on the Ili affair. Visits to the libraries at Oxford and Cambridge were also helpful. In the spring of 1963 I travelled to the Far East, spending three months at the Institute of Modern History, Academia Sinica, on Taiwan and two months at the Tōyō bunko in Tokyo. Only after visits to these centres of learning, libraries, and archives was I able to reconstruct a more complete picture of the subject-matter. The result is the present volume on Sino-Russian diplomacy during the Ili crisis of 1871–81. It should be evident that this work does not purport to cover the details of the Moslem rebellion in north-western China and its suppression by Tso Tsung-t'ang in the 1860's and 1870's. These subjects have been thoroughly examined already,[1] and I content myself with a summary of

[1] Wen-djang Chu, 'The Policy of the Manchu Government in the Suppression of the Moslem Rebellion in Shensi, Kansu, and Sinkiang from 1862 to 1878'. (Ph.D. thesis, University of Washington, 1955.)

these events in Chapter I as a background for the diplomatic study that forms the bulk of this work.

I am grateful to Professor John K. Fairbank of Harvard for his invaluable suggestions, corrections, and comments on my draft manuscript. I am indebted to the Guggenheim Foundation for making possible my research in Europe and Asia. To Professor Francis W. Cleaves of Harvard I am thankful for his assistance in transcribing Mongolian names. Dr. Mark Mancall of Harvard, Dr. Albert Dien of Stanford, Drs. Chauncey S. Goodrich and Phillip W. Damon of the University of California, Santa Barbara, and Mr. Robert Irick read parts or all of the manuscript and made many useful suggestions. Drs. Charles and Barbara Jelavich, now at Indiana University, were very kind in offering me the galley proofs of the Giers–Jomini correspondence, which has since been published under the title *Russia in the East, 1876–1880* (Leiden, 1959). I am grateful to Mrs. Mary Ann Youngren of Wellesley College and Mrs. Jeanne Sollen for editorial and stylistic improvements. Mrs. George Kladnik typed the manuscript with a devotion that is rare among typists. But I alone am responsible for all the inadequacies of the manuscript.

*   *   *   *   *   *   *   *   *   *

A few words about Chinese and Russian names and dates are in order. Chinese names have been romanized according to the Wade–Giles system, except those which have always been known in other forms, i.e. Confucius, not K'ung-fu-tzu. Russian names are spelled according to the Library of Congress system, except those who signed their names in French or German forms, as was the fashion among many Russians in the nineteenth century: thus it is Giers, not Girs, that is used in this volume; Jomini, not Zhomini; and Butzow, not Biutsov. Chinese dates have been transcribed into corresponding dates in the Julian calendar. Russian dates are given together with their Western counterparts; thus 12/24 February indicates 12 February in the old Russian calendar and 24 February according to the Julian system.   I. C. Y. H.

Santa Barbara, California
15 January 1964

Contents

ABBREVIATIONS   XV

INTRODUCTION   I

CHAPTER I.   The Origins of the Ili Crisis   16
  (1) The Ch'ing Administration of Sinkiang   18
  (2) The Moslem Rebellion   22
  (3) The Russian Occupation of Ili   29
  (4) Suppression of the Rebellion   35

CHAPTER II.   Ch'ung-hou and the Treaty of Livadia,   47
  1879
  (1) Ch'ung-hou's Appointment to Russia   48
  (2) The Treaty of Livadia   51
  (3) Chinese Response to the Treaty   59
    (a) *Tso Tsung-t'ang's Attitude*   60
    (b) *Li Hung-chang's Reaction*   63
    (c) *Ch'ung-hou's Defence*   67
    (d) *Chang Chih-tung's Advocacy of War*   70

CHAPTER III.   Ch'ung-hou's Punishment, Reprieve,   78
  and Pardon
  (1) The Punishment   78
  (2) An Interpretation of the Tragedy   81
  (3) Foreign Intervention   84
  (4) The Reprieve and Pardon   89

CHAPTER IV.   The Politics of War and Peace   95
  (1) Tso's Views on War   96
  (2) Li's Views on Peace   100
  (3) An Interpretation of the Controversy   106

CHAPTER V.   Involvement of Foreign Ministers   109

CHAPTER VI.   Gordon's Visit   122
  (1) Gordon's Invitation   122
  (2) Gordon's Relations with London   124
  (3) Gordon in Tientsin   126
  (4) Gordon in Peking   129
  (5) Gordon's Farewell Message   133

CHAPTER VII.   Tseng in Europe: Preparations for His   139
  Russian Mission
  (1) Tseng's Appointment   140
  (2) Tseng's Plight   142
  (3) Tseng's Instructions   145
  (4) Tseng's Preparations   147

CHAPTER VIII. The Opening of the Negotiations in   153
  St. Petersburg
  (1) Russia on the Eve of the Negotiations   153
  (2) The Opening of the Negotiations   159
  (3) The Place of Negotiations   163

CHAPTER IX.   The Treaty of St. Petersburg   171
  (1) The Russian Lack of Policy   171
  (2) Jomini's Plight   176
  (3) The Protracted Negotiations   180
  (4) The Turning-Point   183

CHAPTER X.   The Legacy of the Ili Crisis   189
  (1) China: The Price of Victory   189
  (2) Sinkiang: Change Beyond Tradition   193

BIBLIOGRAPHY   202

GLOSSARY   218

INDEX   223

Maps

Russian Central Asia   3

Chinese Central Asia—Sinkiang   17

Russian Occupation of Ili   31

Tso Tsung-t'ang's Sinkiang Campaign and Supply Lines   40

Territory Ceded to Russia by the Treaty of St. Petersburg   186

Abbreviations

CSL
: *Ta-Ch'ing li-ch'ao shih-lu* (Veritable records of the successive reigns of the Ch'ing dynasty), Tokyo, 1937–8.

F.O.
: Foreign Office documents of Great Britain, Public Record Office, London.

ILTY
: *I-li ting-yüeh Chung-O t'an-hua lu* (A record of Sino-Russian conversations about the treaty on Ili), Shanghai, 1936.

IWSM
: *Chou-pan i-wu shih-mo* (The complete account of the management of barbarian affairs), Peiping, 1930. T'ung-chih period, 1862–74.

Jelavich
: *Russia in the East, 1876–1880*, edited by Charles and Barbara Jelavich, Leiden, 1959.

Li Hung-chang
: *Li-wen-chung-kung ch'üan-chi* (Complete works of Li Hung-chang), Shanghai, 1929:

1. Memorials.
2. Letters to friends and colleagues.
3. Letters to the Tsungli Yamen.
4. Letters relating to the Ts'an-ch'ih Church.
5. Letters to the Admiralty.
6. Telegrams.

D. A. Miliutin
: *Dnevnik* (Diary), 4 vols., Moscow, 1947–50.

Tseng Chi-tse
: *Tseng-hui-min-kung i-chi* (Posthumous works of Tseng Chi-tse), 1893:

1. Memorials.
2. Literary collection.
3. Poetry.
4. Diary.

Tso Tsung-t'ang
: *Tso-wen-hsiang-kung ch'üan-chi* (Complete works of Tso Tsung-t'ang), 1890.

1. Memorials of gratitude.
2. Literary collection.
3. Memorials.
4. Letters.

WCSL
: *Ch'ing-chi wai-chiao shih-liao* (Historical materials concerning foreign relations in the late Ch'ing period, 1875–1911).

USFR
: *Foreign Relations of the United States.*

Unless otherwise indicated, all translations from the Chinese, Japanese, Russian, French, and German are mine.

Introduction

For China the year 1880 was one of anxiety, fear, and uncertainty. The country had been thrown into a state of anger and confusion by an unfortunate treaty regarding Ili signed in Russia the year before by the Manchu diplomat, Ch'ung-hou. Chinese scholars and officials, openly denouncing the treaty as a naked act of aggression and treachery on the part of Russia, advocated outright rejection of the treaty and severe punishment of the signer. The Empress Dowager was said to have burst out in exasperation: 'Ch'ung-hou must die.'[1] Yet beneath the show of anger and protest there was a secret fear of war with Russia as a result of the rejection of the treaty.

To meet this ominous prospect Peking and the provinces were propelled into a flurry of activity. The army was mobilized, and retired officers reactivated; forts were repaired and guns and ships purchased from abroad. Russia retaliated by sending a powerful fleet to China. Would there be a Russian march on Peking and a repetition of the Anglo-French occupation of the Chinese capital in 1860? Indeed, war clouds hung low over China, and no one knew what tomorrow would bring. The mandarins were confronted with a grave emergency, which could develop into a ruinous war for the dynasty. The choice before them was a painful one—a disastrous war or a humiliating peace.

The underlying cause of the crisis was China's dispute with Russia over the control of the Ili Valley in northern Sinkiang. The Russians had occupied the area in 1871 during a period of disorder and Moslem rebellion. They promised to return Ili when Chinese imperial authority was re-established there, but this magnanimous offer was made in the belief that the effete Ch'ing dynasty could never recover Sinkiang. At the time China was in a weak position both internally and externally: the entire North-west was ablaze with Moslem rebellion, the British had refused to ratify the Alcock Convention of 1869, and the Tientsin Massacre of 1870 brought about the mission of

[1] F.O. 418/I/140, Wade to Granville, *confidential*, 2 June 1880, reporting a conversation with Li Hung-chang.

apology to France. Peking was utterly powerless to compel
Russia to evacuate Ili. But in 1878, after nearly ten years of
hard campaigning, Tso Tsung-t'ang succeeded in suppressing
the Moslem rebellion in Shensi, Kansu, Ninghsia, and Sinkiang.
When China asked Russia to honour her promise the Russian
minister in Peking was evasive and dilatory. A Chinese mission
was sent to St. Petersburg in 1878 under Ch'ung-hou to negotiate the return of Ili. He was duped by the Russians into
signing the Treaty of Livadia which restored Ili to China in
name only: seven-tenths of the strategic area, including the
military pass that controlled communication with southern
Sinkiang, was ceded to Russia. Startled by the cession, Chinese
scholar-officials vowed to disown the treaty. Ch'ung-hou was
thrown into prison to await decapitation. Russia reacted by
accusing Peking of bad faith, and by dispatching a fleet of
twenty-three ships under Admiral S. S. Lesovskii to China in a
'naval demonstration'. Peking hurriedly invited Charles Gordon,
the legendary Victorian hero who had made a name during the
Taiping campaign some eighteen years earlier, from India to
help with defence, and Robert Hart, the British inspector-
general of Chinese Maritime Customs, was authorized to enlist
British officers to serve in the Chinese forces.

  Thus Russia and China came dangerously close to war over
the remote area of Ili, several thousand miles from both Peking
and St. Petersburg. The questions naturally arise: Why was Ili
of such significance and what prompted the actions of the two
countries?

  For Russia acquisition of land had always been a cardinal
principle of her policy toward China. By the Treaty of Nerchinsk in 1689 she gained 93,000 square miles of territory from
China, and by the Treaty of Kiakhta in 1727 she secured nearly
40,000 square miles. The Treaty of Aigun of 1858 granted her
185,000 square miles of land on the left bank of the Amur River
down to the Ussuri River, and the Treaty of Peking in 1860
awarded her 133,000 square miles of land east of the Ussuri to
the Pacific.[1] The occupation of some 1,224 square miles of

---

[1] W. A. Douglas Jackson, *The Russo-Chinese Borderlands* (Princeton, 1962), 112,
113, 116. In the Treaty of Peking, 1860, China, in effect, surrendered her claim to
350,000 square miles of land in Central Asia, in addition to the 133,000 square
miles already mentioned.

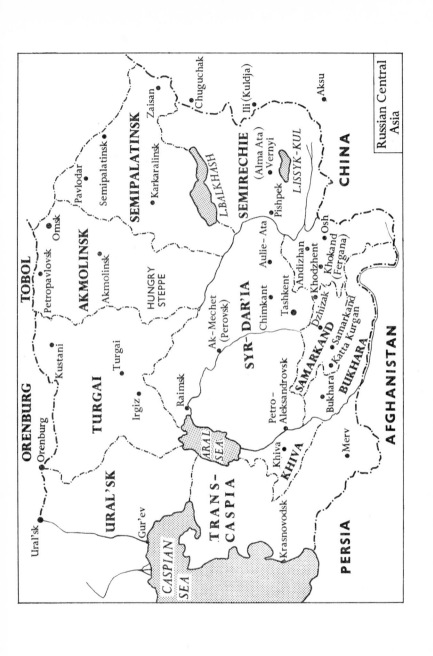

Russian Central Asia

territory in the Ili Valley in 1871[1] was but another step in the fulfilment of Russia's age-old policy of land acquisition from China.

The occupation may also be viewed as an extension of the
steady Russian advance in Central Asia. Peter the Great (1682–
1725) wanted to acquire the gold of Yarkand and to conquer
India, but his dream was shattered by the complete failure of
Prince Bekovich-Cherkasskii's expedition to Khiva in 1717.[2]
Nicholas I (1825–54), however, succeeded in incorporating the
territories of the Kazakh khanates into the Russian empire as
the Ural, Akmolinsk, and Semipalatinsk provinces. By 1854 the
Russians had advanced to the land south of the Ili River, and
the town of Vernyi, now Alma-Ata, was founded.[3] In 1865 the
new province of Turkestan was established, and in 1867 the
governor-generalship of Turkestan was created, with jurisdiction over 'the Turkestan province, the Tashkent district, the
lands seized beyond the Syr-Daria in 1866, and the part of the
Semipalatinsk province lying south of the Tarbagatai range'.[4]
General K. P. von Kaufman was appointed the first governor-
general, with independent power to conduct war and diplomacy
with Central Asian khanates.[5] He vigorously carried out the
Russian advance, and by 1873 all three large khanates of
Central Asia—Khokand, Bukhara, and Khiva—came under
Russian control.[6] It was in this spirit of continuous expansion
in Central Asia that Russia occupied Ili in Sinkiang in 1871. It
is noteworthy that the Russian advance in Central Asia in the
mid-nineteenth century was mostly initiated by ambitious
generals on the frontiers—such as V. A. Perovskii, M. G.
Cherniaev, and K. P. von Kaufman—without guidance from
the central government. St. Petersburg accepted their successes
but disowned their failures.

For the Chinese, Sinkiang and Ili were places whose very
names bespoke mystery, adventure, and military grandeur.
Interest in the area, then known as the *Hsi-yü* (Western Region),[7]

[1] M. A. Terent'ev, *Istoriia zavoevaniia srednei Azii* (A history of the conquest of
Central Asia) (St. Petersburg, 1906), iii. 266.

[2] V. V. Barthold, *La Découverte de l'Asie: Histoire de l'orientalisme en Europe et en
Russie* (trans. by B. Nikitine, Paris, 1947), 235–6.

[3] Richard A. Pierce, *Russian Central Asia, 1867–1917* (Berkeley, 1960), 19.

[4] Ibid. 48.   [5] Ibid. 49.   [6] Ibid. 34.

[7] For general works on the *Hsi-yü*, see Tseng Wen-wu, *Chung-kuo ching-ying Hsi-yü
shih* (A history of China's management of the Western Region) (Shanghai, 1936);
V. V. Barthold, *Four Studies on the History of Central Asia* (English translation by

was first manifested under the brilliant emperor Wu-ti (140–86 B.C.) of the Han dynasty (206 B.C.–A.D. 220). The legendary stories of his emissary Chang Ch'ien's mission to the Wu-sun tribe in the Ili Valley in 138 B.C., Chang's long captivity by the Hsiung-nu (Huns), his epic escape, and his second mission to the Yüeh-chih tribe in 115 B.C., stirred the Chinese imagination for two millennia. In the later Han period (A.D. 26–220), General Pan Ch'ao brought Chinese influence to even greater heights. For thirty years between A.D. 73 and 102 he was active in Central Asia and subjugated some fifty states. In A.D. 97 with 70,000 men he encamped on the shores of the Caspian Sea; his envoy Kan Ying reached as far as the Persian Gulf.[1]

The exploits of the great T'ang (A.D. 618–906) emperors further deepened China's relation with the Western Region. T'ai-tsung conquered the Eastern Turks in 630 and his son Kao-tsung subdued the Western Turks in 658, extending Chinese rule all the way to the Tarim Basin. An *An-Hsi* (Western Pacification) protectorate was set up to take charge of affairs of sixteen states east of Persia. This was a golden era for China in Central Asia.[2]

When the Mongols rose to power in the thirteenth century Sinkiang became part of a Central Asian empire under Chaghadai Khan (Čaɣadai Qan), second son of Chinggis Khan (Činggis Qan).[3] The Ming dynasty (1368–1643) which

V. and T. Minorsky, Leiden, 1956), i. 76–81; *Histoire des Turcs d'Asie Centrale* (adaptation française par Mme M. Donskis, Paris, 1945), 18 ff.; R. Grousset, *L'Empire des steppes* (Paris, 1948); O. Franke, *Geschichte des chinesischen Reiches*, 5 vols. (Berlin u. Leipzig, 1930–52).

[1] C. P. Fitzgerald in his *China: A Short Cultural History* (New York, 1958) claimed that it was not the Persian Gulf but the Black Sea that Kan Ying reached (p. 197). For general information on Han relations with the *Hsi-yü*, see H. Bielenstein, *Emperor Kuang-wu and the Northern Barbarians* (Canberra, 1954); W. M. McGovern, *The Early Empires of Central Asia* (Chapel Hill, 1939); E. Chavannes, 'Les Pays d'Occident d'après le *Heou Han chou*', *T'oung Pao*, viii (1907), 149–234; F. Hirth, 'The Story of Chang K'ien, China's Pioneer in Western Asia', *Journal of American Oriental Society*, xxxvii (1917), 89–136; F. J. Teggart, *Rome and China* (Berkeley, 1939).

[2] For T'ang relations with the *Hsi-yü*, see E. Chavannes, *Documents sur les Tou-kiue (Turcs) Occidentaux* (St. Petersburg, 1903); Liu Mau-ts'ai, *Die chinesischen Nachrichten zur Geschichte der Ost-Türken (T'u-küe)* (Wiesbaden, 1958); F. Hirth, *Die Länder des Islam*, Suppl. to vol. v, 1st ser., *T'oung Pao* (Leiden, 1894); H. A. R. Gibb, *The Arab Conquests in Central Asia* (1923).

[3] For Yüan (Mongol) relations with the *Hsi-yü*, see R. Grousset, *L'Empire mongol (1ère phase)* (Paris, 1941); P. Pelliot and L. Hambis, *L'histoire des campagnes de Gengis Khan (Cheng-wou Ts'in-tcheng Lou)*, vol. i (Leiden, 1951); L. Olschki, *Marco Polo's Asia* (Berkeley, 1960).

overthrew Mongol rule in China won tribute from such king-doms as Khoten, Samarkand, Bukhara, Andijan, and Persia, but was unable to establish military control over them. During the Ch'ing period (1644–1911) Emperors K'ang-hsi, Yung-cheng, and Ch'ien-lung spent the better part of a century conquering the Western Region, and in 1759 the objective was attained.[1] Emperor Ch'ien-lung proudly listed the campaigns among his 'Ten Perfect Achievements'.[2] In 1768 he renamed the Western Region 'Sinkiang', meaning 'New Territory'.

The foregoing survey, brief though it is, clearly indicates China's long-standing interest in Sinkiang. For two thousand years the area was intermittently under Chinese rule, and nearly every ambitious and resourceful emperor cherished the hope of conquering it. Failure to exercise such control was tantamount to an admission of weakness. Hence Ch'ing rulers in the 1870's were naturally unwilling to lose Ili to Russia by default, thereby opening the door to foreign domination of Sinkiang.

The importance of Sinkiang in the Chinese mind is further revealed in several bold historical notions, which suggest that the ebb and flow of dynastic fortunes actually mirrored China's relationship with her frontier areas. During periods of strength and prosperity China could maintain peace and order internally and also hold the barbarian hordes of Central Asia in check. This ideal state of affairs, described as a 'Grand Unification' (*Ta i-t'ung*), was realized under the mighty dynasties of the Han, T'ang, Yüan, and Ch'ing. A less propitious situation, described as a 'Minor Unification' (*Hsiao i-t'ung*), prevailed whenever China, though not strong enough to pacify the nomadic tribes, was able to defend her interior against their incursions—as, for example, during the Northern Sung and Ming dynasties. Yet a third phase developed whenever China was weak and decadent, troubled by internal disorders and foreign invasions. The barbarian invaders were able to make powerful thrusts into the Yellow River Valley in northern China, driving the Chinese dynasty to take refuge in the Yangtze River Valley in the south. Though under constant threat the exiled dynasty could still

[1] For an account of the pacification of Djungaria and Kashgaria in Sinkiang, see Sung-yün, *I-li tsung-t'ung shih-lüeh* (A brief account of the administration of Ili), 1 : 3–19.

[2] Hsiao I-shan, *Ch'ing-tai t'ung-shih* (A general history of the Ch'ing period), revised edition (Taipei, 1962), ii. 145–6.

maintain a shaky existence within a shrunken area. Such a state of affairs, typified by the Southern Sung period, was described as 'Partial Security' (*P'ien-an*). According to these concepts, Chinese history, exclusive of the periods of barbarian conquest, was simply a cyclical alternation of these three dynastic phases.[1]

Quite apart from the validity of these historical notions, one cannot but be impressed with the importance of the *Hsi-yü* to the Chinese. Because North China was vulnerable to attacks by barbarian horsemen from the steppes China's destiny was in a sense linked with the control of the *Hsi-yü*. Resourceful emperors of the various dynasties took this idea to heart and sent count- less expeditions to the *Hsi-yü*. Their actions were interpreted more as necessities for dynastic survival than as attempts at self- glorification. During the Ch'ing dynasty Emperors K'ang-hsi and Ch'ien-lung spared no cost in conquering the *Hsi-yü* in the belief that possession of Sinkiang facilitated the protection of Mongolia and that defence of Mongolia ultimately safeguarded Peking.[2] Even after China's opening to the West in the middle of the nineteenth century, when a totally different type of enemy—not the nomadic horsemen from the steppes, but the seafaring 'barbarians' from Europe and America—appeared on the scene, this traditional strategic concept, though anachro- nistic in an age of sea power, still held sway. In the 1870's, despite military weakness and financial stringency, the Ch'ing court determined to recover Sinkiang from the Moslem rebels at any price and to demand the return of Ili from Russia even at the risk of a disastrous war.

Chinese reaction during the Ili crisis was further influenced by a keen awareness of Russia's privileged position in China. In the early Ch'ing period Emperors K'ang-hsi and Yung-cheng granted Russia a number of favours that were denied to other powers. For instance, Russian prisoners of war, about a hundred in all, taken in the several battles of Albazin (Yacsa or Ya-k'e-sa) in the 1680's, were pardoned and organized into a unit in the Ch'ing army as the Eleventh Company of the Fourth Regiment

---

[1] Ch'en Fang-chih, 'Ch'ing-tai pien-chih shu-lüeh' (A brief account of the frontier governments in the Ch'ing dynasty), *Yen-ching hsüeh-pao* (Yenching Journal of Chinese Studies), 34: 133 (June 1948).

[2] Tso Tsung-t'ang, 'Memorials', 50: 75–77b.

of the Manchu Bordered Yellow Banner.[1] As bannermen they were given the favour of rank and the privilege of living in quarters by themselves. They received annual pensions and were allowed complete freedom of religion. K'ang-hsi even gave them a Buddhist temple, on the site of which they built an Orthodox church, known as the Church of St. Nicolas, later renamed the Church of the Assumption. The Chinese called it *Lo-ch'a miao* (Russian temple); more often it was incorrectly referred to as the Northern Russian Hostel.[2]

The Russian traders were also well treated. Beginning with the Ides mission in 1693 they were allowed to come to Peking every three years in groups of two hundred and to bring their goods in duty-free. They were lodged in the Southern Russian Hostel (the old *Hui-t'ung kuan* of the Ming dynasty), which had been set up for their reception.[3] Although they were legally required to conclude their business and leave Peking within eighty days, the regulations were not strictly enforced.[4] The caravan under Liangusov and Savatiev in 1698 consisted of 289 merchants and 189 secretaries, servants, and brokers, totalling 478 men. Between 1698 and 1718 ten such caravans came to Peking, averaging one every two years instead of every three as officially stipulated, and they were often permitted to remain in the Chinese capital more than eighty days.[5] At times the Chinese government even advanced loans to distressed Russian merchants.[6]

After the Treaty of Kiakhta of 1727 groups of Russian priests were allowed to come every ten years to minister to the Russians in Peking. The Chinese government paid their travelling and living expenses.[7] From 1729 to 1859 thirteen such missions came to China.[8] The priests lived in the Southern Russian Hostel, where they maintained a church called the Convent of

---

[1] Yü Cheng-hsi, 'O-lo-ssu tso-ling' (On the Russian company), in Ho Ch'iu-t'ao (ed.), *Shuo-fang pei-sheng* (A manual of the northern places), 47: 1b–2, 4b. (Hereafter to be cited as *SFPS.*)

[2] Meng Ssu-ming, 'The E-lo-ssu kuan (Russian Hostel) in Peking', *Harvard Journal of Asiatic Studies (HJAS)*, 23: 29–34 (1960–1).

[3] Ibid. 23: 20.   [4] *SFPS*, 12: 5.

[5] Liu Hsüan-min, 'Chung-O tsao-ch'i mao-i k'ao' (A study of early Russo-Chinese commercial relations), *Yen-ching hsüeh-pao*, 25: 165–6 (1939).

[6] Agnes Fang-chih Ch'en, 'Chinese Frontier Diplomacy: Kiakhta Boundary Treaties and Agreements', *The Yenching Journal of Social Studies*, 4: 2: 155–6, 172 (Feb. 1949).   [7] *SFPS*, 12: 3–4.   [8] Meng Ssu-ming, 23: 33.

Candlemas, later, more formally, the Church of the Purification of the Virgin.[1]

The Treaty of Kiakhta also permitted Russia to send students to Peking to learn Chinese and Manchu. In 1728 a language school for the Russians was inaugurated within the Southern Russian Hostel as a separate institution.[2] The students, staying for a ten-year period under Chinese subsidy for travelling and living expenses, were required to wear Chinese clothes supplied by the Court of Colonial Affairs. The Board of Rites provided them with food, and the Imperial Academy (*Kuo-tzu chien*) assigned them Chinese and Manchu instructors.[3]

By virtue of these educational, religious, and commercial privileges, Russia, alone among nations, enjoyed a foothold in Peking from the end of the seventeenth century until the middle of the nineteenth. The Chinese felt that as the recipient of these favours Russia should be thankful to China and refrain from exploiting her during periods of weakness. The occupation of Ili and the imposition of a humiliating treaty were, in Chinese eyes, grave acts of ingratitude. Chang Chih-tung took the lead in expressing this feeling during the Ili crisis.

Thus a number of factors preyed upon the Chinese mind during the Ili crisis: the historical interest in Sinkiang, the dream of Grand Unification, the persistence of the traditional strategical concept, and the annoyance with Russian ingratitude. The mandarins found it difficult to temper emotion with reason, yet responsible statesmanship demanded realistic consideration of the relative power of China and Russia, the hazards of modern warfare, and the prospects of international support. After exhaustive consideration of all the alternatives Peking dispatched a second mission to Russia to revise the treaty, thus shifting the burden of decision to St. Petersburg. Confronted with the ominous choice of war or peace, Russia ultimately realized that peaceful settlement of the dispute was in her best interest, and the Treaty of St. Petersburg was signed in February 1881.

Throughout the Ili crisis Britain played an active role as an

---

[1] Ibid. 23: 28.   [2] Ibid. 23: 34–39; *SFPS*, 12: 5b.
[3] *SFPS*, 12: 3–5. It cost China more than 1,000 roubles and 9,000 pounds of rice annually to support these Russian students and the religious mission in Peking. Cf. Meng Ssu-ming, 23: 37.

interested third party, because of her paramount interest in China and considerations for the security of India and its North-West Frontier. British fear of Russian invasion of India was of long standing. Ever since Peter the Great, she had been haunted by an imaginary Russian advance to her prize possession. Peter's war with Persia in 1722 was considered a step toward capturing Indian trade.[1] In early 1801 Paul I joined Napoleon's 'Grand Project' and ordered 22,000 Don Cossacks to advance into India via Orenburg, Khiva, and Bukhara. The expedition was halted when the Tsar was assassinated in a palace revolution in March 1801.[2] These Russian attempts to reach India, though abortive, left indelible marks on British memories.

The intensification of the Russian advance in Central Asia during the mid-nineteenth century was a source of great anxiety to the British. Those in India who were charged with safeguarding the frontiers in Central Asia decided to meet the Russian thrust themselves with a northward movement from India. Sind was annexed in 1843, and Punjab in 1849. In the years to come, further acquisitions were made, including the khanate of Kalat, along the North-West Frontier of India. Russian generals in Central Asia expressed concern over the British advance, and spoke of Pamirs and Kashmir as natural gateways to India.[3] On the other hand, the British described the Russians as 'within striking distance of the passes leading southward through the Hindu Kush'.[4] Ambitious politicians and expansionists in Britain urged the adoption of strong and preventive measures against Russia. Palmerston stated in 1847 that Persia and Afghanistan must be looked upon as advanced posts of Russia and suggested that such military measures be taken on the frontier as to 'make it plain to everybody that we could not be taken by surprise, that the decisive position could

[1] Harold T. Cheshire, 'The Expansion of Imperial Russia to the Indian Border', *The Slavonic and East European Review*, 13: 37: 89.

[2] M. Pavlovsky, 'La Chine et la Russie en Asie Centrale', *Bulletin de l'Université L'Aurora*, 36: 325 (Oct. 1948); George N. Curzon, *Russia in Central Asia in 1889 and the Anglo-Russian Question* (London, 1889), 323 ff.

[3] M. A. Terentyef (Terent'ev), *Russia and England in Central Asia*, translation by F. C. Daukes (Calcutta, 1876), i. 274, ii. 114. (Hereafter to be cited as *Russia and England*.)

[4] Louis E. Frechtling, 'Anglo-Russian Rivalry in Eastern Turkistan, 1863–1881', *Royal Central Asian Journal*, 26: 471 (July 1939).

neither be snatched from us by a rapid movement nor be wrested from us by a forcible assault'.[1]

After the Crimean War, the British were troubled by the new Russian advance in Central Asia. General Cherniaev reduced Khokand to vassalage in 1865 and General Kaufman detached Samarkand from Bukhara in 1868. Although an agreement was reached between the British and Russian governments in 1869 that Afghanistan be excluded from the Russian sphere of influence, the advance of Russian generals in other parts of Central Asia did not stop.[2] By 1873 all three large Central Asian khanates—Bukhara, Khiva, and Khokand—had come under Russian control. James MacGahan, a British observer of Russian affairs, wrote from the Oxus region in 1876: 'The Russians are steadily advancing toward India, and they will sooner or later acquire a position in Central Asia which will enable them to threaten it. Should England be engaged in a European war, and not show herself sufficiently accommodating on the Bosphorus, then indeed Russia would probably strike a blow at England's Indian power.'[3]

This prediction nearly came true under slightly different circumstances. Stung by British interference in the Russo-Turkish War (1876–8), and by her unfriendliness at the Congress of Berlin, Russia retaliated with an elaborate scheme for invading India in 1878, as a diversionary measure. On orders from St. Petersburg, General Kaufman mobilized 20,000 troops in four columns to carry out the design. Russia thus pressed dangerously close to war with Britain, but a timely settlement at the Congress of Berlin in 1878 saved the peace.[4]

In this heightened atmosphere of Anglo-Russian rivalry in Near East and Central Asia, there was talk in Britain of co-operating with Moslem states to oust Russia from Central Asia, so that Britain would be considered the 'pacificator of Central Asia, the great conservative power bent upon maintaining the status quo for the special benefit of . . . (those) Mohammedan powers'.[5] Clearly, it was in the interest of Britain and the Central Asian Moslem kingdoms alike to form an alliance, since

[1] Alexis Krausse, *Russia in Asia: A Record and a Study, 1558–1899* (New York, 1899), 248.   [2] Cheshire, 13: 37: 91.   [3] Krausse, 165.   [4] Pierce, 39.
[5] Owen Lattimore, *Pivot of Asia: Sinkiang and the Inner Asian Frontiers of China and Russia* (Boston, 1950), 27. (Hereafter to be cited as *Pivot*.)

they were both threatened by Russian expansion. The British therefore encouraged the formation of a Moslem league, and their activity stimulated the development of Pan-Islamism.[1]

Yet Britain at this time was by no means a fixed entity with a single approach to foreign policy. The mid-Victorian politicians may be roughly divided into two schools of thought: the 'Forward School', which maintained that British imperial interests abroad could be effectively defended only by extension of frontiers, and the 'Consolidation School', which held that the same objectives could be achieved by international agreement and informal influence. Although this division of opinion cut across party lines, the Conservatives, because of close connexions with the court and the imperial service, leaned to the 'Forward School', while the Liberals, with its 'Little Englander' wing, leaned more toward the 'Consolidation School'. During the 1870's and the early 1880's, Disraeli and Salisbury were exponents of the 'Forward Policy', while Gladstone and Granville adhered to the anti-expansionist policy of 'Consolidation'. But anti-expansion in the mid-Victorian era did not mean anti-commercial expansion or informal political expansion, but rather opposition to the expansion of imperial frontiers in Asia and Africa beyond the 'protective reach of the British sea-power'.[2] The different outlooks of the two schools made for different emphases in foreign affairs generally, and they were reflected in British policies during the Ili crisis.

The catalyst of the Russian occupation of Ili was a Khokandian adventurer, Yakub Beg, who had entered Sinkiang in 1865 during a Moslem rebellion and established a kingdom there by 1870. The British saw him as a welcome buffer between India and Russia; his rise not only enhanced the prospect of an alliance between Britain and the Moslem league, but also raised the prospects for trade between India and Eastern Turkestan. The London *Times* reported that Indian trade with Turkestan rose from £55,000 sterling in 1867 to £129,000 in 1869.[3] Viceroys Mayo (1868–72) and Northbrook (1872–5) of

[1] Dwight E. Lee, 'The Origins of Pan-Islamism', *American Historical Review*, xlvii: 2: 284–5.

[2] E. A. Benians, Sir James Butler, and C. E. Carrington (ed.), *The Cambridge History of the British Empire* (Cambridge, 1959), iii. 128.

[3] Quoted in Yuan Tsing, 'Yakub Beg (1820–1877) and the Moslem Rebellion in Chinese Turkestan', *Central Asiatic Journal*, vi: 2: 154 (June 1961).

India, though cautious men in regard to foreign involvement and followers of the traditional policy of 'masterly inactivity', were nevertheless encouraged by the commercial possibilities and political usefulness of the new Kashgarian kingdom. They dispatched two missions to Yakub Beg under T. Douglas Forsyth, and the result was the conclusion of a treaty in 1873, by which Britain granted official recognition to Yakub Beg in return for the right of legation and consulate as well as preferential commercial treatment. The British also urged the Chinese to recognize him. Thomas Wade, British minister in Peking, suggested that it might be safer for China to have a weak Moslem state in Sinkiang than to have some powerful Western states established there.[1] Certainly it was the view of the Conservatives who took over the government in 1874 that Yakub Beg should be maintained. Disraeli, aspiring to revive the 'spacious days of Elizabeth', stressed that Britain, not Russia, should be the mistress of the East.[2] The 'Forward Policy' was now in full swing, and his supporters— Foreign Secretary Derby, Indian Secretary Salisbury, and Indian Viceroy Lytton—did their best to discourage Chinese military operations against Yakub Beg and to mediate China's trouble with him. But in spite of these efforts, Yakub Beg succumbed to the merciless attack of the Chinese general, Tso Tsung-t'ang.

Chinese authorities were now re-established in Sinkiang, between Russia and India. They posed no threat to India; in fact they stood in the way of Russia's southward thrust. The Conservatives in Britain therefore supported China's claim to Ili and approved the enlistment of British officers to serve in the Chinese army, before war broke out. However, the 'Midlothian elections' of 1880 deposed the 'Jingo King' and returned Gladstone to government in April 1880. The new Liberal administration followed a policy of 'non-intervention and minimum responsibility abroad'.[3] It disfavoured war between China and Russia because of possible adverse consequences to the British position in China. Russia would doubtless occupy Peking, dealing a severe blow to the British leadership position in China. The Manchu dynasty, with which Britain had

---

[1] F.O. 17/825/136, Wade to Forsyth, 6 Apr. 1876.
[2] Sir A. W. Ward and G. P. Gooch, *The Cambridge History of British Foreign Policy, 1783–1919* (New York, 1923), iii. 77–78.
[3] Benians, Butler, and Carrington, iii. 128.

signed several favourable treaties, might fall, and with it all the British privileges. Moreover, the economically minded Gladstone administration was keenly aware of the fact that such a war would badly affect British trade with China, which was estimated at £70 million annually, about 77·5 per cent. of China's total foreign trade.[1] It was therefore in the British interest that China should not drift into war with Russia, but should strive to solve the Ili problem through peaceful negotiations. To this end, Britain supported China in her diplomatic encounter with Russia, but discouraged the impression that an alliance with Britain or large-scale British military aid would come in the eventuality of war.

For Russia, the whole Ili issue was a Chinese riddle that could not be tackled in a rational, clear-cut manner. The turmoil in Sinkiang had hurt Russian trade, destroyed Russian consulates, increased border raids by Moslem renegades, and caused a large influx of refugees to Russia. Yakub Beg, who had resisted the Russians at Ak Musjid and Tashkent, had now built an empire in Sinkiang. His Moslem kingdom might become a rallying-place for his co-religionists in the Central Asian khanates which had lately come under Russian rule. His friendship with India suggested the possibility of an invasion of the rich Ili Valley under British sponsorship. Yet Yakub Beg's empire was on Chinese soil, and St. Petersburg did not wish to disturb its good relationship with China. Russian generals in Central Asia, however, were impatient with Yakub Beg's potential threat. Kaufman, governor-general of Russian Turkestan, seized the initiative by occupying Ili in 1871, and his general, G. A. Kolpakovskii, on his own authority, declared the area annexed 'in perpetuity'. St. Petersburg had little prior knowledge of the action and had difficulty in defending it. It could not decide either what should be done about Yakub Beg. This indecision may be seen in the fact that on the one hand Russia strengthened his position by signing a treaty with him in 1872, recognizing him as leader of Moslem Sinkiang, and on the other, weakened his position by supplying grain in 1875 to the Chinese army that was sent to fight him.[2]

---

[1] F.O. 17/857/8, Wade to Granville, 18 Feb. 1881.

[2] D. A. Miliutin, *Dnevnik* (Diary) (Moscow, 1947–50), ii. 23; Tso Tsung-t'ang, 'Memorials', 47: 5b–6b, 'Letters', 17: 5.

Although Britain and Russia were rivals in Central Asia, they seemed to agree, at least in 1872–3, that Yakub Beg should be maintained. Britain anticipated greater trade with Kashgaria and the possibility of using Yakub Beg as a buffer between India and Russia. Russia needed him to justify the continuous occupation of Ili. Both Britain and Russia, on the basis of information available to them at the time, had misgivings about China's ability to recover Sinkiang. Tso Tsung-t'ang's victory over Yakub Beg in 1877 came as a total surprise, not only to Britain and Russia, but to many Chinese themselves, including Li Hung-chang.

The fall of Yakub Beg led to the Chinese demand for the return of Ili. Russia was in a dilemma. The generals in Central Asia and the Ministry of War in St. Petersburg were reluctant to relinquish the area, but the Foreign Office and the Ministry of Finance, feeling honour bound and suffering from the ill effects of the Turkish War and the Congress of Berlin, saw the need for conciliation. High officials in the Foreign Office, such as N. K. Giers and A. G. Jomini, were anxious to settle the China affair, but the question was how to do it gracefully and profitably.

Not only in Russia but also in other countries opposing forces could be found at work. In China there was the struggle between Li Hung-chang's preoccupation with the problems of the maritime nations and Tso Tsung-t'ang's insistence on the need for inland frontier defence. Peking was confronted with a difficult choice. In Britain there was opposition between the 'Forward School' and the 'Consolidation School'. Whichever party was in power, the inescapable responsibility remained of balancing the British interest in China with considerations of the security of India, and the questions of policy toward Russia arising from Central Asian, Near Eastern, and European issues. Cross-currents at the national level complicated the already intricate international situation resulting from the changing patterns of behaviour among the powers. But all this makes the Ili crisis a highly interesting chapter in diplomacy.

CHAPTER I

The Origins of the Ili Crisis

SINKIANG, a vast area of some 550,000 square miles about two and a half times the size of France, lies between 75 and 95 degrees longitude and 36 and 50 degrees latitude. It is bounded on the north by Russia and Mongolia, on the east by Mongolia and Kansu, on the south by Tibet and Kashmir, and on the west by Russian Central Asia. The Tien-shan or Celestial Mountains, soaring over 23,000 feet, divide Sinkiang into two unequal halves, the smaller Djungaria in the north and the larger Tarim Basin in the south.[1] The oasis area in the Tarim Basin has often been called Kashgaria.

The seat of the Ch'ing administration in Sinkiang, after Emperor Ch'ien-lung's conquest in 1759, was Ili, situated on the Ili River in the north-western sector of the territory. Western and Russian literature frequently described Ili as a 'province', but it was actually a Chinese prefecture (*fu*) consisting of nine cities, one of which, Ning-yüan (I-ning), was known to the Russians as Kuldja. The population of Ili represented an ethnographic mixture of many groups: the Taranchi (Uighur Moslem agriculturists), the Tungan (Chinese Moslems), the Sibo, the Kirghiz, the Mongols, the Chinese, and the Manchus. Accurate census figures during the 1860's and 1870's are lacking; estimates range from 100,000 to 350,000.[2]

The Ili Valley was the richest region in Sinkiang, with an annual rainfall of ten inches.[3] Grain and cotton were produced in abundance and deposits of oil, coal, iron, copper, and gold were known to exist. Trade with Russia developed toward the end of the eighteenth century, and a Russian mission came in 1811 to investigate the commercial potential of the area. The volume of trade, however, was not significant until the mid-nineteenth century. In 1852 Ili's exports to Russia amounted to £552,000 sterling, and in 1856 the figure rose to £1,016,692.[4]

---

[1] Owen Lattimore, *Inner Asian Frontiers of China* (New York, 1951), 151.
[2] See Note A, p. 197.   [3] Lattimore, *Pivot*, 274.
[4] Liu Hsüan-min, 198–200.

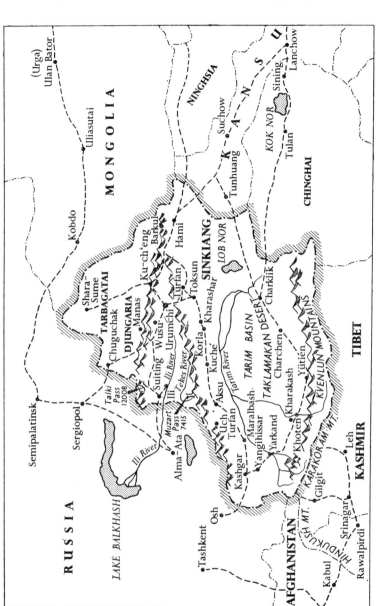

Chinese Central Asia—Sinkiang

Strategically, the Muzart Pass in the southern section of Ili controlled communication with Kashgaria. Possession of Ili therefore facilitated domination of southern Sinkiang, and Western military experts of the nineteenth century reputedly considered Ili a 'fortress of Sinkiang'.[1]

An area of such commercial and military significance naturally attracted the attention of Russian generals in Central Asia, who often referred to the advantages of occupying Ili.[2] The first step in this direction was taken in 1845, when a new road was constructed from Orenburg to Ili. Another significant step followed in 1851, when Russia, by the Treaty of Ili, secured the right to trade duty-free and maintain consulates in Ili and Chuguchak (Tarbagatai); Russian traders were allowed to build homes, warehouses, and churches in these two places. With the founding of Vernyi (Alma-Ata) in 1854, the Russians in Central Asia penetrated the lower Ili Valley and gained access to one of the main routes to Sinkiang. A further important advance was made in 1860, when Russia, by the Treaty of Peking, gained the right to trade and to establish a consulate in Kashgar, as well as a Chinese agreement to demarcate the boundary between Sinkiang and Russian Turkestan along the mountains, great rivers, and existing line of permanent pickets. The resultant boundary Treaty of Tarbagatai of 1864, concluded hastily by the Chinese because of a Moslem revolt in Sinkiang, gave Russia the land south-east of Lake Zaisan and the Tien-shan region north of Lake Issyk-Kul. Ili and Chuguchak, now contiguous to Russian territory, came within easy striking distance of the Russians in Central Asia.[3] Thus, step by step the Russians pressed forward toward Ili until they appropriated it altogether in 1871. The occupation took place during a period of Moslem rebellion, which was caused, in part, by the nature of the Ch'ing administration in Sinkiang.

1. THE CH'ING ADMINISTRATION OF SINKIANG

After the Ch'ing conquest of Sinkiang in 1759, a strict military régime was established to govern the area. In 1760

---

[1] Tseng Chi-tse, 'Memorials', 3 : 2.

[2] A. Kuropatkin, *The Russian Army and the Japanese War* (New York, 1909), i. 70.

[3] Nishida Tamotsu, *Sa Sōdō to Shinkyō mondai* (TsoTsung-t'ang and the Sinkiang question) (Tokyo, 1942), 79–80; Jackson, 37–38.

Emperor Ch'ien-lung dispatched Brigade-General A-kuei to Ili as imperial agent, with 500 Manchu cavalry, 100 Chinese and 300 Moslem troops. They developed military colonies and constructed nine fortified cities in Ili and sixteen around Urumchi.[1] In 1762 a military-governor of Ili, with jurisdiction over both the northern and southern routes of the Tien-shan Mountains, was appointed as the highest authority in Sinkiang. He was stationed in Hui-yüan, one of the nine cities of Ili, with a civilian staff of 468 men and a military staff consisting of an assistant military-governor and six commandants of the forces. Five of these commandants were stationed in Hui-yüan with 4,000 Manchu troops, and one in Hui-ning, another of the nine cities, with 2,140 Manchu soldiers. A variety of troops of different ethnic origins were deployed along the southern shore of the Ili River: 1,000 Sibos, 1,000 Solons and Dahurs—all from Manchuria—1,800 Chakhar and Mongol soldiers from Kalgan, 2,800 Ölöd soldiers, and 600 others. In addition, 3,000 Chinese soldiers and their families were settled in the Ili area to cultivate the land.[2] Altogether about 16,000 soldiers were stationed on the northern route of the Tien-shan Mountains.[3]

Eight big cities and ten smaller ones were built on the southern route of the Tien-shan Mountains. A councillor, in charge of all southern regional affairs, was assigned to the key city of Kashgar. He was assisted by an imperial agent in each of the bigger cities, a commandant of the forces in each of the smaller ones, and some 5,760 soldiers.[4]

The key city of Urumchi in the eastern part was administered by a lieutenant-governor, in command of 3,460 Manchu soldiers. His jurisdiction included Barkul and Ku-ch'eng, each under an assistant commander and 1,000 troops. The frontier city of Chuguchak (Tarbagatai), second in importance to Ili as a military outpost, was placed under the control of an assistant military-governor and two commandants in charge of more than 2,000 soldiers and 540 military colonists.[5]

[1] Ch'i Yün-shih, 'Hsin-chiang yao-lüeh' (An essential outline of Sinkiang), in *Huang-ch'ao fan-shu yü-ti ts'ung-shu* (A collection of geographical works on our imperial dynasty's frontier tribes and tributary states), 24: 2: 9; Sung-yün, 1: 22–24b.

[2] Ch'i Yün-shih, 24: 2: 13; Sung-yün, 1: 22–24.

[3] Wei Yüan, *Sheng-wu chi* (A record of imperial military exploits) (1836), 4: 15b–16b. [4] Ibid. 4: 15b–16b.

[5] *Ch'in-ting Huang-yü Hsi-yü t'u-chih* (An imperial edition of the royal atlas

All high officials and officers in Sinkiang were Manchus, or at least bannermen. A study of the key posts before 1874 reveals that of a total of 234 appointees, 229 were bannermen and only five were possibly Chinese.[1]

Leading officials in Sinkiang before 1874

Post	Chinese	Possibly Chinese	Bannermen	Total
Military-governor of Ili . . .	0	0	25	25
Assistant Military-governor of Ili . .	0	0	17	17
Assistant Military-governor at Tarba-gatai (Chuguchak). . . .	0	0	28	28
Lieutenant-governor of Urumchi . .	0	2	30	32
Imperial Agent at Hami . . .	0	1	9	10
Intendant of Circuit of Barkul and Urumchi	0	0	21	21
Councillor at Kashgar . . .	0	1	23	24
Assistant Military-governor at Yarkand	0	1	23	24
Imperial Agent at Ush. . . .	0	0	18	18
Imperial Agent at Aksu . . .	0	0	8	8
Imperial Agent at Kuché . . .	0	0	8	8
Imperial Agent at Kharashar . .	0	0	13	13
Imperial Agent at Khoten . . .	0	0	6	6
Totals	0	5	229	234

These high Manchu officials did not directly rule the non-Chinese native Moslem population—mostly Turki-speaking, turban-wearing Uighurs (*Ch'an-t'ou hui*)—but functioned through the local Moslem chieftains known as the *begs* (*beks*), who handled such matters as taxes, trade, and justice. The *beg* system had existed in Kashgaria before the Ch'ing conquest. Under the Ch'ing administration, there were thirty-five kinds of *begs* totalling about 270 persons, among whom the following six kinds were the most important: the *hakim beg*, or the chief, who served as a sort of local Moslem governor; the *ishikagha beg*, the assistant governor; the *khazanachi beg* and the *shang beg*,

of the Western Region) (1762), 31: 8b–9; Agnes Fang-chih Ch'en, 'China's Northern Frontiers: Historical Background', *The Yenching Journal of Social Studies*, 4: 1: 83 (Aug. 1948).

[1] Wen-djang Chu, *The Policy of the Manchu Government in the Suppression of the Moslem Rebellion in Shensi, Kansu, and Sinkiang from 1862 to 1878*, Ph.D. thesis, University of Washington (1955), 411. (Hereafter to be cited as *Policy*.) See also his published article, 'Tso Tsung-t'ang's Role in the Recovery of Sinkiang', *Tsing Hua Journal of Chinese Studies*, New Series, 1: 3: 161–2 (Sept. 1958).

two kinds of collectors of revenue; the *haz beg*, the judge; and the *mirab beg*, the superintendent of irrigation and agriculture.[1] They were given the third to the seventh civil service ranks.[2]

The Ch'ing administration in Sinkiang was thus a 'dyarchy' and an indirect rule, stemming from the arrogant notion that the natives were an uncivilized, subject people, beneath the dignity of the Manchu conquerors. The actual task of governing them was left to their own chieftains. High Manchu officials concerned themselves only with policy matters and the ultimate control of Sinkiang. It is thus apparent that Sinkiang was nothing more than a colony of the Manchu overlords. The Ch'ing administration there was maintained by force, not by the consent of those it sought to govern.

When Emperor Ch'ien-lung first conquered Sinkiang, he was careful with the appointment of officials there; only men of ability and integrity were selected. But by degrees the practice became lax, and those chosen for duties in Sinkiang were mostly men who had connexions with the inner court. They went as conquerors, filled with the desire of profiting from the wealth of the land. Each time an army was transferred to Sinkiang, its officers and soldiers cheered at the prospect of gain. The military-governorship of Ili, which normally would have been considered a hardship post on the frontier, was in fact much coveted because it was a lucrative position.[3] Far removed from the watchful eyes of the censors, the officials in Sinkiang led extravagant lives, exacting contributions and forcing irregular levies on the Moslem peasants through their collaborators, the *begs*, who were often all too anxious to exploit their own people in the name of the Manchu overlords. These Manchu officials had absolutely no interest in the local population, whom they treated 'like dogs and sheep'. No effort was made to alleviate the lot of the Moslem people or to understand their language, customs, and problems.[4]

[1] For a study of the *beg* system, see Saguchi Tōru, *Jūhachi-jūkyū seiki Higashi Torukisutan shakaishi kenkyū* (The social history of Eastern Turkestan in the 18th–19th century) (Tokyo, 1963), Chapter 3, 103–92; also H. S. Brunnert and W. V. Hagelstrom, *Present Day Political Organization of China* (Shanghai, 1912), 439–40.

[2] Saguchi, 120, 124.

[3] Ch'in Han-ts'ai, *Tso-wen-hsiang-kung tsai Hsi-pei* (Tso Tsung-t'ang in the North-West) (Shanghai, 1946), 25–26.

[4] Yao Hsin-an, 'Ch'ing-mo Hsin-chiang cheng-ts'e ti shih-te fa-chan' (The historical development of the Sinkiang policy at the end of the Ch'ing dynasty), *Hsi-pei yen-chiu*, 3: 23–24 (Jan. 1932).

Such political apathy and corruption, coupled with the military occupation, provided the Moslems with a strong incentive to rebellion. Their discontent was quickly capitalized upon by the *khojas* (*khwājas*), the religious potentates who had ruled Kashgaria before the Ch'ing conquest.[1] The *khojas* had been banished by the Ch'ing authorities to Khokand, but they were determined to re-establish themselves in Kashgaria. From time to time they organized invasions of Kashgaria in what they termed a 'Holy War' against China. Their co-religionists in Sinkiang were only too ready to conspire with them.[2] As a result, a number of *khoja* invasions and Moslem revolts took place after the Ch'ing conquest of Sinkiang in 1759: the Kashgar rebellion in 1760, the Ush rebellion in 1765, Ziya ud-Din's uprising in 1815, *Khoja* Jihangir's invasions in 1820, 1826, and 1827, *Khoja* Yusuf's attacks in 1830 and 1831, seven *khojas'* invasion in 1847, the Uighur rebellion in Kuché in 1857, and *Khoja* Wāli's invasion of Kashgaria in the same year.[3] In 1864 Sinkiang was ripe for still another major uprising, precipitated by the Tungan rebellion in Shensi and Kansu.

2. THE MOSLEM REBELLION

The Tungans were Chinese-assimilated Moslems who lived largely in Shensi and Kansu; there were six and a half million of them in the former province, and eight million in the latter.[4] Although they had adopted Chinese customs, language, and attire, they retained conspicuous Central Asian physical characteristics and habits. Many of them had high nasal bridges

[1] For information on the *khoja*, see Muhammad Sadiq (Kashghari), *Tazkira-i-khwājagān* (Memoirs of Khoja Muhammad Sadiq of Kashgaria), summarized by Robert B. Shaw under the title *The History of the Khojas of Eastern Turkestan*, edited by N. Elias, supplement to the *Journal of the Asiatic Society of Bengal*, lxvi, part 1 (1897).

[2] Gaimushō Jōhō Chōsajo (Japanese Foreign Office, Bureau of Investigation Report), 'Shimmatsu no tai kaikyō seisaku' (The Moslem policy during the late Ch'ing period), *Kaikyō jijō*, 3: 1: 52 (Mar. 1940); Hung Yüan, 'A-ku-po cheng-ch'üan te pen-chih ho Ch'ing-ping hsi-cheng te i-i' (The very nature of Yakub Beg's régime and the meaning of the western expedition of the Ch'ing army), *Hsin-hua yüeh-pao*, 65: 206 (Mar. 1955).

[3] Saguchi Tōru, 'Shinkyō Uiguru jin no hanran' (The rebellion of the Uighur in Sinkiang), *Hokuri shigaku*, 8: 2 (Nov. 1959).

[4] P. Dabry de Thiersant, *Le Mahométisme en Chine et dans le Turkestan Oriental* (Paris, 1878), i. 38, 40–46.

and wore beards. They eschewed wine, pork, and opium. They married Chinese women but seldom married their daughters to Chinese men. They were fierce fighters but lacked discipline.[1]

The Moslems in China were a minority group despised by the Chinese and Manchus for their religion and their way of life. They suffered from semi-exclusion from high political offices in spite of the announced government policy of equality. Throughout the 268 years of the Ch'ing dynasty (1644–1911), only forty-five Moslems reached positions of distinction, of whom the majority were in military service and only a handful of civilians rose to be governors and governor-generals.[2] Social and political discrimination generated in the Moslems a strong sense of resentment and provided the seed of revolt.

Among the Moslems, the adherents of the New Sect or New Teaching (*Hsin-chiao*) were particularly intransigent and militant. The origin of the New Sect was not conclusively established until recently. The Japanese scholar, Saguchi Tōru, traced the source to one Ma Ming-hsin in 1761–2. Ma, a native of An-ting, Kansu, started to spread the New Teaching in the Salar areas in Hsi-ning after his return in 1761 from a period of religious study in Yarkand and Kashgar. With the help of Su-ssu-shih-san and Hu-ma-liu-hu, he founded the New Sect in 1762, which propagated a mystical ritualism characterized by: (1) loud chanting of the scripture, as opposed to the soft chanting of the Old Sect; (2) prayers with head-shaking and body movement in a dance-like manner—foot-stamping, hand-waving, and face turning up toward heaven; (3) belief in miracles, visions, apparition of spirits, and prediction of good or bad omens; and (4) the worship of saints and their tombs. In ritual the New Sect was definitely related to Sufism.[3] An anonymous work by a Chinese official in Lanchow, Kansu, who took part in the pacification of the Moslem revolt in 1781, sheds further light on the New Sect. Its members were said to: (1) worship with bare feet, (2) believe that death under the 'golden light' would result in better reincarnation, (3) coerce unbelievers into accepting the faith by force, (4) regard faith as more

---

[1] G. Findlay Andrew, *The Crescent in North-west China* (London, 1921), 27–40.
[2] Nakada Yoshinobu, 'Shindai kaikyōto no ichisokumen' (An aspect of Moslem life in the Ch'ing period), *Tōyō gakuhō*, 36: 1: 68–74 (June 1953).
[3] Saguchi, *Jūhachi-jūkyū seiki*, 561–2, 565.

important than family ties, and (5) revere Ma Ming-hsin as the saintly Founder of the Sect.[1]

The adherents of the New Sect were zealous 'reformers' who detested members of the Old Sect for wearing white attire for funeral services and for following the Buddhist and Taoist practice of chanting scriptures for a fee. The reformers would not read the Koran for money or for any other unworthy purpose.[2] They were a group of religious zealots, who maintained two major centres in Chin-chi-pao, Ninghsia, and in Chang-chia-ch'uan, Kansu, in rival existence with the Old Sect stronghold of Hochow.[3] The Old and New Sects quarrelled with each other incessantly in the 1760's and 1770's, and in 1781, Ma Ming-hsin and Su-ssu-shih-san led an attack on the Old Sect. Government investigation of the sectarian warfare led the New Sect to open rebellion in that year, and though it was suppressed, a second revolt broke out in 1783. This revolt too was suppressed and the New Sect proscribed.[4] However, its members were restless and continually sought opportunities to strike. A new revolt broke out in 1862, and one of its most fanatical leaders was Ma Hua-lung, who came from the direct 'apostolic' line of Ma Ming-hsin and who maintained his headquarters in Chin-chi-pao.[5]

The immediate cause of the 1862 rebellion has usually been attributed to the unauthorized cutting of bamboo by a group of Moslems in a Chinese village near Huachow, Shensi.[6] But recent research has cast doubt on the accuracy of this account, because bamboo does not grow in the cold northern province of Shensi. The supposition that the Moslems cut bamboo to make lances is also untenable, because bamboo is too weak for that purpose.[7] The rebellion, apparently, broke out in the following manner.

The Chinese and the Moslems did not mingle socially. But in 1858 a Chinese lad wandered into a Moslem festival at Lin-t'ung, Shensi, without being molested. On the other hand, when a Moslem pedlar went to a Chinese festival, he was badly

---

[1] See Note B, p. 197.   [2] Wen-djang Chu, *Policy*, 243, 361.
[3] Saguchi, *Jūhachi-jūkyū seiki*, 743.
[4] Pai Shou-i, *Hui-hui min-tsu ti hsin-sheng* (The new birth of the Moslem people) (Shanghai, 1951), 46–47.   [5] Saguchi, 252, 744.   [6] See Note C, pp. 197–8.
[7] Wen-djang Chu, *Policy*, 330. See also his published article, 'The Immediate Cause of the Moslem Rebellion in Northwest China in 1862', *Central Asiatic Journal*, 3: 4: 309–16 (1958).

beaten. The Chinese magistrate failed to adjudicate the case justly and the Moslems retaliated by raiding the Chinese village and killing thirteen people.[1] More killing and robbing followed until, in April 1862, the situation reached a crisis in the face of an imminent Taiping invasion of Shensi under Lan Ta-shun. The Taipings did not remain in Shensi long; they attacked Sian and several other cities and moved eastward. After their departure, the Chinese accused the Moslems of harbouring secret sympathy for the Taipings, and tension between the two groups grew to a breaking-point. In May 1862 several Moslems attempted to buy bamboo poles from some Chinese merchants in Huachow. The Chinese raised the price and the Moslems refused to pay. A brawl, resulting in several casualties among the Moslems, flared up but was brought to a halt through the efforts of a few peacemakers. The matter might have rested there had it not been for the fact that the Chinese set fire to the Moslem village at night. In revenge the Moslems plunged into a massacre of the Chinese in Huachow, and their fellow believers in other cities responded by killing Chinese and Manchus indiscriminately. A major uprising was thus born.[2]

The Ch'ing government was preoccupied with the campaign against the Taipings. Only an ineffective general, Sheng-pao, was sent to fight the Moslems, and quite expectedly he achieved no results. In 1863 an able general, To-lung-a, replaced him, and the campaign was carried out much more vigorously. However, To-lung-a's military success was cut short by his death in 1864. Thereafter the rebellion spread like fire until the entire north-west was ablaze.[3]

News of the rebellion in Shensi reached Ili by the end of 1862. The Moslems in Sinkiang were encouraged by the Ch'ing weakness to rise up in sympathetic response. In March 1863 an uprising started near Sui-ting (Suidun), one of the nine cities of Ili, but it was quickly suppressed by government forces. The rebel leaders were executed and more than a hundred Moslems

---

[1] Chang Chi-hsin, 'Lin-t'ung chi-shih' (Events in Lin-t'ung), in *Hui-min ch'i-i*, iii. 17; also Pai Shou-i, *Hui-hui min-tsu ti hsin-sheng* (The new birth of the Moslem people) (Shanghai, 1951), 64–67.

[2] Governor Ying-ch'i's report to the throne, 22 June 1862, in I-hsin (ed.), *Ch'in-ting ch'i-sheng fang-lüeh* (An imperial edition of the strategy in seven provinces) (Preface, 1896), 13: 7–7b.

[3] Wen-djang Chu, *Policy*, 50–51.

arrested. Although order was restored, considerable disquietude prevailed in various parts of Sinkiang. On the night of 4 June 1864 a revolt broke out in Kuché, where Moslem rebels and Chinese bandits killed the imperial agent Sa-ling-a and seized control of the city. A government reinforcement column of 500 men under Wen-yung, acting commandant at Wu-su, was quickly dispatched to Kuché, but it was completely annihilated by the rebels in the desert near Kharashar on 10 July. On 13 July 1864 the Moslems in Urumchi rebelled, taking the Chinese 'city' and besieging the Tartar 'city'. Communication with Ili was cut off.[1]

The Ch'ing administration in Sinkiang was totally unprepared for the rebellion. In rapid succession the Moslems seized the southern city of Manas on 17 July and the northern city on 16 September. The Tartar city of Urumchi fell on 3 October, and Ku-ch'eng was lost on 15 December. In southern Sinkiang the rebels took Yarkand on 26 July, Yangihissa on 29 July, and Kashgar on 30 July.[2] Thus nearly all southern Sinkiang and a large portion of northern Sinkiang were lost.

Ili, headquarters of the Ch'ing administration in Sinkiang, was completely isolated from China proper. Ch'ang-ch'ing, the military-governor whose duty it was to guard Sinkiang for the court, urgently asked for 2,000 troops each from Ming-hsü, assistant military-governor at Chuguchak, and Kuang-feng, assistant military-governor at Kobdo. Ming-hsü came with only a thousand poorly equipped soldiers, while Kuang-feng could not spare any of his 224 men. Ch'ang-ch'ing then requested Peking to dispatch 40,000 men from China proper. What he received was not reinforcement but a notice of dismissal from office and of Ming-hsü's appointment as his successor, effective 1 November 1864. The Moslems in Ili, taking advantage of the unpreparedness of the Ch'ing administration, rebelled on 10 November, electing Mazam Khan (Mai-tzu-tsa-t'e), a *hakim beg* or local governor, their leader. They occupied the outlying areas of Ili, defeating the imperial forces, and then divided their men to besiege the fortresses of Ili and Hui-ning (Bayandai). Ming-hsü raised 1,200 men in an unsuccessful attempt to break the blockade of Hui-ning; on 5 February 1865 Hui-ning fell. The rebels succeeded in persuading the Chahar Mongol military

[1] Wen-djang Chu, *Policy*, 250–2.   [2] Ibid. 256.

colonists to join them, and the Sibo and Solon Manchus to stay neutral.[1]

The siege of Ili went on for a year and a half, causing starvation and pestilence. People lived on horses, dogs, and cats; typhus raged, killing 50 to 100 daily.[2] In desperation, Ming-hsü requested aid from the Russian governor of West Siberia, but to no avail. He also urged Peking to negotiate with the Russian legation for military assistance. Repeated efforts by the Tsungli Yamen (Foreign Office) in late 1865 and early 1866 yielded nothing more than a vague promise from the Russian minister that the Chinese might send relief funds and official dispatches to Ili via Russian territory.[3] Under extreme deprivation, Ili fell on 6 March 1866. Ming-hsü, Ch'ang-ch'ing and their families were all killed. Chuguchak was also lost on 11 April. With the exception of the area near Barkul and Hami in the eastern part, all Sinkiang was taken over by the rebels.[4]

The Moslem rebels, however, were not united. Five leaders vied for power in Sinkiang: (1) *Khoja* Rasheddin proclaimed himself Khan of all Chinese Turkestan, with a capital in Aksu; (2) T'o-ming established himself in Urumchi with the title of Moslem King; (3) Sadiq Beg made Kashgar his headquarters; (4) Mufti Habitulla set up his government in Khoten; and (5) Abderrahman established his régime in Yarkand. Of the five, *Khoja* Rasheddin was the strongest, but he was not of the preferred Āfāq lineage. Sadiq Beg considered him unacceptable and requested Alim Kul, khan of Khokand, to send *Khoja* Büzürg, son of Jihangir and a descendant of the Āfāq family in exile in Khokand.[5] The request was granted, and *Khoja* Büzürg came to Kashgaria in the company of a general, Yakub Beg, in early 1865.[6]

Yakub Beg was born about 1820 in Piskent, fifty miles south

[1] Ibid. 257–63.   [2] Eugene Schuyler, ii. 181.

[3] *CSL*, Mu-tsung period, 162: 5b–6b, edict dated 17 Jan. 1866; also 169: 14b–15.   [4] Wen-djang Chu, *Policy*, 264.

[5] Wu Ch'i-yü, 'Ch'ing-chi Hui-Chiang tu-li chih shih-mo chi ch'i wai-chiao' (The Moslem independence in Sinkiang and its diplomacy during the late Ch'ing period), *Kuo-wen chou-pao*, 11: 11: 2 (19 Mar. 1934); A. N. Kuropatkin, *Kashgaria: Eastern or Chinese Turkistan*, tr. by Walter E. Gowan (Calcutta, 1882), 156–78.

[6] For details of Yakub Beg's adventure, see Yuan Tsing, 'Yakub Beg (1820–1877) and the Moslem Rebellion in Chinese Turkestan', *Central Asiatic Journal*, vi: 2: 154 (June 1961); also T. D. Forsyth, *Report of a Mission to Yarkund in 1873* (Calcutta, 1875), 98, 204–13.

of Tashkent. Rather than follow the religious profession of his father he went to Tashkent to seek his fortune. His sister was married to the governor of Tashkent and his uncle, Sheik Nizamuddin, was very influential. At twenty-five, Yakub Beg became a court chamberlain. Through the influence of his brother-in-law he was appointed to the governorship of Akmasjid, where he remained for five or six years until its seizure by the Russians in 1853. By 1857, when *Khoja* Wāli invaded Kashgaria, he was already in command of the forces at Tashkent and soon afterwards rose to be commander-in-chief of the Khokandian army. He resisted the Russians at Tashkent in 1864, and though defeated his career did not suffer. He was selected by the khan of Khokand to accompany *Khoja* Büzürg to Kashgaria. With sixty-eight men, he set out early in 1865.

Sadiq Beg soon regretted the invitation because of *Khoja* Büzürg's family reputation, but it was too late to turn him back. In a lightning display of military skill and political manipulation, Yakub Beg deposed Sadiq Beg in Kashgar and Abderrahman in Yarkand, and installed *Khoja* Büzürg upon the throne. Once he was king, *Khoja* Büzürg indulged in debauchery. Yakub Beg quickly deposed him and proclaimed himself king of Kashgaria. The coveted title of Atalik Ghazi, 'Champion Father', came to him from the Amir of Bukhara in 1866.[1] During the following year, with the help of his two sons, Yakub Beg subdued Mufti Habitulla and Rasheddin. Now known as the Badaulet, the 'Favourite of Fortune', he turned on T'o-ming, whom he defeated and stripped of the title of Moslem King. When T'o-ming died in 1870, Yakub Beg dominated all southern Sinkiang and part of northern Sinkiang, with a capital in Aksu, and a population of 1,015,000.[2]

Yakub Beg's empire-building met with the approval of Britain, which welcomed a 'common front between Britain and Islam against Russia'.[3] The British tea-planter in India, Robert Shaw, visited Kashgaria in 1868 and returned with a glowing, if exaggerated, report of the commercial potentiality of Yakub Beg's kingdom.[4] Mirza Shadi, Yakub Beg's emissary, then

---

[1] D. Boulger, *Central Asian Portraits* (London, 1880), 100–9.
[2] Forsyth, 62.   [3] Lattimore, *Pivot*, 34.
[4] For the activities of Robert Shaw, see his *Visits to High Tartary, Yarkand and Kashghar* (London, 1871), especially chapter 3.

visited Lord Mayo, viceroy of India, who in return dispatched Sir T. Douglas Forsyth (1827–86) to Kashgaria.[1] The British in India also urged Peking to recognize Yakub Beg, but the Chinese were in no mood to comply.[2] Prince Kung, head of the Tsungli Yamen, informed British minister Thomas Wade that Sinkiang differed basically from such tributary states as Korea and Annam in that it was a part of China, and stated that after the pacification of the rebels in Shensi and Kansu, the Chinese government would go on suppressing the rebellion in Sinkiang.[3] Wade, on the basis of available intelligence, doubted China's ability to recover Sinkiang.[4]

3. THE RUSSIAN OCCUPATION OF ILI

The rise of Yakub Beg posed a difficult problem for the Russian government. Here was a man who was anti-Russian—having resisted the Russian conquest of Khokand a few years earlier—and who now had established himself in Sinkiang. His new Moslem state on Chinese soil might become a rallying-point for the discontented elements in the Central Asian khanates that had lately come under Russian rule. It was even possible that with British blessing his kingdom might ultimately develop into a large Central Asian Moslem empire aspiring to include Russian Turkestan. Thus considered, Yakub Beg was a threat to Russia and an instrument of Britain. Yet he was established on Chinese territory; any official intervention would not only jeopardize Russian relations with Peking but would also arouse British opposition. The situation was distasteful but St. Petersburg could not arrive at a definite policy. A temporary device was adopted: Russia would neither recognize Yakub Beg nor intervene in the affairs of Sinkiang. However, Russian generals in Central Asia, who had charge of border security, became increasingly impatient with the situation.

The turmoil in Sinkiang had caused no small trouble for the Russians. Trade was interrupted and Russian consulates and warehouses in Ili and Chuguchak were destroyed. Moslem

---

[1] F.O. 17/825/136, enclosure, C. M. Aitchison to Thomas Wade, dated 7.6.1870, written at the direction of Viceroy Mayo of India.
[2] F.O. 17/545, Sir Rutherford Alcock to F.O., 4 Feb. 1870.
[3] F.O. 17/548/57, Wade to F.O., 12 Apr. 1870.
[4] F.O. 17/825/136, enclosure, Wade to Forsyth, 6 Apr. 1876.

renegades frequently raided the Russian border and Kirghiz migration to Russia increased sharply in 1869. Many of the migrants engaged in stealing horses and cattle. Two Russian detachments were sent to chastise them, recapturing 15,000 head of cattle during their first attack and 5,000 during the second. Refugees from Sinkiang continued to pour into Russia in large numbers; in 1871 some 1,095 of them accepted the Orthodox faith, while 15,000 migrated to the Valley of Black Irtysh. These occurrences clearly posed new problems for the Russians.[1] In an effort to improve relations with Russia, Abul Oghlan, the new sultan of Ili, dispatched two envoys to Vernyi in 1868, but they achieved no concrete results. Frontier raids continued, and there were mutual complaints and demands for indemnity. In 1870 Baron Kaulbars of the Russian General Staff was sent to Ili to settle the charges and counter-charges, but again the mission was a failure.[2]

Added to these annoyances was the Russian fear of Yakub Beg's invasion of Ili under British sponsorship, which seemed the more possible after the visits of Robert Shaw and Douglas Forsyth to Kashgaria in 1868 and 1869. General K. P. von Kaufman, governor-general of Russian Turkestan, who had independent powers to conduct war and diplomacy with Central Asian khanates, decided to strike first. A carefully prepared report was sent to St. Petersburg to justify the need for the occupation of Ili.[3] In August 1870 he dispatched an army to occupy the descent of the strategic Muzart Pass and make Ili indefensible. In May 1871 he sent a task force under Major Balitskii to Ili on the pretext of punishing the Moslems for their raids on the Russian border. Meanwhile, the armed forces at Borokhudzir on the border were strengthened under the command of General G. A. Kolpakovskii, governor of Semirechie. On 24 June Kolpakovskii swept across the border with a striking force of 65 officers and 1,785 soldiers. On 28 June they defeated 4,000 Moslem troops at Alim-tu, and on 1 July they occupied Sui-ting. Abul Oghlan surrendered on 3 July 1871.[4] He came to Kolpakovskii's camp and declared: 'If it is the will

[1] Terentyef (Terent'ev), *Russia and England*, i. 232, 241, 242, 246, 272–3.
[2] Schuyler, ii. 183, 186.
[3] Ibid. ii. 186.
[4] M. A. Terent'ev, *Istoriia zavoevaniia . . .*, ii. 50–51.

of Heaven that the Russians, not I, should possess Kuldja, I
will offer my sultandom to the Russians. . . . Only I am guilty
of fighting you; my people are not. Punish me but spare my
people.'[1] Kolpakovskii accepted the surrender and ordered him
to hand over all weapons. On the following day the Russians

Russian Occupation of Ili

triumphantly entered Ili in the company of the deposed
chieftain, and Kolpakovskii on his own authority declared Ili
annexed 'in perpetuity'. The Russians occupied a total of
1,224 square miles of territory in Ili.[2] Although St. Petersburg
did not direct the activities of Kaufman and Kolpakovskii, it
accepted the fruits of their conquest.

The occupation went unnoticed by the outside world for
some time. More than three weeks passed before Sir Andrew
Buchanan, British ambassador in St. Petersburg, could give

[1] Ibid. 51.
[2] Ibid. iii. 266. For details of the occupation, cf. ibid. ii. 23-58.

London any inkling of Russian activities in Ili.[1] It was not until 23 August that he was able to inform London officially of the Russian occupation.[2] Thomas Wade was unaware of the event until he was notified by the Foreign Office in December 1871.[3]

The Chinese themselves, having been cut off from Sinkiang for years, did not know of the Russian occupation until they were notified by the Russian minister, General G. Vlangaly, on 1 September 1871. The laconic Russian diplomatic communication made no reference to Ili's being occupied 'in perpetuity'; it merely stated that General Kolpakovskii had 'recovered' Ili from the Moslem rebels and had captured their chieftain.[4] Peking quickly ordered Yung-ch'üan, acting military-governor of Ili in exile at Kobdo, Mongolia, to proceed to Ili to negotiate the return of Ili; a fund of 200,000 taels was provided for the mission.[5] Yung-ch'üan, however, was fearful of the assignment; after much procrastination and a stern warning from the court, he reluctantly undertook the journey.[6] He had hoped to raise a force of one thousand soldiers to accompany him, but was able to gather only a little more than a hundred.[7] Troop movement in winter was extremely difficult; the soldiers had to dig their way out of heavy snow in order to proceed, and half the camels and horses died on the way. After many trials and tribulations, Yung-ch'üan and his men finally reached Chuguchak, on 20 January 1872; the road to Ili was completely blocked by snow.[8]

The Russian government appointed Colonel Boguslavskii of the Ministry of Home Affairs to negotiate with Yung-ch'üan, with the following instructions:

1. Explain the conditions in Ili and the measures Russia had taken to protect it for the benefit of China;
2. Declare that Russia could not return Ili before the arrival of sufficient Chinese troops;
3. Ascertain the measures the Chinese government proposed to adopt for the administration of Ili;

---

[1] F.O. 65/822/162, Buchanan to Granville, 26 July 1871.
[2] F.O. 65/822/193, same to same, 23 Aug. 1871.
[3] F.O. 17/590/279, Wade to Granville, *confidential*, 29 Dec. 1871.
[4] *IWSM*, T'ung-chih period, 82: 7.
[5] *IWSM*, 83: 27.   [6] *IWSM*, 83: 31b-32; 82: 38b, 41.
[7] *IWSM*, 83: 53.   [8] *IWSM*, 85: 34b.

4. Refrain from discussing reparation of military expenses;
5. Refrain from discussing the demarcation line between Russia and China.[1]

Boguslavskii and Yung-ch'üan met on 15 May 1872 in a place called Se-erh-ho-o-lu-le (Zharbolak?), near Chuguchak. The Chinese were anxious to effect Russian withdrawal from Ili, but Boguslavskii evaded the issue by incessantly questioning the strength of the Chinese force. Upon learning that Yung-ch'üan had come with only a hundred soldiers, he dismissed the question of evacuation with the brisk comment that the Chinese had too little strength to hold Ili. He intimated that settlement of the issue would best be left in the hands of the Russian minister in Peking and the Chinese court. Boguslavskii was obviously playing a delaying game, and Yung-ch'üan, with his thin force, could not press the issue. He returned to Chuguchak without achieving any results.[2]

When informed of the state of negotiations, Prince Kung, head of the Tsungli Yamen, questioned the Russian minister in Peking repeatedly about Boguslavskii's attitude. Vlangaly explained that the occupation of Ili was undertaken in order to safeguard the Russian border from Moslem raids. Yung-ch'üan's small force could not be expected to hold Ili. Any premature return would only tempt the Moslem rebels to retake it and once again threaten the security of the Russian border. In that case, Russia would be forced to occupy Ili a second time. Why return Ili when China was not prepared to hold it? He insisted that no discussion of Ili could take place until China recovered Kashgar and Manas, thus freeing the Russian border from further disturbances.[3] In September 1872 Boguslavskii himself came to Peking and repeated the same argument to Prince Kung. After having blocked settlement of the issue, he returned home.[4]

Peking became convinced that argument was useless, and it decided to recover Manas and Urumchi by force, so that China could negotiate from a position of strength.[5] Yung-ch'üan was ordered to prepare his troops for the task, but he requested

---

[1] Terentyef (Terent'ev), *Russia and England*, i. 252–3.
[2] *IWSM*, 86: 36–40.
[3] *IWSM*, 87: 7b–9b.
[4] *IWSM*, 88: 12.
[5] *IWSM*, 89: 25.

permission to resign on grounds of kidney trouble. The court asked him to nurse his ailment in the camp at Chuguchak, and allowed him a month of rest but no resignation.[1]

Russia proudly announced to the world that her stewardship of Ili was an act of kindness to China during a period of internal disorder, and that she would return the territory as soon as Chinese imperial authority was re-established in Sinkiang.[2] Vlangaly assured foreign diplomats in China that the Russian government had no intention 'to annex or occupy territory in Turkestan'.[3] Such magnanimous declarations were of course made in the belief that the effete Ch'ing government could not reconquer Sinkiang. The Russians now discovered that activities which tended to prolong disorder in Sinkiang would ensure their retention of Ili. Yakub Beg, formerly a thorn in Russia's side, suddenly took on new significance, and Captain Baron Kaulbars was sent to him. They negotiated a commercial treaty of five articles on 9 April 1872, by which Russia recognized Yakub Beg as leader of Moslem Sinkiang, and Yakub Beg allowed Russian traders a low import duty of 2·5 per cent. *ad valorem* and freedom of trade in his domain. Sa'id Yakub, a nephew of Yakub Beg and envoy to Tashkent and St. Petersburg, was courteously received by the Russians.[4]

The British in India were worried about Russian activities. Viceroy Northbrook, who succeeded Mayo after his assassination in 1872, for once abandoned his usual cautious attitude of 'masterly inactivity' and received Sa'id Yakub warmly in March 1873. He dispatched Sir Douglas Forsyth on a second mission to the Kashgarian state in October 1873. The mission, consisting of three hundred men, brought Yakub Beg a letter from the Queen, and several thousand old-style muskets from the viceroy of India. The result was the conclusion of a commercial treaty of twelve articles, by which the British granted Yakub Beg official recognition in return for the right of legation and consulate, as well as preferential commercial treatment in his kingdom.[5]

[1] *IWSM*, 89: 11b–13b.

[2] F. Martens, *Le Conflit entre la Russie et la Chine* (Brussels, 1880), 69, 71.

[3] F.O. 17/626/2, Wade to Granville, *confidential*, 6 Jan. 1872.

[4] Wu Ch'i-yü, 11: 11: 6.

[5] For Forsyth's mission and the treaty, see T. D. Forsyth, *Report of a Mission . . .* and H. W. Bellew, *Kashmir and Kashghar: A Narrative of the Journey of the Embassy to Kashghar in 1873–74* (London, 1875).

To strengthen his international position further, Yakub Beg established diplomatic relations with Turkey, which he honoured as a superior state. The Sultan of Turkey sent him three thousand rifles, thirty cannon, and three officers—one each from the infantry, the artillery, and the cavalry—to help train his troops.[1] A private British organization called the Central Asian Trading Company also supplied him with weapons.[2]

With all this diplomatic and military support, Yakub Beg, the soldier of fortune, seemed firmly established in Kashgaria. The Chinese found the situation distasteful but were unable to cope with it, for they could not reach him before suppressing the Moslem rebels in Shensi and Kansu. Yakub Beg was therefore free from Chinese attack until General Tso Tsung-t'ang swept into Sinkiang in 1876.

4. SUPPRESSION OF THE REBELLION

Tso Tsung-t'ang (1812–85), scholar, soldier, statesman, and hero of the Taiping campaign, was appointed governor-general of Shensi and Kansu in 1866, with the specific assignment of suppressing the Moslem rebellion in these provinces.[3] But before assuming the position he was ordered by the court to fight the Nien rebels;[4] so it was not until after the pacification of the Nien rebellion in summer 1868 that he was able to carry out the earlier assignment.

The government campaign against the Moslem rebels had made no progress; there was no definite policy towards the rebels, and officers in charge of the campaign—such as Sheng-pao, To-lung-a, En-lin, and Hsi-lin—wavered between the extremes of militant extermination and cowardly appeasement. Tso's arrival in Sian, Shensi, on 26 November 1868 marked a turning-point. By efficient leadership and good strategy Tso,

---

[1] F.O. 17/826, India Office to Foreign Office, 25 Jan. 1879, forwarding a narrative of events in Kashgaria by one of the three Turkish officers sent to Yakub Beg by the Sultan of Turkey.

[2] Louis E. Frechtling, 'Anglo-Russian Rivalry in Eastern Turkistan, 1863–1881', *Royal Central Asian Journal*, 26: 477, 479, 483 (July 1939).

[3] See Note D, pp. 198–9.

[4] For details of the Nien rebellion, see Siang-tseh Ching, *The Nien Rebellion* (Seattle, 1954), 159 pp., and S. Y. Teng, *The Nien Army and Their Guerrilla Warfare* (The Hague, 1960), 240 pp.

despite initial reverses, cleared Shensi of the rebels in autumn 1869. He then moved his forces to Kansu and Ninghsia, and in early 1870 his general, Liu Sung-shan, launched a powerful attack on the rebel centre Chin-chi-pao in Ninghsia, the base of Ma Hua-lung. The rebels resisted stubbornly; Liu was killed in action, and his nephew Liu Chin-t'ang, then twenty-six, was given command of the army. Seventy-one battalions were lost before Chin-chi-pao was taken in 1871. The next major victory came when the rebel Ma Chan-ao surrendered Hochow on 6 March 1872, and half a year later Tso entered Lanchow victoriously. The crowning success of Tso's five-year campaign came in November 1873 when Ma Wen-lu, the rebel in the last stronghold of Suchow, capitulated. However, the wily Shensi rebel Pai Yen-hu escaped to Sinkiang to join forces with Yakub Beg.[1] The government had spent forty million taels on the campaign thus far, and intended to pursue it to its logical conclusion in Sinkiang.[2]

At this juncture China found herself involved with Japan in the Formosa crisis; a settlement was reached only after paying the aggressor half a million taels.[3] Shocked by China's unpreparedness to meet the Japanese threat, the court at Peking realized the urgent need for creating a naval force to guard China's coasts. The question then arose: Could China support a naval programme while conducting a costly campaign in Sinkiang? A great debate ensued on the relative urgency and importance of coastal defence and frontier defence.

In general, high officials in the coastal provinces supported the naval programme. They felt that the threat of Japan was more immediate than that of Russia in Central Asia. Li Hung-chang, the grand secretary and governor-general of Chihli, pointed out to the court: 'Japan is right on our threshold, capable of spying out our weakness or preparedness. She is China's most important permanent problem.'[4] As for Sinkiang, Li spoke disparagingly: 'The various cities in Sinkiang first came under our control in the Ch'ien-lung period. Quite apart from the great difficulty of winning these cities, we spent more than three

---

[1] For details of his Shensi and Kansu campaign, see Ch'in Han-ts'ai, 68–72; also Bales, 212–93.   [2] Tso Tsung-t'ang, 'Memorials', 45: 38–39b.
[3] For details of the Formosa incident, see my *China's Entrance into the Family of Nations: The Diplomatic Phase, 1858–1880* (Cambridge, Mass., 1960), 172–4.
[4] *IWSM*, 99: 32b.

million taels annually on military expenses in peace (just to keep them). We have taken several thousand *li* of open space at the price of a (pecuniary) drain that will continue hundreds and thousands of years. It is not worth it.'[1] He boldly asked the court to stop the Sinkiang campaign and shift its funds to the naval programme, which called for the purchase of foreign ships and guns, the training of officers and sailors, the recruitment of talented personnel by a new 'foreign affairs' examination, the opening of mines, the manufacture of munitions, and an increase in customs duties on opium imports to help pay for naval expenses. The total cost was estimated at ten million taels annually.[2] Other high officials in coastal areas such as Ting Jih-ch'ang, ex-governor of Kiangsu, Wang K'ai-t'ai, governor of Fukien, and Wen-pin, acting governor of Shantung, echoed Li's view and urged the creation of a navy of forty-eight ships, which were to be divided into three equal squadrons and stationed in the north, central, and south China coasts respectively.[3] In sum, the advocates of maritime defence made five arguments: (1) frontier defence was not as important and urgent as maritime defence, in view of Peking's proximity to the coast and Sinkiang's great distance from the capital; (2) financial exigency and the uncertainty of victory on the difficult terrain of Sinkiang compelled re-examination of the advisability of the Western campaign; (3) Sinkiang, a vast piece of barren land, was of little practical value to China and was not worth the cost of recovering it; (4) Sinkiang was surrounded by strong neighbours and could not be effectively defended for long; and (5) to postpone the recovery of Sinkiang was not unfilial—the withdrawal of troops for the time being was not renunciation of territory conquered by Emperor Ch'ien-lung, but simply a sensible way of preserving China's strength for the future.[4]

Nevertheless, there were many officials who, while not disputing the importance of naval defence, argued that it should not be made at the expense of defending the frontier, and that the rebels in Sinkiang had to be suppressed and the lost land recovered, regardless of the naval programme. Wang Wen-shao,

---

[1] *IWSM*, 99: 23b–24b.   [2] *IWSM*, 99: 15, 24b.
[3] *IWSM*, 98: 24–27, 31–34b, 44b–45.
[4] *IWSM*, 99: 14–32b; Tseng Wen-wu, 331–2.

governor of Hunan, argued that the peace of China really hinged on a successful campaign in Sinkiang, because coastal trouble was likely to flare up if China failed in the north-west:

> If our troops fall behind a step, the Russians advance a step. If our troops lose a day, the Russians gain a day. There is nothing more urgent than this affair. The several nations of Britain, France, and the United States also may exploit the situation to their advantage and take action. Any progressive worsening of the Russian affair will inevitably bring on the maritime problem, and our defence will be hard put to the double challenge. As a result the general state of Chinese foreign relations in the future will be unthinkable.

It was therefore necessary, he said, to bring all Chinese power to bear on the Sinkiang campaign, in order to check the Russians and to prevent Western nations from making troubles on the coast.[1]

A somewhat similar view was expressed by Ting Pao-chen, governor of Shantung, who argued that Russia was a much greater threat than Japan or any Western nation, since Russia and China had common frontiers and therefore Russia could reach China by land as well as by water. Japan, though near, could only reach China by water, and the Western nations, though capable of reaching China by sea, were far away. Therefore neither of these powers was so menacing as Russia. Besides, the Russians repeatedly used the trick of playing both ends against the middle—posing as a mediator between China and the Western states and profiting from both. 'In your minister's view', Ting contended, 'the trouble of the various (maritime) nations is like the sickness of the limbs which is distant and light, whereas the trouble of Russia is like the sickness of the heart and stomach, which is near and serious.' He feared a Russian back-door thrust to Peking from Manchuria, in which case Japan and the Western states might also take advantage of the situation to stir up trouble on the coast. For this reason, defence of the inland frontier against Russia was a matter of the greatest urgency.[2]

Having received all these memorials, the court solicited Tso Tsung-t'ang's opinion on the issue. Tso responded on 12 April 1875 with a powerful and persuasive state paper, stating that

---

[1] *IWSM*, 99: 60b–70b.   [2] *IWSM*, 100: 41–41b.

the Sinkiang campaign had to be carried to total victory regardless of what became of the naval programme. Western nations, he asserted, driven primarily by the desire for trade profits, fought for harbours and ports, not for territory. Russia, on the other hand, had territorial as well as commercial designs. It was therefore essential that China block the Russian advance and recover Sinkiang. He impressed upon the court the following points: (1) Sinkiang was the first line of defence in the northwest. It protected Mongolia, which in turn protected Peking. If Sinkiang were lost, Mongolia would be indefensible and Peking itself threatened; (2) there was no immediate danger of invasion from Western nations, but there was the danger of Russian advance in Sinkiang; (3) the funds for frontier defence should not be shifted to coastal defence, which already had its own standing fund; the tight budget for frontier defence allowed no borrowing; (4) the land conquered by the founders of the dynasty should not lightly be given up; and (5) such strategic spots as Urumchi and Aksu should be recovered first.[1] He concluded his argument with a warning that to stop the Sinkiang campaign now was to lose by default and pave the way for foreign domination of the area.[2]

Although the arguments of Li and Tso were both cogent and well reasoned, it was nevertheless apparent that there was no immediate maritime trouble along the coast, but there was a rebellion in Sinkiang which required suppression. China's historical interest in Sinkiang and the concept of Grand Unification undoubtedly exercised an additional influence on the court, which finally came to the conclusion that interruption of the Sinkiang campaign at this point would hamper frontier defence without helping coastal defence. On 23 April 1875, on the recommendation of the Grand Secretary Wen-hsiang, the court appointed Tso imperial commissioner in charge of military affairs in Sinkiang. The old practice of using only Manchus in that military 'colony' was broken; for the first time since the Ch'ing conquest in 1759, a Chinese was installed as the leading official in Sinkiang.[3] The stage was thus set for the Sinkiang campaign.

---

[1] Tso Tsung-t'ang, 'Memorials', 46: 32–35b; Tseng Wen-wu, 332–3.
[2] Tso Tsung-t'ang, 'Memorials', 46: 36b–37.
[3] Ibid., 46: 53.

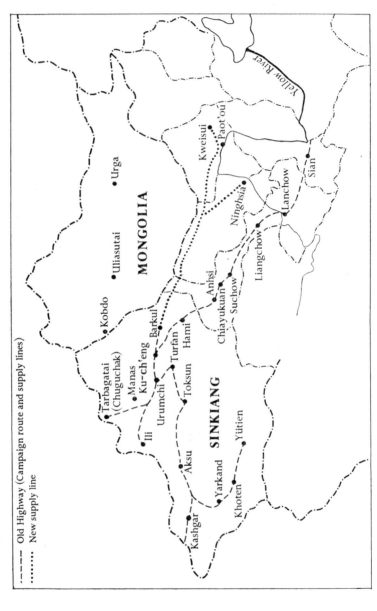

Tso Tsung-t'ang's Sinkiang Campaign and Supply Lines

- - - - Old Highway (Campaign route and supply lines)
· · · · · New supply line

Tso established his headquarters in Lanchow, Kansu, and began reorganizing the army, raising funds, and meeting the problem of logistics. By early 1876 his preparations were nearly complete. In March of the same year he moved his headquarters to Suchow, with a plan to attack Pai Yen-hu on the northern route of the Tien-shan Mountains first and then turn to Yakub Beg on the southern route.[1] Tso's troop movement was extremely rapid by existing standards. By 15 July Liu Chint'ang and his army had penetrated several hundred miles of extremely rough country to capture the important city of Ku-ch'eng, whence they advanced to Fukang, north-west of Urumchi, on 28 July. They took Urumchi on 18 August, after long-drawn-out siege operations against the rebel Ma Jen-te. Pai Yen-hu, however, escaped south. Liu continued his attack and, although he met strong opposition at Manas, the city fell to the Chinese army on 6 November 1876. With this victory the whole of Djungaria was pacified.[2] The first part of the Sinkiang campaign had come to a quick and successful end. Tso rested his troops on the northern route, waiting to attack the south in the following spring.

Yakub Beg, apprehensive of the imminent Chinese attack, sent Sa'id Yakub to London to seek British mediation. The Kashgarian envoy indicated through Sir Douglas Forsyth that Yakub Beg's state would accept the status of tributary to China, like Burma.[3] Disraeli's government, which had come into power in 1874, was receptive of the idea. The 'Jingo King' had always believed that Britain, not Russia, should be the mistress of the East. In the spirit of the 'Forward Policy', Salisbury of the India Office decided that it was 'desirable' for Britain to offer mediation, and on 13 June 1877 Wade was authorized by the Foreign Office to bring the Chinese minister and the Kashgarian envoy together.[4] News of Chinese advances in Kashgaria arrived in London; Sa'id Yakub intimated secretly that the Amir would 'accept any position that China may assign him, anything short of expropriation'.[5] On 7 July Lord Derby of the Foreign Office

[1] For a succinct study of Tso's Sinkiang campaign, see Wen-djang Chu, 'Recovery of Sinkiang', op. cit. 136–65; also Bales, 325 ff.
[2] C'hin Han-ts'ai, 100–2, also Bales, 358.
[3] F.O. 17/825, Wade to Derby, *confidential*, 24 May and 4 June 1877.
[4] Ibid. India Office to Foreign Office, 8 June 1877.
[5] Ibid. Wade to Derby, 25 June 1877.

formally sent the Chinese minister, Kuo Sung-tao, a proposal of mediation, recommending the following three conditions as the basis for an 'honourable and lasting settlement':

1. A recognition by Amir Yakub Khan of the suzerainty of China. The Amir to be left in complete control over the country he now holds, but would, periodically, send embassies bearing presents or tribute to Peking and would address his Imperial Majesty the Emperor of China as his superior.

2. A definite demarcation of boundaries between the kingdom of Kashgar and China.

3. An agreement to be entered into as to the assistance to be rendered by either power to the other in case of need.[1]

Kuo, who had never been sympathetic with Tso's Sinkiang campaign, was in favour of the British mediation, but to suggest it to Peking at a time when the Chinese forces in Kashgaria were winning was impolitic. Nevertheless, he confided to the British Foreign Office that he would risk his reputation to give the British proposal 'his strong support'.[2] To Li Hung-chang, the arch-advocate of maritime defence, he wrote that China should not lose this opportunity of British mediation to end the Sinkiang campaign.[3] To the court, he advised that China should not endlessly continue to spend money conquering remote territories but should instead act humanely toward outer tribes; that if Yakub Beg agreed to disband his Moslem rebels, surrender a few cities, and ward off the Russian advance, he should be spared. Kuo intimated that Tso was senile and should be kept from the hardships of the frontier.[4] Li Hung-chang, with the rest of the maritime-defence party, were of course encouraged by the British offer of mediation. But Tso Tsung-t'ang energetically argued against it, pointing out that the British offer was designed less to benefit China than to keep Russian influence out of India. Britain, he contended, was motivated by the fear that Yakub Beg's extinction would draw Russia and China closer together, at the expense of the British

---

[1] F.O. 17/825, Foreign Office memorandum, 7 July 1877.

[2] Ibid. Foreign Office memorandum on Kuo's visit to Lord Tenterden, 14 July 1877.

[3] Kuo Sung-tao, *Yang-chih shu-wu ch'üan-chi* (Complete works from the Knowledge-Cultivating Hall), 'Literary Collections', 11: 8b.

[4] *WCSL*, 11: 1–5b.

position in Central Asia. China must not fall into the trap. If Britain wanted to favour Yakub Beg, she could find a place for him on British or Indian soil, but not in Sinkiang. The problem of Ili could be solved only when Yakub Beg was destroyed.[1] The court accepted his reasoning, which was strengthened by his continued victories in Sinkiang. Prince Kung therefore informed Hugh Fraser, British chargé d'affaires in Peking, that Kuo had no authority to negotiate the Kashgarian question in London; only General Tso could settle the problem in Sinkiang.[2]

While all this diplomatic manœuvring was in process, Tso's army was striking with amazing speed into the heart of Kashgaria. Three columns under Generals Liu Chin-t'ang, Chang Yao, and Hsü Chan-piao advanced from Urumchi, Hami, and Barkul respectively. Yakub Beg's army made a poor showing. The Chinese forces took Toksun on 24 April 1877 and Turfan on 16 May. Defeated in war and despairing of his future, Yakub Beg remained in Korla in a state of despondency. On 29 May blood suddenly poured from his nose, and although there was no evidence of sickness he became entirely prostrated and died. The Turkish officer who served with him believed that he was poisoned.[3] Tso also attributed his death to suicide by poisoning,[4] while the Russians believed that he was killed in a fight with his treasurer, Sabir Akhun.[5] The news of his death reached London on 16 July 1877, at the very time Wade was bringing the Chinese minister and the Kashgarian envoy together in his house. The British still hoped to save what was left of the Amir's kingdom, but the internecine and fratricidal strife within Kashgaria itself doomed the project.[6] Hak Kuli Beg, the Amir's second son, was killed by his elder brother, Beg Kuli Beg, in a struggle over the succession.[7] The Kashgarian kingdom was disintegrating from within; only a minor blow from without was needed to consign it to the oblivion of history.

[1] Tso Tsung-t'ang, 'Letters', 17: 30b.
[2] F.O. 17/825, Hugh Fraser's telegrams to F.O., 23 and 24 Sept. 1877.
[3] F.O. 17/826, India Office to F.O., 25 Jan. 1879, enclosing letter No. 247 from the Indian government, giving an account of occurrences in Kashgaria by Muhammad Yusaf Effendi, one of the three Turkish officers sent by the Sultan in 1873 to train Yakub Beg's army. He served in the Amir's army until after Yakub Beg's death.   [4] Tso Tsung-t'ang, 'Memorials', 50: 71b–72.
[5] A. N. Kuropatkin, *Kashgaria*, 248–9.
[6] F.O. 17/825, Wade to Derby, 25 July 1877.
[7] F.O. 17/826, India Office to F.O., 25 Jan. 1879.

Liu Chin-t'ang, the brilliant young general, began to move again in mid-September. He defeated Pai Yen-hu and entered Aksu on 25 October. Kashgar was taken on 25 December 1877, only ninety-five days after he left Turfan.[1] Beg Kuli Beg fled to Russia, as did the elusive Shensi rebel Pai Yen-hu. The Chinese troops pursued Pai all the way to the Russian border, just in time to see him cross the frontier on 28 December and be disarmed by the Russian guards. Tso's disappointment can be imagined; the escape left a loophole in what would otherwise have been a perfect success.[2] The pacification of Sinkiang was nevertheless the crown of Tso's arduous ten-year campaign which had begun in Shensi-Kansu. In grateful appreciation of his victory, the emperor made him a marquis and Liu Chin-t'ang a baron.[3] Prouder than ever, Tso called his accomplishment 'a truly great feat seldom seen since the Ch'in and Han dynasties'.[4] The imperial authority of China was thus once again established in all Sinkiang except for a small pocket in Ili, which was still under Russian occupation, and Peking was now ready to demand its return.[5]

The Russians were caught unprepared by the rapid turn of events in Chinese Turkestan. When they had promised in 1871 to return Ili to China as soon as law and order were restored there, they had not for a moment believed that the Ch'ing government could re-establish its rule in Sinkiang. On later occasions they had declared that they would consider the restitution of Ili after China had reconquered Urumchi and Manas.[6] Yet when Tso satisfied that condition in 1876, Eugene K. Butzow (Biutsov), Russian minister in Peking, stated that Ili was not to be returned until a satisfactory adjustment of the regulations governing overland trade between China and Russia had been made.[7] There was little doubt that the Russians were stalling, and Peking became increasingly impatient. On 20 June 1877 the court asked Tso to 'make a general plan and express his frank opinions quickly and confidentially in a memorial'.[8] Tso responded on 28 July 1877, stating that when they pacified the distant territory of Sinkiang, the founders of

[1] Ch'in Han-ts'ai, 104–5; also Bales, 374–5.
[2] Tso Tsung-t'ang, 'Memorials', 52: 30b.
[3] Ibid. 52: 49–49b.   [4] Tso Tsung-t'ang, 'Letters', 20: 30.
[5] See Note E, p. 199.   [6] *IWSM*, 87: 7b–9b.
[7] *WCSL*, 10: 29.   [8] Tso Tsung-t'ang, 'Memorials', 50: 65–65b.

the dynasty had been guided by a desire to strengthen the position of Mongolia, and the belief that to protect Mongolia was indirectly to protect Peking. Therefore China's position in Sinkiang had to be strengthened, especially in view of the Russian expansion eastward. Russia, he said, was at war with Turkey and a bitter rival of Britain; she could not afford not to return Ili. China had a just cause in demanding its restitution and should insist on it firmly. He summarized by saying: 'The land should not be given up, and the army movements should not be stopped.' To give China a truly strong hold on Sinkiang, he suggested making it a province and an integral part of the empire.[1]

Peking's irritation over Butzow's dilatory tactics was further aggravated by his refusal to extradite the rebel chief, Pai Yen-hu, who had fled to Russia. Repeated communication and conference with him in May 1878 elicited only a non-committal suggestion that Tso get in touch with the governor-general of Russian Turkestan, General K. P. Kaufman, about the matter.[2] Continuously baffled by the evasive attitude of the Russian minister, the Tsungli Yamen decided to send a diplomatic mission to Russia to negotiate directly with the government in St. Petersburg.

The swiftness of this decision may seem a little puzzling, but actually the principle of sending permanent diplomatic missions abroad was approved by the court in May 1875. Chinese missions were sent to England in 1876, to Germany in 1877, and to France, the United States, and Japan in 1878.[3] A mission would have been sent to Russia to establish the Chinese legation, with or without the Ili issue. The intransigence of the Russian minister in China prompted the Ch'ing court to give such a mission the additional task of negotiating the return of Ili. Doubtless precedents of past diplomatic missions to Russia under Tulisen in 1714 and T'o-shih in 1731 and 1732 facilitated this decision.[4] The experiences of the more recent *ad hoc* missions to the West also lent encouragement. Burlingame's resounding success and the speedy settlement of the issues at stake by the missions of apology to France and England in 1870 and 1876 contributed to the feeling that foreign governments seemed

---

[1] Ibid. 50: 75–77b.
[2] *WCSL*, 13: 12–13.
[3] Hsü, *China's Entrance*, 176.
[4] See Note F, pp. 199–200.

more amenable than their servants in China. The transfer of negotiations from Peking to St. Petersburg was therefore a test of the validity of this impression. Successful management of the case would vindicate the Yamen's wisdom in establishing legations abroad. In this sense, the mission to Russia was sent with the hope that it would establish a precedent for future Chinese diplomacy.

CHAPTER II

Ch'ung-hou and the Treaty of Livadia, 1879

FOR the mission to Russia, the court at Peking seems to have first considered Marquis Tseng Chi-tse, son of the great statesman Tseng Kuo-fan, but on the recommendation of the grand councillor Shen Kuei-fen the appointment, to Tseng's chagrin, went to Ch'ung-hou, military governor of Mukden.[1] Ch'ung-hou (1825–93), a Manchu of the Wanyen clan and a member of the Bordered Yellow Banner, took his *chu-jen* degree in 1849. After a number of minor posts, he made his début in foreign affairs in 1858 when assigned to the staff of the famous Mongolian general Seng-ko-lin-ch'in, who was charged with coastal defence in Tientsin against the invading Anglo-French armies under Lord Elgin and Baron Gros. When peace returned in late 1860, he was recommended by Prince Kung to fill the new post of Superintendent of Trade for the Three Northern Ports, in which capacity he directed negotiations of treaties and trade regulations with Denmark, Holland, and Spain in 1863, with Belgium in 1865, with Italy in 1866, and with Austria in 1869. His career in foreign affairs was enhanced by his appointment as chief of the Mission of Apology to France in 1870 as a result of the Tientsin Massacre. After many months of delay due to the siege of Paris during the Franco-Prussian War, he was able to present, on 23 November 1871, the Emperor's letter of regret to the French President Thiers at Bordeaux, the provisional seat of the government, thus officially concluding the case of the Tientsin Massacre.[2] Upon his return to China in early 1872 he was rewarded with the posts of senior vice-president of the Board of War and minister of the Tsungli Yamen. In this latter capacity he participated in the first audience granted to foreign diplomats by Emperor T'ung-chih on 29 June 1873. Thus,

---

[1] W. A. P. Martin, *A Cycle of Cathay* (New York, 1896), 385. (Hereafter to be cited as *Cycle*.)

[2] For a study of Ch'ung-hou's mission to France, see Knight Biggerstaff, 'The Ch'ung Hou Mission to France, 1870–1871', *Nankai Social and Economic Quarterly*, 8: 635–47 (1935–6).

with his wide experience in foreign affairs, it was quite understandable that Peking should choose him for the Russian mission.[1] Foreigners generally liked him; they considered him 'an accomplished gentleman of an agreeable personality' and politer than most mandarins.[2] Sir Thomas Wade, British minister to China, described him as a 'pleasant man' but 'never remarkable for ability'.[3]

I. CH'UNG-HOU'S APPOINTMENT TO RUSSIA

At the time of his appointment, Ch'ung-hou was in Manchuria as military governor of Mukden, a post he had inherited from his deceased brother in 1876. In announcing the appointment the court took special notice of his past performances in an edict dated 22 June 1878:

> Sinkiang has now been pacified, but Ili is still occupied by Russian soldiers and has not been returned. The rebel leader Pai Yen-hu and accomplices, having fled to Russia, have not been handed over either, and questions of treaty revision with the state in question [Russia] have remained unsettled for a long time. Ch'ung-hou, who has always ably discharged his duties and is well acquainted with Chinese foreign affairs, is hereby specially appointed to proceed to [Russia] and stay there to manage affairs according to the circumstances. Let the general in question turn over clearly all the tasks of his present incumbency and come to the capital for an audience in accordance with this edict.[4]

At the audience he was admonished by the Empress Dowager Tz'u-hsi to be doubly cautious with the Russians.[5] Because of the 'delicate' nature of his assignment,[6] he was appointed first-class imperial commissioner, i.e. ambassador, with 'full powers to act as he sees fit'.[7] This special authority, though also given to Ch'i-ying in 1842 when he negotiated the Treaty of Nanking

---

[1] Hummel, i. 209–10.

[2] E. V. G. Kiernan, *British Diplomacy in China, 1880 to 1885* (London, 1939), 40; H. B. Morse, *The International Relations of the Chinese Empire* (Shanghai, 1910–18), ii. 332.

[3] F.O. 418/I/111, Wade to Granville, *confidential*, 19 May 1880.

[4] *WCSL*, 13: 28b.

[5] Weng T'ung-ho, *Weng-wen kung-kung jih-chi* (The diary of Weng T'ung-ho), 18: 92b–93b.

[6] *China: Dispatches*, 48: 22, Chester Holcomb to William M. Evarts, 3 July 1878. (National Archives, Washington, D.C.)

[7] *WCSL*, 13: 28b.

with Sir Henry Pottinger and to Kuei-liang in 1858 when he
negotiated the Treaty of Tientsin with Lord Elgin and Baron
Gros, was not given to other Chinese diplomats abroad, who
were all second-class imperial commissioners, i.e. ministers.
Thus Ch'ung-hou was the only Chinese diplomat abroad who
enjoyed such a high rank and such authority. Tso Tsung-t'ang,
when apprised of the appointment, was well pleased with the
choice and the wide discretionary powers allowed Ch'ung-hou,
hoping that such liberality would facilitate his negotiations.
Tso suggested, however, that while the negotiations might be
carried on in Russia, the treaty be signed in Ili by Ch'ung-hou
and a specially deputed Russian official.[1] Should the diplomatic
mission fail to bring about a desirable outcome, Tso confidentially and confidently told the Tsungli Yamen, he could
settle the issue on the battlefield.[2] 'At present our military might
is at its peak. We can fight if we want to fight. What do we
fear? But we border on Russia in the north-east and north-
west, and once war breaks out, there will be no end to it.'[3]
Tso therefore sternly warned his generals not to provoke a
war, in order to deny the Russians excuse for complaint or
hostility.[3]

Ch'ung-hou planned to take the easy sea route to Russia
rather than the difficult land route via Ili. Chang P'ei-lun, a
reader in the Hanlin Academy, was quick to warn the court
that a negotiator for the return of Ili must be familiar with its
topography to avoid the errors of ignorance in a settlement. To
go to Russia by sea without personal knowledge of the subject-
matter of the negotiations, Chang said, would be like pre-
scribing medicine to a patient without first taking his pulse. He
urged the court to make Ch'ung-hou go by land and consult
with Tso Tsung-t'ang in Sinkiang before proceeding to Russia.
He also protested vigorously against the vast discretionary
powers vested in Ch'ung-hou:

I have heard that Ch'ung-hou is an imperial commissioner with
full powers to act as he sees fit. I have examined Western customs
and practices (and found that if an envoy) is given full powers and
special authority to act as he sees fit, his powers (in practice) are not
limited to a single issue. In case there should be some very important

---

[1] Tso Tsung-t'ang, 'Letters', 21: 15b, 21: 18b.   [2] Ibid. 21: 35.
[3] Ibid. 20: 42b.

matters whose merits and demerits have not been investigated by our envoy, and in case the Russians force him to an immediate answer of 'yes' or 'no', what would happen to the general situation, even if the envoy were to take the blame [for the bad decision]? The British and French ministers represent big nations, but neither has the power to act as he sees fit. Ch'ung-hou's newly added title of Senior Assistant Chamberlain of the Imperial Bodyguard is honourable enough to be in accord with the general rule of international law that envoys who are exchanged be of comparable rank. I humbly submit that an envoy to a distant land be given full powers in substance but not in name. I sincerely pray that your Imperial Highness will review the case with the greatest care and withhold from Ch'ung-hou the authority [lit. name] of full powers to act as he sees fit. When confronted with vital and unprecedented issues, he should memorialize at once for imperial guidance; in this way his position may be somewhat eased. [Otherwise] any matter, no matter how rashly handled by him, will be binding once an agreement is reached. Remorse after an initial recklessness would be of no avail![1]

But the court was not troubled by this warning. It reassured Ch'ung-hou of his authority to act as he saw fit and allowed him to take the sea route to Russia.[2] He was accompanied by about thirty persons, including two Russians: M. Hagan, professor of Russian at Tungwen College, and M. de Poggio, a member of the Russian legation in China.[3] They left Peking on 23 October 1878 and sailed from Shanghai on 8 November 1878, reaching Marseilles on 17 December. After a courtesy call at the French Foreign Office on 21 December he left for Berlin by train and reached St. Petersburg on 31 December 1878.[4]

Ch'ung-hou had come to Russia with the special mission of recovering Ili for China, but he had made virtually no preparations for the task. In Paris, when asked by Minister Kuo Sung-tao about his tactics for the negotiations, he demonstrated complete ignorance of the issues at stake and of the topography of Ili. Apart from declaring that Ili must be returned to China, he could say nothing and was rather displeased with Kuo's questioning. Kuo secretly predicted his failure.[5]

[1] Chang P'ei-lun, *Chien-yü chi* (Works of Chang P'ei-lun), 1: 63–64.
[2] *WCSL*, 15: 31.   [3] F.O. 418/I/1, Hugh Fraser to Salisbury, 23 Oct. 1878.
[4] *WCSL*, 15: 5–6b, H. B. Morse, ii. 332.
[5] Kuo Sung-tao, 'Literary collections', 11: 22b–26.

2. THE TREATY OF LIVADIA

Long before the arrival of Ch'ung-hou, the Russians had been preparing themselves for the Ili issue. By their own admission, it is clear that, when they promised in 1871 to return Ili, they never for a moment believed China could defeat Yakub Beg and regain control of Kashgaria.[1] But as Tso Tsung-t'ang's army advanced within striking distance of Ili in the spring of 1878, the Russians were forced to second thoughts. General G. A. Kolpakovskii, commander in Ili, alerted General K. P. von Kaufman, governor-general of Russian Turkestan, in regard to China's intention of invading Ili from four directions. Though confident that he could defeat the Chinese Kaufman wanted to avoid war, because of the extreme dearth of China experts in his headquarters and because many of his experienced officers and soldiers had been transferred to the Turkish war.[2] He was therefore inclined to advise that Ili be returned to China for a high price. Colonel A. N. Kuropatkin, head of the Asiatic Section of the General Staff in 1878 and a protégé of Kaufman, submitted with his patron's blessing a memorandum to the Chief of the General Staff, Count F. L. Heyden (Geiden), in which he made clear the strategic value of Ili and the desirability of asking £10 million as the price for returning it to China. This vast sum could then be used for the construction of the Siberian railway.[3]

To be sure, the Russian military party headed by Count D. A. Miliutin, minister of War, was opposed to the restitution of Ili on the ground that 'the Asiatics will attribute generosity, or even justice, solely and simply to incapacity to retain what had been taken'.[4] But the Tsar and the Foreign Office considered the return of Ili a debt of honour, and feared that any conflict between Russia and China could only serve Britain.[5] The Tsar ordered the creation of a special committee to study the problem, with Miliutin as chairman, and the following members:

[1] A. N. Kuropatkin, *The Russian Army and the Japanese War* (New York, 1909), i. 92. (Hereafter to be cited as *Japanese War*.)
[2] V. S. Kadnikov, 'Iz istorii Kul'dzhinskago voprosa' (From the history of the Kuldja problem), *Istoricheskii vestnik*, cxxiv. 902 (1911).
[3] Kuropatkin, *Japanese War*, i. 93.
[4] F.O. 418/I/10, Plunkett to Salisbury, 24 Sept. 1879.
[5] C. de Cardonne, *L'Empereur Alexandre II: vingt-six ans de règne, 1855–1881* (Paris, 1883), 617.

N. K. Giers (Girs), assistant minister in the Foreign Office; Admiral S. A. Greig, minister of Finance; Generals Kaufman and Obruchev, and Colonel Kuropatkin.[1]

Kaufman formally recommended to the committee that Ili be returned to China for 120 million roubles, which would be used to construct the Siberian railway. Although stron-gly supported by Kuropatkin, the plan met opposition from Giers and Greig. Both felt that Russia was bound by her pledge to return Ili. Admiral Greig maintained also that Russia was in no particular need of money.[1] On 4/16 March 1878 the committee decided that Russian dignity demanded the restitution of Ili to China, but not before settlement of commercial and border problems between the two countries, including China's pardon of Tungan rebels in Ili.[2]

When Ch'ung-hou arrived in St. Petersburg, the Russians were at first uncertain whether he should be treated as an ambassador or a minister, because his official title, First-class Imperial Commissioner, was not a diplomatic rank. But they soon decided to accord him a flattering welcome. An ostentatious reception considered appropriate for the Orientals was staged for him. 'He was fetched from his hotel in an imperial carriage drawn by six horses, his suite following likewise in an imperial carriage drawn by four horses, and attended by the customary officers of the court.'[3] After the audience with the Tsar on 20 January 1879 a luncheon was served, and then they were conducted back to the hotel in the same manner as they had been conveyed to the palace. Russian high circles continued to give Ch'ung-hou receptions of a 'caressing nature'.[4] There could be little doubt that the Russians were trying to dupe him. Ch'ung-hou, a polite man of pliable disposition rather than a shrewd diplomat, readily fell into their trap. Overwhelmed by Russian cordiality, he expressed himself to F. R. Plunkett, first secretary in the British embassy, as having been much pleased with his reception.[5] He told Peking that he could only

---

[1] Kuropatkin, i. 93.   [2] Miliutin, iii. 124.

[3] F.O. 17/826/40, A. Loftus to Salisbury, St. Petersburg, 28 Jan. 1879.

[4] F.O. 17/826/628, Edwin H. Egerton to Salisbury, Vienna, *confidential*, 2 Oct. 1879, reporting the description of Russian treatment of Ch'ung-hou by Count Kalnóky, Austrian minister in Russia: 'the caressing nature of the reception which the Chinese Embassy has met with in high quarters at St. Petersburgh'.

[5] F.O. 17/826/516, Plunkett to Salisbury, 10 Oct. 1879.

repay Russian courtesy with 'sincerity' in negotiations and assured them repeatedly that 'whatever is beneficial to both countries can certainly be agreed to and put into practice'.[1]

The negotiations on the Russian side were conducted by A. G. Jomini (Zhomini), senior counsellor in the Foreign Office, and E. K. Butzow (Biutsov), minister to China, who had been recalled from Peking to assist in the negotiations. Prince A. M. Gorchakov, officially chancellor and foreign minister, had suffered a political eclipse since the Russian defeat in the Congress of Berlin, and N. K. Giers, the assistant foreign minister, was, for all practical purposes, head of the Foreign Office. Since Giers was accompanying the Tsar on his annual trip to Livadia, the actual burden of negotiations fell on Jomini and Butzow.

In his first telegraphic messages to the Tsungli Yamen on 14 and 16 April 1879 Ch'ung-hou reported hopefully that the Russians did not dispute China's right to repossess Ili but they wanted new trade regulations, border adjustments, and settlement of damages to Russian traders. He also reported his agreement to expand trade and compensate Russia for military expenses in Ili, although the exact sum had not yet been set. The Tsungli Yamen was quite pleased with the early progress of the negotiations, readily admitting that the Russian demand for repayment of occupation expenses was to be expected. It cautioned Ch'ung-hou, however, that the Russians might not easily give up Ili because of its several hundred thousand taels of annual tax income.[2]

On 14 May another message from Ch'ung-hou reached the court, explaining that Moslem rebel leaders like Pai Yen-hu, who had fled to Russia, were not being encouraged by the Russian government; on the contrary, it had agreed to tighten border controls to prevent their return to China to make trouble. If they did cross the border, the Chinese were free to send punitive expeditions against them without incurring Russian ill-feeling. Ch'ung-hou, however, relayed the Russian request for Chinese amnesty to Moslem rebels, so as to make unnecessary their flight into Russia. He stressed the importance of pardoning them if China did not want to receive an Ili empty of people. He also suggested that a high official be appointed to

[1] *WCSL*, 15: 31–32.   [2] Ibid. 15: 16–17, Memorial of 21 Apr. 1879.

confer with a high Russian official about the details of taking over Ili and the settlement of its borders.[1]

The Tsungli Yamen, having long been frustrated by Russian dilatory tactics, was excited by the rapid progress of the negotiations and the good prospect of recovering Ili, although it suspected a Russian ruse. To prepare for taking over Ili and settling its borders, it recommended to the court that a high official known to the Russians be appointed.[2] For this position, Hsi-lun, councillor at Chuguchak, was selected. He was ordered to consult, before meeting with the Russian representatives, with Tso Tsung-t'ang and Chin-shun, the military governor of Ili, about the repossession of Ili. On 27 May 1879 Tso was ordered by the court to be merciful toward the Moslem population of the cities he would take over, and not to kill anyone except the leaders of the rebels.[3]

The Russians too were quite satisfied with the early progress of the negotiations. Jomini reported to Giers on 17/29 May: 'The Chinese negotiation is going on slowly but well. Butzow is not losing sight of the amnesty.'[4]

The Russian special committee on Ili met again on 18/30 June to discuss the terms for the restitution of Ili. Kaufman, Obruchev, and Kuropatkin, having just returned from a trip to Ili, now recommended Ili's return at the price of sixty million roubles on condition that the Sino-Russian frontiers be left as they were.[5] Giers and Admiral Greig found the suggestion of such a huge sum damaging to Russian dignity, and the latter furiously stated that Russia should not imitate British commercialism. Kaufman sarcastically drew an analogy between the admiral's prideful poverty and the vanity of the proverbial Spanish lord who wore an empty money-bag, full of holes, underneath an embroidered coat.[6] After some heated debate, most of the committee members concluded that China was not in a position to pay so large a sum, and decided to set five million roubles instead as the price for the return of Ili.[7]

---

[1] *WCSL*, 15: 25–26b; 15: 27–28.   [2] Ibid. 15: 27–28.   [3] Ibid. 15: 28.
[4] Jelavich, 91, Jomini to Giers, 17/29 May 1879.
[5] Miliutin, iii. 149.
[6] Kadnikov, 907.
[7] Ibid. According to a Russian general's estimate, the total cost to Russia of occupying Ili from 1871 to 1881 amounted to no more than 2,265,400 roubles. See M. A. Terent'ev, iii. 254.

The committee decided further that Russia should keep part of Ili for strategic reasons, and seek new commercial privileges and border readjustments.[1] All in all, the Russians were determined to secure an impressive spoil in China to compensate for their loss at the Congress of Berlin.[2]

Ch'ung-hou telegraphed to Peking on 11 and 13 July transmitting the Russian request for an immediate relaxation of the trade ban. The Yamen would not comply with it before the settlement of the Kashgaria border and the Russian occupation expenses, apprehensive as it was that once the Russians were given the trade privilege they might delay the restitution of Ili. The Yamen was willing to lift the trade ban simultaneously with the return of Ili, but not before.[3] Tso Tsung-t'ang was instructed by the court to refuse admission of Russian traders before the actual recovery of Ili.

In St. Petersburg Butzow continued to play his 'caressing' game with Ch'ung-hou, intimating constantly that Russian occupation expenses, though unfixed, would not be large. In hearty appreciation of what he took to be generosity, Ch'ung-hou again urged Peking to lift the trade ban immediately. The Yamen was somewhat nettled; it cautioned him against rash action, saying bluntly that the suggestion was 'tantamount to not getting Ili back or even worse'. The Yamen took pains to point out that 'foreigners are wholly unfathomable by nature. Often we have carried out our commitment on what is beneficial to them, but they refuse to carry out what is beneficial to us'. It called for prudence and stressed the advisability of simultaneous settlement of all issues: trade, boundaries, occupation expenses, and the return of Ili. The court instructed Ch'ung-hou to hold firm and not to give in on the first three items before the restitution of Ili.[4]

At this point a message came from Ch'ung-hou which shocked Peking immeasurably. The Russians now demanded revision of the boundaries in Kashgaria, Ili, and Tarbagatai set by General Ming-i and the Russians in 1864. A Russian map showing the proposed frontiers was attached to Ch'ung-hou's message, and the Yamen was astonished to discover that

---

[1] Kadnikov, 908.
[2] For Russia's defeat at the Congress of Berlin, see Chapter VIII, section 1.
[3] *WCSL*, 15: 33–34.
[4] Ibid. 15: 35–36b.

hundreds of square *li* of territory in the southern and western part of Ili were to be ceded, leaving the main part of Ili entirely isolated from the other eight cities in the south. Ili would thus be bounded by Russian territory on three sides and become indefensible. The Yamen considered this Russian demand 'utterly inadmissible', advising the court that this kind of restitution was no better, and possibly even worse, than no restitution at all.[1] Tso Tsung-t'ang, when apprised of the situation, urged that China should insist not only on the return of all Ili but also its spacious outskirts for defensive purposes. He suggested that Ch'ung-hou concern himself only with the general principles of the boundaries without making any detailed arrangements, which should be decided by special Chinese and Russian officials on the spot. In a sarcastic vein he remarked: 'Our envoy has stated that he wanted to move them [the Russians] by sincerity, but I am afraid that Butzow's greedy and crafty heart cannot be moved by sincerity.'[2]

From all sources, it seems that Ch'ung-hou was in a great hurry to conclude his assignment. On 27 August the Yamen learned from him that reimbursement for occupation expenses had been fixed at five million roubles and that the Russian government had ordered General Kaufman to hand over Ili to China. When Ch'ung-hou once again urged the court to lift the trade ban, the Yamen reluctantly assented to his plea, to forestall any Russian excuse for delaying the restitution of Ili. The court thereupon approved the resumption of trade with Russia.[3]

Ch'ung-hou's anxiety to leave Russia may be seen in his acceptance of the Russian claim to the five million roubles compensation without a fight. He also accepted, after some perfunctory debate, the Russian request for navigation rights in the Sungari River up to 600 versts at Potuna.[4] When a draft treaty was prepared, he asked for a telegraphic reply from Giers in Livadia on whether the Tsar would sanction it. Jomini reported to Giers on 31 August/11 September: 'The Chinese ambassador is in a great hurry to be finished with it!'[5] On 9/21 September

---

[1] *WCSL*, 16: 2–3b, Memorial of 27 Aug. 1879.
[2] Ibid. 16: 4–8.   [3] Ibid. 16: 10–11b.
[4] Jelavich, 92, Jomini to Giers, 21 Aug./2 Sept. A *versta* is nearly two-thirds of a mile.   [5] Ibid. 94, Jomini to Giers, 31 Aug./11 Sept.

Jomini again reported to Giers about Ch'ung-hou's haste to be off: 'The Chinese keeps hoping to leave by Saturday.'[1] Giers could not have secured a better treaty, for it gave Russia practically everything she wanted. Upon learning of the Tsar's approval of the draft treaty, Ch'ung-hou set out for Livadia to sign the treaty. Giers, perhaps with the guilty conscience of one who has deceived a gullible foreigner, conceded: 'The arrival of the Chinese frightens me a bit.'[2]

On 22 and 30 September and 2 October Ch'ung-hou repeatedly telegraphed to Peking of the completion of his mission and his imminent return to China. The general contents of the treaty were reported by him as follows:

1. Russia consents to return Ili.
2. China consents to pardon the inhabitants of Ili.
3. The transfer of Ili is to be conducted by General Kaufman and Tso Tsung-t'ang.
4. The Tekes Valley and the passes in Tien-shan leading to Kashgar and Khokand are to be ceded to Russia.
5. China agrees to pay an occupation fee of five million roubles.
6. China grants Russia permission to establish consulates at Hami, Turfan, Urumchi, Kobdo, Uliasutai, Ku-ch'eng, and Chia-yü-kuan.
7. Russian merchandise is to be free of duties in Mongolia and the north and south sides of the Tien-shan ranges.
8. Russian traders may transport their goods to and from Chia-yü-kuan, Kalgan, Tientsin, and Hankow by way of Sian, Han-chung, and Tungchow.
9. Ratifications of the treaty are to be exchanged in St. Petersburg within one year.[3]

The ministers of the Tsungli Yamen were dumbfounded and appalled to find that their experienced man Ch'ung-hou had made such excessive concessions without the express consent of his government. The Yamen hurriedly cabled to Ch'ung-hou that the terms could by no means be accepted, whereupon he replied by telegraph: 'The treaty having been clearly settled, it is absolutely impossible to re-negotiate.'[4]

[1] Ibid. 95, Jomini to Giers, 9/21 Sept.
[2] Ibid. 149, Giers to Jomini, 11/23 Sept.
[3] *WCSL*, 16: 25–28, English text in *USFR* (1879–80), 266.
[4] *WCSL*, ibid.

On 2 October 1879 Ch'ung-hou, on his own authority, without the prior approval of his government, signed the Treaty of Livadia and three other documents: (1) a code of trade regulations, (2) an agreement regarding the payment of the five million roubles through Messrs. Baring Brothers, and (3) an agreement with respect to the Russian right of navigation on the Sungari River up to Potuna.[1] Even before all this information had reached Peking, Wade was able to surmise from the ministers of the Yamen that 'they did not seem to be satisfied with it'.[2] Ch'ung-hou himself, however, was so confident of Peking's acceptance of the treaty that he assumed the ratifications would be exchanged within four months.[3] He apparently did not realize what he had done. As he left Russia he thanked the Tsar and the Russian Foreign Office for their 'high consideration', their 'confidence' and 'goodwill'.[4] The London *Mail*, in an article entitled 'The Kuldja Question', was quick to comment caustically: 'Kuldja has been regained, and that in the eyes of the Chinese is worth a great price; but when it is perceived that Russia will still hold the province practically under her authority, it is much to be doubted if either the generals in Central Asia or the Ministers in Pekin will deem that there is much cause to feel grateful to the Czar.'[5] The author cast doubts on the acceptability of the treaty to Peking, stressing the cession of the Tekes Valley and the indemnity of five million roubles. Ch'ung-hou left St. Petersburg by train on 11 October 1879 for Germany and France, and then returned by boat to China.[6]

The Russians were of course overwhelmed by the favourable terms of the Treaty of Livadia, but after the initial elation had subsided they began to have doubts about the Chinese ratification. Jomini confided to Giers that 'after all, a treaty is definitive only after the ratification'.[7] It was indeed a question whether Peking would accept the treaty!

---

[1] F.O. 418/I/265, Plunkett to Granville, *secret*, 21 Sept. 1880.

[2] F.O. 17/826/88, Wade to Salisbury, telegram, 2 Oct. 1879.

[3] F.O. 418/I/9, Plunkett to Salisbury, 20 Sept. 1879.

[4] F.O. 418/I/143, Consul A. W. Hewlett, in Canton, to Lord Tenterden, 10 July 1880, inclosure 9, Ch'ung-hou's communication to the Russian government.

[5] This article is enclosed in *China: Dispatches*, 52: 578, Seward to Evarts, 30 Jan. 1880.   [6] *WCSL*, 18: 1–1b.

[7] Jelavich, 96, Jomini to Giers, 30 Sept./11 Oct.

3. CHINESE RESPONSE TO THE TREATY

The Tsungli Yamen, upon learning the general contents of the treaty from Ch'ung-hou's telegrams of 22 and 30 September and 2 October, was greatly alarmed by the cession of the Tekes Valley and the Muzart and Talki Passes. Such territorial loss would isolate Ili and cut away the two main lines of communication with the eight southern cities. From the military standpoint it meant in effect the end of China's control of Ili, hence of Sinkiang. Other items, such as Russian retention of business and properties in Ili after its restitution, and establishment of Russian consulates and storehouses in seven key places, were certain to create untold troubles and complications in the future. Apart from the occupation expense of five million roubles or 2·80 million taels, which the Yamen was resigned to accepting without quibbling, the treaty was found totally unacceptable and impracticable. But the Yamen feared that an outright rejection of the treaty would bring forth a Russian accusation of Chinese bad faith.[1] China was in a dilemma, and the Yamen described it at great length to the court on 8 October 1879:

Your ministers have stated in their previous memorials that restitution of Ili (in this way) was like non-restitution or even worse. Our anxieties proved to be not unwarranted. Ch'ung-hou has been engaged in foreign affairs for years and is well informed on border and commercial affairs. There is no reason to suppose that he has not struggled hard to keep whatever is beneficial and harmless to China. His agreement to the treaty, it can be imagined without saying, must have been caused by insatiable Russian demands. When your ministers received his letters on border arrangements, they immediately telegraphed him: '(Arrangements) in your letters will hurt the whole situation in Moslem Sinkiang', and 'Too many concessions have been made in your outlined report; they definitely cannot be permitted', whereupon Ch'ung-hou sent a telegraphic reply, saying: 'The treaty having been clearly settled, it is absolutely impossible to re-negotiate.'

Your ministers humbly submit that others may make demands but it is up to us to consent or not. Although it is important that Ch'ung-hou recover Ili, when there are so many damaging points in the border and commercial settlements he should have deliberated and arranged them prudently. It is utterly beyond comprehension how

[1] *WCSL*, 16: 25–28, Memorial of 8 Oct. 1879.

he could have concluded negotiations with [the Russians] so care-
lessly.

Although Ch'ung-hou's telegrams and letters that have been sent
to us contain such phrases as 'all arrangements must be approved
(by the Emperor) before they can be put into practice,'—a condition
which we may fall back on—yet in view of the vast differences
between Chinese and foreign conditions, we have no assurance at all
(that we can do so). We know that the revised British treaty of 1869
[the Alcock Convention], which has not been ratified by them [the
British government], has not been put into practice even today.
Since the present Russian treaty has the stipulation that it is operative
only after the ratification, it seems that we may also brush it aside
and make it inactive. Nevertheless, if we agree first and reject later,
we are at fault. Assuming (the Russians) as an enemy, (we may
expect them) to use this occasion as an excuse not only for not
returning Ili at all, but also for making a lavish number of (extra-
neous) demands and threats, on the pretext of treaty revision and
border settlement. Foreigners see only profit. They incessantly fight
for profit even when China has not agreed to give. How will they
give up something that China has already agreed to give?[1]

The Yamen submitted to the court for comparison a Chinese
map of Ili and a Russian map that Ch'ung-hou had sent back.
It stressed the fact that the long frontier between China and
Russia made effective defence extremely difficult. Rejection of
the treaty might result in Russian invasion, but acceptance
would create untold future complications. There was no way out
of this dilemma, and the Yamen requested the court to ask for
suggestions from Tso Tsung-t'ang, Li Hung-chang, Chin-shun,
and Hsi-lun. The court accordingly ordered them to find out
whether the important strategic passes had been ceded away;
if they had been, China would definitely reject the treaty. Tso
was further instructed to be prepared to defend the border.[2]

(a) Tso Tsung-t'ang's Attitude

When the contents of the treaty were made generally known,
there was an uproar in Chinese officialdom. Tso Tsung-t'ang
feared that the fruit of his labour was about to be snatched
away. In fact, even before he learned of the general contents of
the treaty, he had grown dissatisfied with Ch'ung-hou's work.

---

[1] *WCSL*, 16: 25–28.   [2] Ibid. 16: 28b–29.

The Tsungli Yamen had sent him records of conversations between Ch'ung-hou and Butzow, and Tso was struck with the former's pliability. In a letter to his leading general, Liu Chint'ang, he wrote: 'Our envoy takes no firm stand and grants (concessions) too readily. Little did he know that when these people [the Russians] are given an inch they want a foot. It is hardly proper to take a conciliatory stand, for it can only invite arguments. When our envoy was first sent, I told the Tsungli Yamen in a letter that the mission could not be accomplished by too hard or too soft (a method). But what has happened is exactly what I feared.'[1] He offered to tell the Russians: 'We have a just cause; you cannot deceive us.'[1]

When apprised of Ch'ung-hou's cession of the Tekes Valley in violation of his instructions, and his refusal to reopen the negotiations for the simple reason that the treaty had already been copied out, Tso burst out. To his friend and confidential assistant, Yang Shih-ch'üan, he wrote:

> Our emissary Ch'ung-hou has absurdly and ridiculously concluded the negotiations and talks about a quick return home. This is just his way of getting out of the assignment. Although he may sign a treaty with their [the Russian] government, it is effective only after our Imperial Highness's approval. Much can still be done during the interval and (the case) is completely different from 'agreement first, rejection later'. Speaking practically, the whole thing hinges on how strong or how weak we are. If we are strong we can make justice out of injustice; if we are not strong our justice will be taken as injustice. It has been so in ancient as well as in modern times. The life and death, ebb and flow of a state depend on force and not totally on justice. Now that our emissary has signed a treaty in violation of his instructions, the imperial edicts have already disputed (his authority) and disowned (his act). (The treaty) naturally will not be ratified. This is not a case of bad faith.[2]

To strengthen China's military position, Tso offered to move his headquarters to the advanced Hami outpost. On 26 September 1879 he recommended to the court that it compensate liberally for Russian occupation expenses and constructions in Ili in the old tradition of benevolent treatment of alien tribes, but that it reject outright the border and

[1] Tso Tsung-t'ang, 'Letters', 23: 9, 10b-11.
[2] Ibid. 23: 32b; 23: 40-40b.

commercial arrangements. He urged that the Sino-Russian frontiers be maintained as stipulated in the Ming-i treaty of 1864, that no Russian consulate be permitted in Chia-yü-kuan, and that no Russian trade be allowed to extend beyond it.[1]

When the full text of the treaty, as opposed to the outline of its contents which he had received so far, was sent to him by the Tsungli Yamen on 19 November 1879, Tso was further outraged. He furiously condemned the Russian annexation of the southern and western portions of Ili as an intolerable act of naked aggression. The loss of the southern area would isolate Ili, he contended, and the loss of the western area would deprive Ili of its two major reinforcement routes. Militarily, Ili's position would become indefensible, lying helplessly at the mercy of the Russian forces.[2]

Tso launched another vehement attack on the treaty on 4 December 1879, when he responded to the 8 October edict asking for comments from several leading officials. To recover Ili in the manner prescribed by the Ch'ung-hou treaty, he pointedly remarked, was to obtain an empty city with some barren suburbs, which were liable to be lost to Russia at any time. 'When a state is devoid of military strength, cession of territory and begging for peace may be in order. But without firing a shot (Ch'ung-hou) has abruptly decided to give away important territory to satisfy their [Russian] greed. It is like throwing a bone to a dog; when the bone is finished with, it [the dog] will bark again. The immediate dangers being so obvious, how much more so would be the future ones! This is a matter of bitter regret and profound disappointment.' He warned of Russia's territorial designs and insisted on the disavowal of the border arrangements at all costs.[3]

As a way out of the dilemma, Tso suggested the combined use of diplomacy and force. 'We shall first confront them with arguments, in a specious and contriving way, and then settle it on the battlefield, with resolute fortitude to gain the final victory.'[4] He offered once again to advance his headquarters to Hami and deploy his troops on the two sides of the Tien-shan Mountains. 'With one mind in the whole state, standing firm

[1] Tso Tsung-t'ang, 'Memorials', 55: 3–9.   [2] Idem, 'Letters', 23: 46b.
[3] Idem, 'Memorials', 55: 31–40; *WCSL*, 18: 2–8.
[4] Tso Tsung-t'ang, 'Memorials', 55: 38

and steadfast, we can keep the general situation under control.' To sustain his military arrangements, he asked Peking to remind the treasury and the provinces of their allotted contributions to his army, totalling five million taels annually. As to the restitution of Ili, he said it should not be effected under the miserable conditions of the treaty. China had better postpone its return until the territorial arrangements had been satisfactorily settled.[1]

Thus, we see, the old soldier Tso was not single-mindedly advocating war as the only way to lift China from its predicament. He wanted diplomacy first; only when diplomacy had failed would China resort to war. In this sense he was not a war-monger, as many foreigners liked to depict him. The court found his dual policy of diplomacy and war highly acceptable, and his catchwords, 'First confront them with arguments . . . then settle it on the battlefield', became the guiding principle in state planning.[2] Appreciatively, the court approved Tso's military arrangements on the two sides of the Tien-shan.

(b) *Li Hung-chang's Reaction*

Li, the grand secretary and governor-general of Chihli, was the leading spirit of maritime defence against Japan and a strong advocate of peace and friendship with Russia. From the start he was not sympathetic with Tso's campaign in the north-west; nor did he favour the policy of pressing Russia for the return of Ili. In response to the court's request for comment on the treaty, Li expressed his views in a long memorial which reached the court on 15 November 1879. To safeguard his position he started out with an accusation of Russian duplicity and intrigue, but all along he indicated or implied that what had transpired was exactly what he had expected. 'Chinese scholar-officials are accustomed to viewing foreign missions with misgivings. In time of peace few ever study Russian affairs. . . . Making plans for the Western Region in the past, your minister feared most that the recovery of the lost land might be only in name and not in reality.'[3] Thus he implied that China's lack of international experience and sufficient knowledge of Russia presaged Ch'ung-hou's failure. It was also

---

[1] Ibid.   [2] Ibid. 55: 39b–40.   [3] *WCSL*, 17: 16–19.

a polite way of vindicating his policy of not insisting on the return of Ili. But since Ch'ung-hou had performed badly, Li felt compelled to pass judgement on him: 'Probably Ch'ung-hou considered his chief duty to be the restitution of Ili. When he fulfilled his mission of recovering the territory, he did not bother to examine carefully the advantages and disadvantages of the other issues. He was indeed too reckless!' With this mild and politic reprimand to Ch'ung-hou, Li felt more secure in defending the treaty in an artful way. The monetary compensation of five million roubles was not found excessive, and he surmised that Ch'ung-hou must have been so overwhelmed by the modesty of the sum demanded that he relaxed his watchfulness on the other issues. Although Li conceded that loss of the southern area would isolate Ili from the other eight cities on the southern side of the Tien-shan Mountains, he did not feel that the cession of western Ili was too harmful. While he agreed with the Tsungli Yamen that restitution of Ili in this way was tantamount to non-restitution, and predicted that Tso Tsung-t'ang would never agree to it, Li did not favour outright rejection of the treaty:

The present mission of Ch'ung-hou had its origin in an imperial edict which endowed him with full powers to act as he saw fit. We cannot say that he had no power to negotiate a treaty settlement. If we agree first and reject later, we are at fault. In international relations since time immemorial, the first essential is to decide whether a cause is just. If our cause is unjust, we only ask for insult. The way of the militarist also considers the just or unjust nature (of war). If our cause is unjust, our army cannot be strong. In Sino-Western relations today, it is especially important that we place ourselves in a completely just position without even (a shred) of injustice. If after losing Ili we further incur the opprobrium of being unjust, we shall be ridiculed by foreign nations, and suffer even more. Furthermore, (the Russians) inevitably will put us under pressure from time to time on pretexts of border demarcation and treaty revision. Continual pressure will lead unavoidably to war.

Once war broke out, he believed, defence of the long frontiers of China was impossible. Japan, with her designs on the Liu-ch'iu islands, might take advantage of the situation, and Britain and France might also fish in the troubled waters of China to demand treaty revision. Li thus warned that rejection of the treaty might produce even greater evils than would acceptance.

Li thereupon suggested two remedies for these difficulties. First, he recommended arguing for revision of the treaty's border and commercial stipulations just before exchange of ratifications took place, and if this proved futile, to ask Tso Tsung-t'ang to take charge of the situation in view of his geographical proximity to the scene of dispute. Second, he suggested a pool of talents in the Tsungli Yamen and the provinces to draw up safe trade regulations and appoint able men as trade superintendents at Kalgan and on the frontiers. In short, Li's twofold approach was to 'establish (good) regulations and appoint (able) men'. The long state paper was concluded with a careful reservation that Ch'ung-hou's telegrams were too simple to permit full comments, which could be made only when the complete text of the treaty and Ch'ung-hou's personal explanations were available.[1]

By this time Ch'ung-hou had returned to China. Hearing about the uproar against him, he went to Paoting to see Li before going to Peking to report his mission. He took pains to point out that the treaty, though imperfect, was the result of half a year's bargaining with the Russians. He maximized the strong opposition of the Russian officers and civilians to the return of Ili because of its strategic value. He indicated that it was entirely the result of his hard work and the kind consideration of the Tsar, mindful of the two-hundred-year-old Russo-Chinese friendship, that all Russian opposition to its restitution was finally overruled. Li listened with a sympathetic ear and warned the Tsungli Yamen of the inadvisability of rejecting the treaty: 'We have now fortunately settled (the dispute) once and for all. If we propose changes in a treaty that has already been settled, certainly they will not agree to it. If the exchange of ratifications does not take place at the appointed time, we shall fall right into the original trap of the Russians; there will be untold future troubles.' Li relayed Ch'ung-hou's defence of the territorial loss in the treaty: the land north of Chuguchak had virtually been lost to Russia long ago and could not be considered newly ceded by Ch'ung-hou, while the old boundaries of Kashgaria were still as they had been. The only territory,

[1] *WCSL*, 17: 16–19.

therefore, that China lost under the treaty was the barren land between the two mountains south of Ili. Li attempted to strengthen his plea for peace by quoting letters from Generals Liu Chin-t'ang and Chang Yao, leading lieutenants of Tso, to show that they also favoured an early peace and retirement from the frontiers. With these as support Li was encouraged to state in direct language: 'Our military (morale) is not vigorous. It may be outwardly strong but inwardly [it is] dried up. Any break with Russia will create great trouble. I sincerely hope that your Yamen will take charge of important policy and not be swayed by irresponsible public opinion. If this can be done, it will indeed be fortunate for all concerned.'[1]

The comments by Tso and Li on the treaty reflected their old feud over the relative importance of inland defence and maritime defence. Their views on war and peace also revealed their personal conflict. Knowing full well that Tso advocated rejecting the treaty, Li sarcastically wrote to the Yamen: 'His Excellency Tso insisted on rejecting the border arrangement and wanted to move his headquarters to Hami to threaten the Russians, hoping to make them reduce or change some of the treaty stipulations. This will never work.'[1] Tso, always arrogant and ready to launch a counter-attack, had no kind words for Li either. He impressed upon the court that the more China retreated the more Russia would advance, and that the inevitable future troubles would not be limited to north-western China. Li's advocacy of peace and acceptance of the treaty he likened to the prescription of a quack doctor: 'A man who is sick with abdominal swelling from constipation cannot be cured by a mild and sweet-tasting medicine. A quack doctor sees only what is before his eyes and dares not prescribe a powerful drug. The swelling disease and the patient will end together, and there will be no day when the disease will go and the man recover. Is the Sino-Russian relation today any different from this case?'[2]

Shen Pao-chen, governor-general of Liang-Kiang, also spoke strongly against the treaty. The cession of new territory to compensate for the return of Ili was described as 'cutting away a sound part of the body to cure an inflamed ulcer'. Rejection

---

[1] Li Hung-chang, 'Letters to Tsungli Yamen', 10: 17–17b.
[2] Tso Tsung-t'ang, 'Memorials', 55: 41–42b, dated 14 Dec. 1879.

of the treaty was not bad faith, since ratification of the treaty by the sovereign was recognized by the general rules of international law as well as by the treaty itself. He argued:

> If the worst comes to the worst, it would still be better for us to make an honourable declaration that we will not demand Ili, so as to block the multitudinous (Russian) demands and intrigues. I am thoroughly aware that we should not give up a foot or even an inch of our ancestors' (land); how do I dare to risk the bad reputation of asking for an abandonment of territory? But since our gain is compromised by our loss, it [my proposal] is nothing more than exchanging one plan for another. When the gain does not compensate for the loss, the gain is only nominal without reality, not to mention the unpredictable future troubles. There is the saying, 'Between the two evils, choose the lesser one,' and also, 'When a poisonous snake bites the hand, the courageous man cuts off the wrist.' A good chess-player will never spoil the whole game by favouring one piece.[1]

Shen recommended that, failing an outright rejection of the treaty, it would be advisable to sacrifice Ili to recoup the other losses. Kuo Sung-tao, ex-minister in London and Paris, recommended rejection of the treaty and a delay in repossessing Ili so that the Russian attempt to make China cede new territory would be blocked.[2]

(c) Ch'ung-hou's Defence

After his meeting with Li, Ch'ung-hou fearfully went to Peking. To the court he magnified the difficulties he encountered in Russia, exaggerating the intransigence of Giers and Butzow. He contended, as he had earlier to Li, that he had been able to secure the treaty only after half a year of hard bargaining at several dozen meetings with the Russians. 'Your minister argued exhaustively on those issues that he knew they would not agree to, and compromised a little on those issues that were not objectionable.' He reminded the court of the old promise of the late Grand Secretary Wen-hsiang to the Russian ex-minister in Peking, General Vlangaly, that China would give a 'handsome reward' for the return of Ili. It was in this spirit, Ch'ung-hou stated, that he had agreed to pay Russia five million roubles for its occupation expenses. As to Russian navigation in the

---

[1] *WCSL*, 17: 6b–7b.
[2] Kuo Sung-tao, 'Memorials', 12: 13 ff.

Sungari River, the stipulation permitting it first appeared in the Treaty of Aigun in 1858; it was not he who had made the promise. On the contrary, he had succeeded in limiting Russian shipping in the Sungari to Potuna. He implied that he should not be held responsible for the two stipulations on monetary compensation and navigation in the Sungari.

The sensitive issue of territorial cession was defended very cleverly by Ch'ung-hou. He maximized, as he had with Li, the opposition of the Russian military personnel and public opinion to the restitution of Ili because of its high strategic value, and emphasized that only his persistent pleading and the age-old friendship between China and Russia finally had moved the Tsar to overrule all opposition and agree to return it. However, the Russians felt that their position after the restitution would be drastically weakened; hence the need to acquire some Chinese territory to consolidate their boundaries. Ch'ung-hou piously hoped that his treaty, whatever its merits or demerits, might have the beneficent effect of restoring Ili to the dynasty, improving the livelihood of the border peoples, and maintaining friendly relations with a neighbouring state.[1]

The court instructed the Tsungli Yamen and Li Hung-chang to examine Ch'ung-hou's defence. The Yamen reported first: 'The original purpose of Ch'ung-hou's mission to the West [Russia] this time was to negotiate for the return of (Ili). When the Russians promised to return Ili, Ch'ung-hou thought that he had recovered our old territory and had not wasted his journey. Consequently in the trade issue he settled with them too rashly and hastily, and in the boundary issue he compromised too much.'[2]

Li Hung-chang's review of Ch'ung-hou's defence reached the court on 21 January 1880. Having now examined the complete text of the treaty, he also concluded that Ch'ung-hou had been duped. No longer so conciliatory as before, he recommended that four items in the treaty be definitely rejected: (1) the territorial arrangements in Ili, Kashgaria, and Chuguchak, (2) the trade arrangements in Sinkiang, Inner and Outer Mongolia, (3) the transportation of Russian merchandise directly to Hankow, and (4) navigation of Russian ships to

---

[1] *WCSL*, 17: 20–24b.
[2] Ibid. 17: 27–27b.

Potuna. He advised that the Tsungli Yamen resolutely take up these issues with the Russians before the exchange of ratifications. The objective would be to solve the long-range problem of Russian-Chinese hostility and war rather than to limit attention to a piecemeal and temporary solution of the present problems. Li explained that his suggestions, though they might sound vague and high-flown, should not be regarded as a device to shift the burden of solution to the Yamen. Rather they had been made solely to benefit the general planning.[1]

The Empress Dowager Tz'u-hsi was exasperated with the terms of the treaty. She was said to have cried out in a fit of anger: 'Ch'ung-hou must die.'[2] It was only after some very tactful remonstrance by her brother-in-law Prince Ch'un and the Grand Secretary Pao-yün—in view of the danger of shocking foreign sympathies—that she did not kill Ch'ung-hou at once.[3] On 21 January 1880 she called a grand conference of forty-five high officials to study the treaty,[4] and announced:

> We have unjustly suffered from this case for a long time but never did we expect that (the Russians) would force the issue in such an utterly unbearable way. If we accept it (the treaty), we cannot face our ancestors above, nor can we face our people below. . . . (The issue of) border demarcation must be definitely rejected, and the existing trade conditions need not be changed. . . . Before Ch'ung-hou took leave I repeatedly instructed him that he should only accept what could be granted and reject what could not. I had not expected that he would turn out to be so ridiculously absurd. Let his crime be carefully examined along with (the treaty).[5]

In response to this call, a barrage of memorials poured into the court from all quarters of the empire. Ting Pao-chen, governor-general of Szechwan, memorialized that if war was

---

[1] Ibid. 18: 23–25b.

[2] F.O. 418/I/140, Wade to Granville, *confidential*, 2 June 1880, reporting a conversation with Li Hung-chang.

[3] Ibid. Li told Wade: 'You know a woman's temper.'

[4] These officials included (1) princes of the first and second order, (2) three ministers of the Presence, (3) five members of the Grand Council, (4) nine members of the Tsungli Yamen, (5) six members of the Grand Secretariat, (6) presidents of the Six Boards: Civil Office, Revenue, Ceremonies, War, Punishments, and Public Works, (7) six members of the Censorate, and (8) Prince Chün, father of the boy Emperor. (F.O. 418/I/33, Wade to Salisbury, 8 Feb. 1880, Inclosure 2.)

[5] Weng T'ung-ho, 18: 92b–93b.

unavoidable, he would volunteer as a special emissary to Russia, to argue with the Russians in order to gain time for Chinese military preparations. He also offered 300,000 taels annually from the Szechwan treasury to finance military action.[1] Chin-shun, military-governor of Ili who assisted Tso in his campaign, was exasperated by the cession of the Tekes Valley and the Muzart Pass. He vigorously warned that China should not allow Russia 'to choke her throat and climb on her back'. On the one hand, he urged that the Tsungli Yamen and Tso Tsung-t'ang continue to argue with the Russians without a halt. On the other, he offered to station strong forces in Urumchi and Kashgar, and train soldiers and local populations in farming and military colonization to prepare for a long war of attrition.[2] His colleague, Hsi-lun, councillor at Chuguchak (Tarbagatai), recommended postponing the restitution of Ili, urging the need for strengthening border defences first.[3]

(d)   Chang Chih-tung's Advocacy of War

The most outspoken and eloquent critic of the treaty was a rising young scholar, whose incisive arguments and fine prose style projected him into the centre of the political arena overnight. Chang Chih-tung (1837–1909), a humble librarian of the Supervisorate of Imperial Instruction, in an eloquent memorial using all the literary skills at his command, recited a number of compelling reasons for rejecting the treaty: permission for Russians to trade and transport goods in inland China would enable them to penetrate deep into the recesses of China; allowing Russian navigation in the Sungari River in the homeland of the Manchu dynasty would encourage other foreign nations to demand the same; exemption of Russian traders from taxes in Sinkiang and Mongolia would extend the same right to other foreign traders through the most-favoured-nation clause in the several treaties; establishment of Russian consulates in Hami, Urumchi, and elsewhere would place the whole of Sinkiang under their influence, and if other foreign powers invoked the most-favoured-nation treatment, then all

---

[1] Ting Pao-chen, *Ting-wen-ch'eng-kung tsou-kao* (Memorials of Ting Pao-chen), 18: 34–38.
[2] *WCSL*, 18: 32b–35, 9 Feb. 1880.   [3] Ibid. 19: 17–19, 24 Mar. 1880.

China would be filled with foreign officials; and payment of
five million roubles for a useless, empty Ili was ridiculous.

In beautifully balanced and parallel sentences, he argued
against the ratification of the treaty:

> The Russians must be considered extremely covetous and truculent
> in making the demands, and Ch'ung-hou extremely stupid and
> absurd in accepting them. The Empresses Dowager and the Emperor
> have been extremely perspicacious and resolute in their righteous
> anger, in their reprimand of the envoy, and in their calling for a
> collective deliberation (of the case) by court officials. From the
> councillors of state, the Tsungli Yamen, the princes and great
> ministers down to the hundreds of petty officials, everybody knows
> that (the treaty) should not be ratified, yet no one dares openly
> suggest changing it. Indeed, they fear that rejection of the treaty will
> bring about war at once, but your minister thinks this is nothing to
> be feared. If we insist on changing the treaty, there may not be
> trouble; if we do not, we are unworthy to be considered a state.[1]

In this humiliating crisis, Chang suggested four steps to be
taken. First of all, China should take the decisive step of
immediately beheading Ch'ung-hou to demonstrate to Russia
her resoluteness. Secondly, high morale and a swing of world
public opinion against Russia could be achieved by exposing
Russian duplicity and treachery in foreign newspapers. Exhausted after the Turkish war, Russia was in no position to fight
China. In fact, Russian internal disorder could lead to an assassination of the Tsar at any moment. Thirdly, he advocated
superior reasoning in diplomacy: postponing the restitution of
Ili would be a reasonable way out of the predicament. Russia
would be in no position to be critical of China's non-ratification
of the treaty, since this was recognized practice in international
law and diplomacy. Fourthly, he unfolded a grand strategy:
China was to guard the three important areas of Sinkiang,
Manchuria, and Tientsin. Tso Tsung-t'ang was to defend
Sinkiang and Western China, while assigning his troops of
Manchurian origin to defend Manchuria, the home base of the
ruling dynasty. Since St. Petersburg was some twenty thousand *li*
from Manchuria, the Russians could not possibly penetrate it for
any sustained period. To defend Tientsin was the inescapable

---

[1] Ibid. 18: 18–22b, 16 Jan. 1880.

duty of Li Hung-chang, who had been given millions of taels each year for building up the fleet and the army. Now was the time for him to prove himself. China also might use the five million roubles indemnity to employ foreign officers to fight Russia. If there had to be a war, he said, let it be now rather than later, for in a few years able men like Tso Tsung-t'ang and Li Hung-chang would be too old and useless. If China did not fight on the frontiers today, she would have to fight in her heartland in the future.

To conclude his long memorial, Chang stated pointedly: 'In sum, military preparations must be made, whether the treaty can be re-negotiated or not. Restitution of Ili must be delayed, whether the treaty can be changed or not. Ch'ung-hou must be killed, whether the treaty can be changed or not. This is the impartial consensus of opinion of all the officials in the country, not the private view of your minister alone!'[1] Chang was thus the first official to demand Ch'ung-hou's death.

This bombastic state paper won its author fame overnight. People admired his literary style—his beautiful diction, his balanced prose—and his incisive judgement of the critical situation. His memorial became the one most widely read and he became the hero of the hour. The court was impressed with his work.

Encouraged by his initial success, Chang submitted a supplementary memorial on 6 February 1880. Chinese diplomacy, he argued, should be based on military preparedness: army training, fund-raising, and full use of available talents. Military training should begin with the recruitment of Mongolian, Moslem, and Manchurian armies, simultaneously with the enlistment of sailors in the Fukien–Canton area. Fund-raising should include the levying of an opium tax to support military expenditures and the appointment of good economists and financiers to key positions in the government. Wise employment of talents meant proper use of able men: Tso Tsung-t'ang should be transferred to the central government, leaving his

---

[1] *WCSL*, 18: 18–22b. An English translation of this memorial was first made by Mr. Parker, as assistant in the British Consulate in Canton, before 15 May 1880; he paid $50 to procure the document. (F.O. 418/I/87, Consul A. R. Hewlett of Canton to Salisbury, *secret*, 15 May 1880.) Ironically, on the very day this translation was forwarded to London as a secret paper, the *Shanghai Courier* printed a full translation of this memorial.

present assignment on the frontiers to his deputies. Mongolian forces should be commanded by Mongol princes, and Manchurian defence entrusted to high-ranking officers from the provinces. Tseng Chi-tse, minister in London, should be instructed to seek British help to checkmate Russia. 'With these arrangements we can fight, but your minister knows that the government does not intend to fight. He does not speak to promote war. None the less, only when we have the will to fight and real weapons to fight with can we find room for diplomacy!'

In diplomacy Chang urged that Russia must be reminded of the unique position she enjoyed in China:

> Ever since Emperor K'ang-hsi we have maintained relations with Russia for a long time, treating her neither as a dependency nor as an outlandish barbarian state. When our troops besieged Albazin, the Russians were hard pressed. Unable to bear (the sight), Emperor K'ang-hsi lifted the siege and stopped the attack. . . . This was our first favour to Russia.
>
> We did not kill the hundred-odd captured Russians including I-fan [Ivan?], but instead allowed them the privilege of living in the capital and organizing them into a unit (of their own). This was our second favour to Russia.
>
> During the time of Emperor Yung-cheng, official Russian students arrived. We established the Russian Hostel (for their quarters) and offered them knowledge. When they wanted to learn medicine, we sent Mongolian doctors (to teach them), and when they wanted to learn the Lama scriptures we assigned the Bu-erh-fan monks (to teach them). This was our third favour to Russia.

For all these privileges Russia should be grateful to China and restore Ili gracefully, instead of taking advantage of her in her hour of trouble. China should oblige Russia to honour the old boundaries established by the Supplementary Treaty of Peking of 1860 and by the revised treaty of 1864. Russia must be warned that trade would be cut off and Khokand and Ili invaded, if she attacked Manchuria, and that if she attacked Sinkiang, the Chinese would invade Nerchinsk. Chang argued that with all her internal troubles Russia was in no position to make a sustained drive into China. Even if China should lose a battle, she might recoup her losses in several ways: she might urge Turkey on to attack Russia in Europe; she might induce Japan to attack Sakhalin and reward her with land in Formosa;

she might persuade Britain and Germany to checkmate Russia and repay them with handsome rewards, and she might stir up internal strife in Russia. If all these measures worked, Chang predicted that St. Petersburg soon would cease to be Russian.

To resolve the crisis by methods short of war, Chang suggested that China might have recourse to any one of the following alternatives: pay Russia more for the restitution of Ili, or give her some remote, barren land in Sinkiang in exchange for Ili, or demand the extradition of the rebel chief Pai Yen-hu rather than the restitution of Ili to gain a moral victory and psychological satisfaction.[1]

The court was so impressed with Chang's pithy arguments that it broke precedent to order him, however low in status, to participate in all future meetings of the princes and ministers in the Tsungli Yamen and to take part in the formulation of government policy.[2] In the twinkling of an eye Chang shot to fame and became the idol of many. Experienced politicians bowed in admiration and frustrated scholars sighed with envy. His meteoric rise was indeed a phenomenon, possible only within the framework of the old order. Without support of an electorate or public media of communication, he was able to make his influence felt primarily by appealing to the rulers and by winning acclaim from the *literati*; in the hands of both, he knew, the fate of the state and society lay. A master of political psychology and of the inner mechanism of the imperial bureaucracy, he knew that the hour of crisis provided the best opportunity for capturing the attention of these two groups.

The country had been driven into a quandary by the question of war or peace. To accept the treaty and sacrifice Ili would hurt Chinese pride and spoil the myth of 'Grand Unification'. To lose the land won by Emperor Ch'ien-lung was unfilial and unworthy of history. Yet, to wage war over Ili was to court disaster. On the other hand, to accept peace on Russian terms was unbearably humiliating. The whole country was in a dilemma, anxiously awaiting someone to show the way. At this delicate moment Chang made his appearance. His fast pen, his forceful argument, his powerful reasoning, and his beautiful prose created an immediate impact on the scholars and officials. The sensation he created was in itself a welcome

[1] *WCSL*, 18: 25b–32.   [2] Ibid. 18: 32.

relief to the distressed court and society. Whatever the practical wisdom of his suggestions, he fulfilled his countrymen's expectation by providing an answer to the almost impossible question. In urging the execution of Ch'ung-hou and taking a strong stand against Russia, he was appealing to Chinese pride and reasserting the imperial authority to do what it pleased, regardless of foreign pressure. He spoke what the court liked to hear, and wrote what the *literati* liked to read. Few who read his memorials today can fail to be impressed. The combination of political opportunism, quick judgement, and literary talents catapulted him into the front of the political arena.

Because Chang expressed the feelings of many like him, his voice became the voice of public sentiment. Politicians flocked to his doors to echo his views, and endless memorials were sent to the court, demanding the punishment of Ch'ung-hou and the rejection of the treaty. They clamoured for war to uphold China's territory and dignity. The suppression of the Taiping, the Nien, and the Moslem rebellions was cited as proof of China's ability to defend her honour against Russia, and in such a just war of self-defence was seen the opportunity to sweep away once and for all China's humiliation by the West.[1] Their demands for war and their high-sounding pronouncements filled the air, creating an intense atmosphere of bellicosity. So powerful was this public sentiment that even the court, desirous of peace as it was, dared not ignore it.[2] The Tsungli Yamen was forced to revise its original position of rejecting part of the treaty.[3] It had to take a much stronger stand than it was willing to take. George Seward, an American minister and a shrewd observer of Chinese politics, was quick to discover the plight of the Yamen. He reported to Washington:

(Chinese statesmen are) very sensitive in regard to national prestige and very much disposed [indisposed?] individually to open themselves to any imputation of carelessness or weakness in this regard. . . . Statesmen charged with the duty who should neglect to defend the national prestige would be made the object of grave

---

[1] Hsü Chi-ying, 'Tseng Chi-tse yü Chung-O I-li chiao-she' (Tseng Chi-tse and the Sino-Russian negotiations over Ili), *Ta-kung pao* (Tientsin), 26 Mar. 1937, p. 3.

[2] Li Hung-chang, 'Letters to friends and colleagues', 19: 18b–19, Letter to Tseng Chi-tse, 25 Apr. 1880.

[3] Tseng Chi-tse, 'Literary collection', 3: 15b, Letter to Ting Jih-ch'ang, 25 Mar. 1880.

attack. The Foreign Office [Tsungli Yamen] in particular is as sensitive as foreign offices generally, and its members would not willingly encounter the charge that they have abandoned any of the interests committed to them.[1]

If the Tsungli Yamen was subject to the strong pressure of *literati* public opinion, so was the court, which had to make the final decision. The court was trapped between the ringing manifestoes of the vociferous scholar-officials and the ominous prospects of a disastrous war with Russia. There was no way to save 'face' and avoid war simultaneously. The decision was indeed a very difficult one. The all-powerful Empress Dowager Tz'u-hsi became sick of a liver ailment and was unable to attend to court affairs for a month. The other Empress Dowager, Tz'u-an, was more renowned for her private virtues than for her ability to manage the affairs of state.[2] Thus in the critical months of early 1880 China was in a quandary.

The court finally decided that the crucial issue of war or peace should be debated by all the important officials of China —princes of the blood, the adjutant generals, the grand councillors, the grand secretaries, the ministers of the Tsungli Yamen, the presidents of the Six Boards and the Nine Courts, and the members of the Censorate. On 19 February Prince Li, the presiding officer, reported the findings:

We, your ministers, have examined and read all the memorials (relating to the Treaty of Livadia). Although their manners of expression are different, their ideas do not exceed the three categories of not approving the treaty and (trade) regulations negotiated by Ch'ung-hou, inflicting punishment on him for his mismanagement, and making plans for war and peace. . . . We, your ministers, have deliberated unceasingly. Since the treaty concluded lately by Ch'ung-hou and the foreign ministry in the Russian capital cannot be approved, can we not dispatch another emissary to explain, discreetly, reasonably, and earnestly, to the Russian emperor and officials, how Ch'ung-hou had negotiated the treaty, the (trade) regulations, and the protocols in excess of his authority and in violation of his instructions, and how all the officials in China—high and low, inside and outside the capital—refuse to accept them?

[1] *China: Dispatches*, 55: 23, Seward to Evarts, 12 Jan. 1880.
[2] Li Hung-chang, 'Letters to friends and colleagues', 19: 22b, Letter to Tseng Chi-tse, 13 May 1880. The Dowager's liver disease was of long standing. See Weng T'ung-ho, 19: 42, 19: 72b, 20: 4.

It is hard for us to predict whether they will not raise many (new) threatening demands. Nevertheless, upon judging the present situation, it seems more advisable to send another emissary, (to show that) on our part we have considered (the issue) from the standpoints of both reason and human feeling. On their part they may also utilize the occasion to make a graceful exit.

Should it meet the approval of Your Imperial Highness, we request that a high official thoroughly conversant with foreign affairs be appointed to Russia, bringing with him personally a Letter of Credence, to explain to and argue with (the Russians) in detail about the basic reasons for our objection to the points at stake. Whether or not they promise to return Ili in the future, he should not conclude matters with them lightly, in order (not to) mismanage (the affair) again![1]

The court approved the recommendation and appointed Tseng Chi-tse, minister in London and Paris, as the new envoy to St. Petersburg to re-negotiate the Treaty of Livadia.

[1] *WCSL*, 19: 1–3.

CHAPTER III

Ch'ung-hou's Punishment, Reprieve, and Pardon

ALONG with their clamorous protest against the Treaty of Livadia, the scholar-officials also pressed for the punishment of its signer, Ch'ung-hou. Most vociferous on this point were the members of the Hanlin Academy, who considered themselves guardians of propriety in Confucian society. Huang T'i-fang, a reader in the Academy, demanded on 2 January 1880 that stern justice be meted out to Ch'ung-hou for his double crime of disloyalty to the state and disrespect for the Emperor:

In sending envoys abroad the government has the purpose of maintaining good relations with other states. Misrepresentation (by an envoy) is not permissible; an unauthorized act is even less permissible. (Of all the diplomats) in historical records and of all the envoys that have been sent abroad, none has so irrationally injured the state as Ch'ung-hou. . . . His heart knows fear only of the enemy state but not of the Empresses Dowager and the Emperor. He made concessions of great importance on his own without first requesting imperial authorization, and returned home without waiting for an imperial summons. Furthermore, (after his return to China) he lingered in Shanghai and other places one after another, hoping for the gradual cooling of Imperial anger, and then requested an audience. Your minister has also heard that after reaching the capital gate, Ch'ung-hou had the audacity to hide himself away, and did not appear in the capital to pay respect (to the Emperor). As an envoy he is disloyal. As a reporter on his mission, he is disrespectful. Our state has standard punishments for disloyalty and disrespect. Your minister humbly prays that Your Imperial Highness will exercise your special powers in ordering the court officials to examine (the case) and severely punish his offences, so as to warn other officials against committing unauthorized acts to the detriment of the state.[1]

I. THE PUNISHMENT

On that very day, 2 January 1880, the court dismissed Ch'ung-hou from his post of senior president of the Censorate,

[1] WCSL, 18: 9b-10.

on the ground of his unauthorized return to China. It turned him over to the Board of Civil Offices, which was to recommend a punishment.[1] Thus disgraced, Ch'ung-hou fearfully awaited the decision. Shen Kuei-fen, the grand councillor who had recommended his appointment to Russia, was now so regretful of his action and so fearful of public condemnation through association of his name with Ch'ung-hou's that he fell ill and soon died.[2]

On 17 January 1880 the Board of Civil Offices reached the verdict that Ch'ung-hou was to be dismissed from all posts. The court was not satisfied with the recommendation, and ordered the Board of Punishments to pass a heavier sentence.[3] On 26 February Fan Tseng-hsiang, a bachelor in the Hanlin Academy, echoing Chang Chih-tung's view, urged that Ch'ung-hou be put to death:

> The man who negotiated the treaty must be killed, because, if he is spared from death, we cannot but accept his treaty. There is no neutrality in this matter and we cannot have both [his life and rejection of treaty]. . . . What is known in foreign countries as violation of instructions is what we call disobedience to imperial edicts. What is known in foreign countries as 'acts in excess of one's powers' is what we call 'injury to the state by unauthorized acts'. . . . With no regard for his Emperor and his father, Ch'ung-hou has injured the state with an offence one hundred times worse than Ch'i-ying's.[4] Apart from death by beheading there is no other treatment that can be applied.[5]

The memorialist took pains to point out that severe punishment for Ch'ung-hou could serve the double purpose of demonstrating to the Russians China's resoluteness and of warning Tseng Chi-tse against similarly disgracing his country.

The court ordered that Ch'ung-hou be handed over to a special council for trial. Some forty memorials poured into the court demanding his head; ordinarily, five unfavourable

---

[1] Ibid. 18: 10.
[2] Li Hung-chang, 'Letters to friends and colleagues', 19: 22b–23.
[3] *WCSL*, 18: 22b–23.
[4] Ch'i-ying was sent by the court to negotiate with Lord Elgin and Baron Gros in Tientsin in 1858. Found unacceptable to the foreigners, he left Tientsin without imperial authorization. He was then taken to Peking in chains, and after a trial, executed. For detail, see my *China's Entrance*, 37–45.
[5] *WCSL*, 19: 5–7.

memorials could remove a man from office, and fifteen to twenty could send him to death.[1] The prevailing sentiments in the capital as well as in the provinces were so strongly against him that no one dared to speak on his behalf.[2] Thus on 3 March 1880, on the recommendation of Prince Li, the court threw Ch'ung-hou into prison, having sentenced him to death by beheading after the Autumn Assizes.[3]

In all fairness, Ch'ung-hou was punished not so much for his unauthorized return to China, which the edict made much of, as for the failure of his mission: he had signed away territory he had no authority to sign away. His greatest mistake appears to have been his complete ignorance of the affair he was called upon to deal with. He had made no attempt to acquaint himself with the geography of Ili. He had ignored Chang P'ei-lun's suggestion that he go to Sinkiang to see at first hand the local situation and that he consult Tso Tsung-t'ang on the strategy for the negotiations. His sea voyage might not have been such a blunder if he had thoroughly familiarized himself with the topography of the area in dispute and had mapped out a clear approach to the problem beforehand. In Paris, when met by Kuo Sung-tao and asked about his methods for dealing with the Russians, he was vague and evasive on all issues except that Ili had to be recovered. Kuo had been dumbfounded by his lack of preparedness and had foretold his failure.[4] In a letter to Tseng Kuo-ch'üan, governor of Shansi, Kuo spoke disparagingly of Ch'ung-hou's impudence, recalling that before he [Kuo] had gone to London as China's first minister in 1876, he had asked Ch'ung-hou about European conditions because the latter previously had led an apology mission to France in 1870. Ch'ung-hou at that time had talked fearfully about the power of Western ships and guns; possibly, Kuo felt, Ch'ung-hou had been predisposed by that venture to fear the Russians in this case of Ili.[5] Kuo attributed Ch'ung-hou's failure in Russia to four causes: first, his complete ignorance of the geography of Ili and his neglect of all maps; second, his failure to distinguish between vital issues and peripheral ones by fixing his attention

---

[1] Kiernan, 53.

[2] F.O. 418/I/111, Wade to Granville, *confidential*, 19 May 1880, reporting Li's view on the situation.   [3] *WCSL*, 19: 11b.

[4] Kuo Sung-tao, 'Literary collections', 11: 22b–26, Letter to Li Hung-chang.

[5] Ibid. 11: 30b.

solely on the recovery of Ili to the neglect of all other important issues; third, his predisposition to fear Russia, and finally, his perfunctory performance of duty. But Kuo was not in favour of punishing Ch'ung-hou, since he did not want to arouse the Russians and give them a pretext for further disturbances.[1]

2. AN INTERPRETATION OF THE TRAGEDY

Ch'ung-hou was an agreeable and mild-mannered person, but too easily swayed by flattery or bullying. Although for many years he had been a minister in the Tsungli Yamen and at the same time the superintendent of trade for the Three Northern Ports, and although he had directed a number of treaty negotiations with such small European states as Denmark and Holland, he had done all this with the help and guidance of colleagues and other government officials. He had not been alone in charting the course of action. But in Russia, though assisted by the legation staff, he was left to himself to make the final decisions, and there he was lost. Russian wine, food, hospitality, and flattery overwhelmed him. His excessive concessions even inspired speculation that he had been bribed,[2] but Sir Thomas Wade, British minister in Peking, disputed this, saying 'He is too rich to have been bribed'.[3] Russian sources revealed no bribery either, but they did speak of Ch'ung-hou's great anxiety to complete his assignment and return home.[4] Giers considered him a pleasant man but not prudent or careful.[5] Other motives than bribery were also assigned to him: Tseng Chi-tse, minister in London and later his successor in Russia, spoke of Ch'ung-hou's yearning to be free to attend to his family affairs in China,[6] and Ting Pao-chen, governor-general of Szechwan, mentioned his unusual fear of Russian threats and Russian power.[7] From Russian records of negotiation

---

[1] *WCSL*, 20: 15–21; also Kuo Sung-tao, 'Memorials', 12: 23 ff., 25 Jan. 1880.

[2] *China: Dispatches*, 54: 683, Seward to Evarts, 8 May 1880.

[3] F.O. 418/I/242, Wade to Granville, *very confidential*, 25 July 1880: 'Whether Ch'ung-hou was cajoled or terrified I cannot ascertain. He is too rich to have been bribed.'

[4] Jelavich, 94–95, Jomini to Giers, 31 Aug./11 Sept. and 9/21 Sept. 1879.

[5] *ILTT*: 215–16, Giers to Tseng, 19 Jan. 1881.

[6] Tseng Chi-tse, 'Literary collection', 3: 15–15b, Letter to Ting Jih-ch'ang, 25 Mar. 1880.

[7] Ting Pao-chen, 'Memorials', 18: 35, dated 28 Feb. 1880.

with Ch'ung-hou, it is clear that he had never engaged in any heated debate with Butzow, Jomini, or Giers. Wade said that Ch'ung-hou was 'so hard pressed by the Russian negotiators that he fairly lost his wits'.[1] Probably he was terrified by their imposing presences. All these factors—his lack of a knowledge of Ili, his anxiety to return home, and his fear of the Russians—contributed to his decision to conclude the treaty in a hurry.[2] But what made him dare to ignore the Yamen's warning against the treaty was probably his misunderstanding of his institutional position; here we see the tragic influence of the past.

Ch'ung-hou's official title was imperial commissioner first class, envoy to Russia, with full powers to act as he saw fit. The Tsungli Yamen understood the title to confer the traditional powers of an imperial commissioner without the restrictions and qualifications entailed on a Western diplomat. An imperial commissioner did not receive instructions from anyone; as the Emperor's high emissary, he was given great discretionary powers to perform a specific mission. He could do practically anything in the name of the Emperor. If he needed guidance, he could send for it from time to time, but so long as he succeeded, nobody questioned his methods in discharging his duties. Thus his fate depended on the result of his performance rather than on strict observance of a prescribed set of instructions as in the West.[3] For this reason the Yamen issued him no instructions at the outset. In fact, no Chinese diplomats—Kuo Sung-tao in London and Paris, Ch'en Lan-pin in Washington, Liu Hsi-hung in Berlin, Hsü Ch'ien-shen in Tokyo—were ever provided with definite instructions when they were sent abroad. They were given nothing but letters of credence for accreditation. This lack of instructions posed no problem to these regular resident ministers, whose main duty was to set up Chinese legations abroad rather than to engage in active diplomatic negotiations. But Ch'ung-hou's mission to Russia was entirely different: in addition to establishing the legation, he was to

---

[1] F.O. 418/I/111, Wade to Granville, *confidential*, 19 May 1880.

[2] Li Hung-chang, 'Letters to friends and colleagues', 19: 22b, Li to Tseng Chi-tse, 13 May 1880.

[3] For a discussion of the role of imperial commissioner, see my *China's Entrance*, 31–37, and John K. Fairbank, *Trade and Diplomacy on the China Coast* (Cambridge, Mass., 1953), i. 96.

negotiate for the return of Ili, and such a mission was not a simple administrative one. It is surprising that the Tsungli Yamen did not see the difference and so provide him with definite instructions to guide him. In this way the Yamen was remiss in its duty; Ch'ung-hou himself was not entirely to blame.

Apparently, Ch'ung-hou too understood his powers in the light of 'imperial commissionership' rather than in the Western sense of 'ambassadorship'. He was untroubled by the lack of instructions. As imperial commissioner empowered to act as he saw fit, he probably believed that he had the power to sign the treaty as long as Ili was recovered. Most likely he also was prompted to take a liberal view of his authority by the very fact that he was the only first-class imperial commissioner outside China; all other Chinese diplomats were second-class imperial commissioners, or ministers plenipotentiary in the Western sense. His one consideration was to recover Ili; all other issues were minor.

It is interesting to note that when the Yamen instructed him at the last minute to reopen negotiations with the Russians rather than accept the treaty, he replied that it was too late because the text of the treaty had already been copied out. One cannot understand his temerity in flouting the Yamen's warning without taking cognizance of the peculiar triangular relationship between the court, the Yamen, and the envoy abroad.[1] The Yamen and the envoy were equal and parallel organs of state under the Emperor, one inside and one outside China. Neither enjoyed a hierarchical superiority over the other. The envoy was not responsible to the Yamen and was not obliged to obey it. He could report direct to the Emperor without the knowledge of the Yamen, although he normally would acquaint the Yamen with his reports to the court. Some Chinese diplomats never bothered to send reports to the Yamen at all, and it was therefore not surprising that Ch'ung-hou dared to ignore the Yamen's warning.

Ch'ung-hou must have believed that his powers in Russia would be the same as those he would have had in China. An imperial commissioner in China, with authorization to act as

---

[1] For a discussion of the relationship between the Yamen and the envoy, see my *China's Entrance*, 191–3.

he saw fit, could 'kill first, report later' (*hsien-chan hou-tsou*);
Ch'ung-hou apparently believed analogously that he too could
'sign first, report later'as long as he recovered Ili. Little did he
realize that his authority to act as he saw fit was nothing more
than the 'full powers' of the Western ambassador which empowered him to negotiate, but not to accept every condition his
opponent proposed. This delicate technicality eluded even so
well-informed a man as Li Hung-chang, who remarked that
Ch'ung-hou, with his special authorization, could not be said
to be without the power of signing the treaty.[1] In the eyes
of foreign observers, Ch'ung-hou truly 'believed himself empowered to do what he did'.[2] For this misunderstanding of his
functions, natural as it was, Ch'ung-hou paid the high price of a
humiliating treaty. China had entered the family of nations as
a new member by 1880, but her mind was still shackled by the
practices of the past. She had to learn a new way of life in a
strange new world, and every step was a struggle. Her diplomats
made many blunders, but Ch'ung-hou's was the worst. In the
eyes of traditionalist China, giving away land which the great
Emperors K'ang-hsi and Ch'ien-lung had spent a century to
conquer was a fatal sin. Ch'ung-hou must pay with his head.
Filial piety to the founding fathers of the dynasty forbade any
punishment less severe.

3. FOREIGN INTERVENTION

Ch'ung-hou's arrest and death sentence caused no little stir
in the diplomatic corps in China. Foreign diplomats exhibited a
general concern and sympathy for the fallen Manchu official.[3]
They felt that he was 'being sacrificed because of the cry raised
against him by officials who have no responsibility in foreign
affairs'.[4] They believed that Ch'ung-hou had been in constant
telegraphic contact with the Tsungli Yamen during the whole
course of the negotiations and that a large part of his work was
known and approved of in advance. The Yamen could have
prevented his return in good time. Thomas Wade, British
minister in China, said: 'The fallen Ambassador is the most

[1] *WCSL*, 17: 16–19, Li's memorial received at court on 15 Nov. 1879.
[2] *China: Dispatches*, 55: 23, Seward to Evarts, 12 Jan. 1880.
[3] Ibid. 52: 575, same to same, 29 Jan. 1880.
[4] Ibid. 52: 586, same to same, 6 Feb. 1880.

cautious of men, and I cannot doubt held no powers but such as were carefully bounded by his instructions.'[1] Wade considered it impossible that Ch'ung-hou 'would go one hair's breadth beyond his instructions'.[2] George Seward, the American minister, also wrote: 'We entertain no doubt that the late Ambassador did his duty to the best of his ability, and that his return to China was nothing more than the natural consequence of the completion of his work.'[3] Foreign ministers in Peking took the position that Ch'ung-hou deserved nothing more than a reprimand or censure, and they resented the application of a harsh Oriental punishment in China's new diplomacy.[4] Seward wrote movingly: 'We cannot expect to see him again, for a considerable period, at any rate, in the foreign office, and this is much to be regretted.'[5] There was some general feeling that Ch'ung-hou's punishment was a manifestation of xenophobia, which, though superficially limited to Russia, was actually directed against all foreign nations having relations with China.[6]

Foreign diplomats, feeling that they could not remain silent during a great tragedy involving a brother diplomat, met to discuss steps to be taken. They concluded that they should inform the Tsungli Yamen that 'foreign powers cannot disregard the question of humanity which is involved, and the effect of this and other hostile demonstrations upon our [their] general interest'.[7] The German minister, Max von Brandt, however, stated that he did not want to interfere with the internal affairs of China. Yet he reluctantly concurred in the general decision of protest to the Yamen.[8]

No identical notes were sent; each foreign minister wrote to Prince Kung in the way he thought best suited to the occasion. Seward, in reporting his action to the American Secretary of State, William M. Evarts, stated: 'I am free to confess that I have been actuated more by a desire to do my duty in a humanitarian

[1] F.O. 418/I/22, Wade to Salisbury, 25 Jan. 1880.
[2] F.O. 418/I/25, same to same, 9 Mar. 1880.
[3] *China: Dispatches*, 53: 586, Seward to Evarts, 6 Feb. 1880.
[4] Ibid. 52: 557, same to same, 12 Jan. 1880; 53: 618, 8 Mar. 1880.
[5] Ibid. 52: 557, same to same, 12 Jan. 1880.
[6] The Russians in particular played up this sentiment. Cf. Martens, 70–71.
[7] *China: Dispatches*, 53: 586, Seward to Evarts, 6 Feb. 1880.
[8] China, No. 2, Vol. 2, Conf. Vol. 3, Brandt to German Foreign Office, No. 26, 6 Feb. 1880. (Politisches Archiv d. Auswärt. Amts, Bonn.)

point of view than by considerations of dangers to our interests.
. . . A foreign representative does not discharge his responsibility in such a country as this if he fails to do what he reasonably may to call a halt to barbarous ways.'[1] Evarts endorsed his intercession for Ch'ung-hou.[2]

Although the notes of the United States, Britain, France, and Germany were not identical, they contained similar ideas. The following excerpts from the British note of 6 February 1880 accurately represented the common sentiments of the foreign ministers:

It is with much delicacy that the Undersigned approaches the subject on which he is about to speak; he feels at the same time that it is impossible for him to be silent. . . .

In foreign countries, an agent returning home after completing the negotiations in which he had been specially commissioned to engage, would possibly not be thought to have committed a very grave offence, if indeed any offence at all. . . . While the offence indicated in the Imperial decrees is simply the Minister's unauthorized return to China, a rumour prevails that his negotiations with Russia have been made the subject of grave charges against him. . . .

It is in the recollection of the Undersigned that when in 1858 a Chinese minister [Ch'i-ying], for returning from Tientsin to Peking without permission was put to death, his punishment was universally reprobated abroad, and if in now punishing its envoy, but if [either?] for his return to China without authority, or for his negotiation of an unsatisfactory treaty, the Imperial government were to go the same length, the Undersigned is certain that its act would be severely condemned, not by the British government alone, but by every government in the Western world.

In a recent interview with the ministers of the Yamen, the Undersigned took upon himself to state his apprehension of the consequence that might attend the infliction of severe punishment in the case of the Imperial envoy. He repeats his opinion now only in the interest of China, and he will be well pleased to find that His Imperial Highness and Their Excellencies do not regard his intervention as officious.[3]

---

[1] *China: Dispatches*, 53: 586, Seward to Evarts, 6 Feb. 1880.

[2] *China: Instructions*, 3: 369, Evarts to Seward, 1 May 1880.

[3] F.O. 418/I/34, Wade to Salisbury, 8 Feb. 1880, enclosures of notes of all four foreign ministers in China. The same four notes may also be found in American, French, and German archives, Cf. *China: Dispatches*, 53: 589 enclosures; *Chine*, 58: 42 enclosures; and *China*, No. 2, Vol. 2, Conf. Vol. 3, No. 26.

In protesting to the Tsungli Yamen, the foreign ministers, of course, had no knowledge of the last-minute exchanges between Ch'ung-hou and the Yamen before the treaty was concluded. They did not know that Ch'ung-hou had signed it with no regard to the Yamen's warning and disapproval. Prince Kung did not feel called upon to divulge the exchanges at this point. In his customarily polite way he thanked the foreign ministers for their concern over China's future, assuring them of China's sincere wish to adopt 'a reasonable and satisfactory course' in the Ch'ung-hou case.[1] On 15 February, as previously mentioned, Tseng Chi-tse was appointed to reopen negotiations in Russia. This encouraged Seward to remark: 'While the fate of Ch'ung-hou is yet unknown, it seems to me that the determination reached by the government to reopen negotiations with Russia and the knowledge that extreme measures in this case would cause general dissatisfaction and affect prejudicially their future representations at St. Petersburg, indicate that the moment of gravest danger has passed.'[1] Yet the disquietude and tension arising from the punishment of Ch'ung-hou was not totally gone. As a precaution Seward told Admiral Patterson to be prepared to protect the United States' nationals and interests in China.[2]

At this point Wade received a telegram from London which read: 'The Queen is much shocked to hear of Chung How's [*sic*] condemnation to death. If you think that a strong personal appeal from Her Majesty to the Emperor will be to the advantage of the condemned man, you are instructed to make it.'[3] Wade felt that a direct approach to the Yamen might incur the retort that the punishment of an official was an internal affair of China that admitted of no foreign interference. And thus the best of intentions on the part of Britain might lead directly to an affront to the Queen's dignity. Wade therefore did not approach the Yamen but broached the subject instead to Li Hung-chang in Tientsin, requesting his good offices. If Ch'ung-hou's sentence could be commuted to banishment and hard labour in the north-west, Wade suggested, he would then be pleased to tell London that the Queen's wishes had been met. In appreciation,

---

[1] *China: Dispatches*, 53: 605, Seward to Evarts, 23 Feb. 1880.
[2] Ibid. 53: 619, same to same, 9 Mar. 1880.
[3] F.O. 418/I/28, Sir Julian Pauncefote to Wade, telegram, 25 Mar. 1880.

Wade continued, the Queen most likely would be willing to use her influence to persuade the Russians to reopen negotiations with Marquis Tseng, but China must first pardon Ch'ung-hou as a sign of her truly peaceful intentions toward Russia.[1] Li had harboured a suspicion that it was Russia that had asked the Queen to plead for Ch'ung-hou's life, but Wade assured him that the Queen had acted independently.[2] Tseng Chi-tse, in London, also wrote to Li to request the commutation of Ch'ung-hou's sentence, in order to save Russian pride. Li, who had been sympathetic to Ch'ung-hou all along, was thus encouraged to prevail upon the Yamen to exert its influence at court for Ch'ung-hou's pardon. He wrote to the Yamen: 'Ch'ung-hou himself is of no consequence, but the general security (of our country) is of the greatest importance. I presume that you too are anxiously aware of this.'[3]

The Yamen was well aware that any request for Ch'ung-hou's pardon would run the risk of imperial displeasure and public attack; it sharply replied to Li that he should write directly to the court about the Queen's offer to intercede. Li bravely accepted this burden, and asked Wade to provide him with a note that would assure his own memorial the foundation of the Queen's request. He found, however, that international usage did not permit foreign diplomats like Wade to enter into direct communication with local officials, but only with the foreign office of the central government. Li, of course, was glad to be spared the unpopular move of asking for Ch'ung-hou's pardon, but he did continue his good offices for Wade. After having been assured by Li of a friendly reception by the Yamen, Wade addressed a formal note to Prince Kung, expressing the Queen's wish.[4] The new French minister, M. A. Bourée, also made a plea for Ch'ung-hou's life on behalf of the French President and urged China not to let slip the chance for Anglo-French mediation of her trouble with Russia.[5]

The Yamen was being pressed not only by Wade, Li, and Bourée, but also by several others. Liu K'un-i, newly appointed

---

[1] Li Hung-chang, 'Letters to the Tsungli Yamen', 11: 2–4; also F.O. 418/I/72 and 112, Wade to Salisbury, *confidential*, 19 and 24 May 1880.

[2] Li Hung-chang, 'Letters to the Tsungli Yamen', 11: 6, 27 May 1880.

[3] Ibid. 11: 2–4.

[4] Ibid. 11: 4–5, 23 May 1880.

[5] *Chine*, 58: 210–211, Bourée's telegram to Paris, 10 June 1880, and Paris's reply.

governor-general of Liang-Kiang who was also in charge of the coastal defence in the south, arrived in Peking in time to witness the crisis. Upon learning that the Manchurian defence had been entrusted to Solon soldiers who were good at bows and arrows but untrained in modern firearms, he ruefully remarked: 'When I heard this, I did not know whether I should cry or laugh. After much deliberation (I knew that) the only way out was to accept the Anglo-French mediation and retrieve Ch'ung-hou's sentence, so as to relieve the immediate pressure and avoid the crisis of 1859 (i.e. Anglo-French advance to Peking in 1860).'[1] Kuo Sung-tao, the former minister to Britain and France, also urged that Ch'ung-hou's punishment be reduced to confiscation of his property for military expenses.[2] So exhorted from all sides, the Yamen felt compelled to ask W. A. P. Martin, president of Tungwen College and an expert on international law, for an advisory opinion on Western practices in similar cases. Martin replied that Christian states normally penalized their envoys for diplomatic failure by nothing heavier than dismissal, but that Turkish envoys frequently had been shot.[3]

4. THE REPRIEVE AND PARDON

The pressure from the leading diplomats in China, as well as from high provincial authorities like Li and Liu, was hard to resist. On 15 June 1880 the Yamen made the unpopular move of pleading for the pardon of Ch'ung-hou, reviewing for the court the whole sequence of events from the first protests of the diplomatic corps to the intercession of the British Queen and the lenient views of Li and Liu. It also stressed the need for quieting Russian irritation over the punishment of Ch'ung-hou, in order to pave the way for the Russian reception of Marquis Tseng. Furthermore, it pointed out, British mediation would not begin until Russia was pacified first by the pardon of Ch'ung-hou. The Yamen also relayed to the court the disquieting information, from the French minister Bourée, that Max von Brandt and the Russian chargé d'affaires, Koiander,

---

[1] Liu K'un-i, *Liu K'un-i i-chi* (The posthumous works of Liu K'un-i) (Peking, 1959), iv: 1932–6, v: 2482, also *WCSL*, 21: 2–4.
[2] Kuo Sung-tao, 'Memorials', 20: 15b–21b.
[3] Martin, *Cycle*, 384–5.

were conspiring together to stir up a war. The French intelligence warned against playing into their hands. The Yamen moreover feared that China's refusal of British and French mediation might goad them both into the Russian camp, with the result that China would face not one enemy but three, and the future would be bleak. On the other hand, granting Britain and France their request for Ch'ung-hou's pardon could win their sympathy and keep them from the Russians. This was too good a chance to be missed for China to turn world public opinion to her favour. 'All in all', the Yamen said, 'the Russian affair is unpredictable. Even though our move may not foil the Russian plot, it may realistically win British and French good will. We do not expect to profit from it but to avoid further loss. In the future, even if there should be successive complications, foreign nations will not wholly disregard us and we shall not stand helplessly alone. In this way the general situation may yet be managed. Because of the importance of this matter, your ministers have been in constant correspondence with Li Hung-chang; it so happens that Liu K'un-i has arrived in the capital in time to hold several confidential conversations with us about this matter. He shared our conclusion and his language is even more emphatic.'[1] Tso Tsung-t'ang, as well as these others, also urged the Yamen to comply with the British and French request for the pardon of Ch'ung-hou.[2]

Those who had once asked for Ch'ung-hou's punishment could not of course countenance any move for a pardon. Huang T'i-fang, now supervisor of imperial instruction, who had earlier recommended a heavy punishment for the Manchu diplomat, chided the British and French ministers for giving an empty promise of mediation without any assurances that the treaty would be altered. He also attacked Li and Liu, the two governor-generals in charge of the northern and southern fleets, for having engrossed huge sums of defence money for years, without being able now to defend the country in time of need. Punishment of Ch'ung-hou, he warned, had been the consensus of all the officials a short while ago; any sudden about-face would make the Chinese concept of justice the laughing-stock of the world. Therefore, for the dignity of China, no pardon should be granted.[1] On 19 June the court referred the issue to the leading officials for examination.

On 23 June Chung P'ei-hsien, sub-director of the Court of Imperial Stud, protested against an outright pardon on the ground that there was no assurance that, after the pardon, Russia would pay any attention to British and French mediation. She might still demand the explicit execution of the treaty, in order to provoke a war. So that China might not be duped by foreigners, the pardon should be granted only if Britain and France agreed to intervene so vehemently that Russia would have to give up the treaty. Otherwise, war would be inevitable and Ch'ung-hou, the source of all these troubles, would have to pay with his life.[2] Hu P'ing-chih, a reader of the Grand Secretariat, and Wang Hsien-ch'ien, a libationer of the Imperial Academy of Learning, recommended a compromise: Ch'ung-hou would be temporarily spared from death but would still be kept in prison, pending the completion of Tseng's mission. If Tseng succeeded in revising the treaty, Ch'ung-hou might be freed as a special mark of imperial favour; if not, he would be killed to pay his debt to the state.[3] This suggestion made sense to Prince Ch'un, who memorialized on 23 June to support it, arguing that in unusual times China should break away from usual judicial practices and adopt fitting, if unconventional, measures. British and French friendship was important at this moment of crisis; hence their plea for the pardon of Ch'ung-hou should not be ignored. To delay Ch'ung-hou's sentence until after the completion of Tseng's mission would meet at least partially the British and French request and would maintain their friendship.[4] On 29 June Wang Jen-k'an, a first-class compiler in the Hanlin Academy, cautioned the court against creating a precedent of invoking foreign aid in trouble.[5]

Chang Chih-tung, the bright new star of Chinese officialdom who had now become a reader in the Hanlin Academy, offered two plans. First, China should proclaim publicly that in punishing Ch'ung-hou she had no intention of insulting Russia. The British and French ministers might be decorated for their offer of mediation. They might also be asked to inform the Russians that China was willing to increase her payment for Russian

[1] *WCSL*, 21: 5b–6b.   [2] Ibid. 21: 6b–7b.   [3] Ibid. 21: 7b–8.
[4] Ibid. 21: 8–10b.   [5] Ibid. 21: 10b–11b.

occupation expenses in Ili and to delay her demand for the return of Ili, and that China did not object to the whole treaty but only to a few difficult articles. Second, Ch'ung-hou might be pardoned if he contributed a million taels for military expenses and went to Russia to assist Tseng in reopening the negotiations. If the treaty could not be revised and war broke out as a result, Tseng should be ordered to decapitate Ch'ung-hou then and there. Chang openly attacked Li Hung-chang and Liu K'un-i, for their fear of war and their inability to relieve the Emperor's anxieties. Both of them, he said, should be severely reprimanded for their dereliction of duty if Ch'ung-hou was to be pardoned.[1]

On 26 June Prince Li came to the conclusion, on the basis of all these views, that while the act of pardon was a prerogative of China which allowed no foreign interference, the request of the British Queen had been made with the best of intentions and should therefore be granted. He recommended a commutation of Ch'ung-hou's sentence, to show the grace of the Emperor and the Empresses Dowager as well as to dissipate foreign suspicion.[2] On the same day, 26 June, Ch'ung-hou was given a reprieve by the court but was kept in prison to await the outcome of Tseng's mission. The British Foreign Office was notified that the remission of the sentence was made 'out of deference to the wish of the Queen' but that Peking did not want it to be known publicly because 'the Russian government might view with disfavour such a commutation having been granted to another power rather than to them'.[3] Wade had advised the Chinese government that in its decree announcing the reprieve, no reference to the Queen should be made.[4] Peking officially notified Russia of the move as a concrete expression of China's desire for peace.[5]

The court made the decision most reluctantly. In spite of all rationalization, the fact remained that it had been forced by foreign pressure to renounce what it still believed to be the right course. To vent its wrath, the court followed the suggestion of Chang Chih-tung and administered a stern rebuke the following day to the three officials in charge of coastal defence in the

[1] *WCSL*, 21: 13–15.   [2] Ibid. 21: 11b–12b.
[3] F.O. 418/I/97, Lord Tenterden's memo, dated 3 July 1880.
[4] F.O. 418/I/201, Wade to Granville, *confidential*, 28 June 1880.
[5] *WCSL*, 21: 15–15b.

north and south: Li Hung-chang, governor-general of Chihli and leader of the northern fleet, Liu K'un-i, governor-general of Liang-Kiang in charge of the southern fleet, and Wu Yüan-ping, governor of Kiangsu and acting governor-general of Liang-Kiang:

Ch'ung-hou's offence has been forgiven simply because our coastal defence is not completely dependable. We have therefore conde-scended to comply with their [the Anglo-French] request, but when-ever we think about it we become bitter and resentful. At present the re-negotiation of the treaty is an important issue involving many difficult conditions that we cannot accept under any circum-stances, and it is hard to say that war will not break out. Li Hung-chang long has been entrusted with the important assignment of defending the capital area and the coast, and Liu K'un-i and Wu Yüan-ping are engaged in the defences of the north and south, all with inescapable responsibilities. They must plan for defensive measures well in advance in their respective areas to relieve My anxieties. If they dare to drift and put up a show (of preparedness) while letting opportunities slip, it is to be feared that, when respon-sibility is assigned, the governor-generals in question will not be able to face the heavy punishment![1]

The foreign diplomatic corps was informed of Ch'ung-hou's reprieve.[2] While the American Acting Secretary of State William Hunter expressed gratification over 'the humane action' of the Chinese government,[3] the British Foreign Secretary Lord Granville considered the reprieve not 'an acceptable method of approaching the Russian government'.[4] As expected, Russia was not satisfied with China's partial concession; they demanded a complete pardon of Ch'ung-hou. Marquis Tseng, arriving in Russia in early August, again requested Peking to show further leniency toward Ch'ung-hou to remove the last obstacle to the negotiations. His telegram reached Peking on 11 August. In response, an edict was issued: 'Now that the Russians have received our envoy and agreed to re-negotiate the treaty, the issue of whether Ch'ung-hou should be killed or not is no longer important. Even if he is not killed, where can he flee? Let him be pardoned and released.'[5] On 12 August Ch'ung-hou was

---

[1] Ibid. 21: 16–16b.   [2] *China: Dispatches*, 54: 718, enclosure.
[3] *China: Instructions*, 3: 47.
[4] F.O. 418/I/102, 107, Granville to Wade, *confidential*, 5 and 9 July 1880.
[5] Weng T'ung-ho, 19: 41b.

granted complete freedom. It was stated that once freed he did not stay at home grieving and penitent as custom demanded but instead went about the city to visit friends, and received numerous congratulations to celebrate the occasion.[1] He was pardoned, and a free man, but he was never again given an official appointment.

[1] *WCSL*, 22: 19b–20.

CHAPTER IV

The Politics of War and Peace

ALL through the heated discussion of the treaty and the fate of Ch'ung-hou, the court was trying desperately to fortify China's defence, because, although a new mission to Russia had been appointed, there was no assurance that the Russians would agree to re-negotiate. War might still break out at their pleasure. To prepare for this forbidding future, the court on 1 March 1880 put Tso Tsung-t'ang in complete charge of the defence of the north-west. He was ordered to raise new troops, refit his veterans, and submit a progress report in one month. Tseng Kuo-ch'üan, who had captured Nanking from the Taipings in 1864, was sent to Manchuria to guard the home base of the ruling dynasty, and the fierce, illiterate general Pao Ch'ao was ordered to raise ten thousand troops to be stationed between Tientsin and Shanhaikuan.[1] Liu K'un-i, governor-general of Liang-Kiang, was charged with the defence of the southern coastal areas including Fukien, Formosa, Amoy, Kiangsu, and Shanghai; in addition he was to plan for the defence of the Yangtze area in co-operation with Admiral P'eng Yü-lin. Li Hung-chang, governor-general of Chihli and leader of the Huai army and the northern fleet, was ordered to deploy his ships in Chefoo and Dairen to guard the gateways to North China, and to station troops in Fengt'ien and Newchwang. Some of his Huai troops were to be transferred to Tientsin.[2] With these measures the court hoped to meet the ominous crisis.

It can readily be seen that the court relied heavily on the Hunan personnel for defence: Tso Tsung-t'ang in the north-west, Tseng Kuo-ch'üan in Manchuria, Pao Ch'ao in Shanhaikuan, Liu K'un-i and P'eng Yü-lin in the southern coastal and Yangtze areas. All of them were veteran Hunan soldiers who had distinguished themselves under Tseng Kuo-fan during the Taiping campaign. Even the new envoy to Russia, Marquis Tseng,

---

[1] *WCSL*, 21: 30b; 32: 7. [2] Ibid. 11: 8.

was an illustrious descendant of the founder of the Hunan army.

On the other hand, Li Hung-chang and his Huai followers were given only the token assignment of defending Tientsin and a limited area in the north. This arrangement may have stemmed from the court's doubt that Li, who advocated appeasement of Russia, would fight wholeheartedly, but it was also made necessary by the peculiar structure of the Hunan and Huai commands. Co-operation between the two was next to impossible. Officers of each army would take orders only from their own superiors, and soldiers would obey only their own officers.[1] It was therefore a matter of practical necessity to rely on one of the two groups. Since most of the Hunan personnel took a strong stand on the treaty, the court gave them nearly all the important assignments, leaving only a limited area to the Huai personnel. This uneven distribution of commands—and power—caused no small amount of jealousy and resentment. The relations between Li Hung-chang and Liu K'un-i, prominent figures of the two cliques, were described as incompatible, like 'fire and water'.[2] Li's conflict with Tso Tsung-t'ang, needless to say, was even worse.[3]

1. TSO'S VIEWS ON WAR

Tso Tsung-t'ang dispatched his progress report to Peking on 2 April 1880, assuring the harassed court that while he would not be the first to open fire, he was absolutely ready if war began. He would invade Ili from three directions. The eastern flank of the army would be commanded by General Chin-shun, military-governor of Ili, the central route by General Chang Yao who would strike from Aksu along the Tekes River into Ili, and the western flank by General Liu Chin-t'ang who would advance from Uch Turfan into Ili. Tso himself planned to move his headquarters to Hami to take charge of the general command.[4] On 26 May he left for Hami, his coffin with him, to

---

[1] Lo Erh-kang, *Hsiang-chün hsin-chih* (A new study of the Hunan Army) (Changsha, 1939), 232.   [2] Liu K'un-i, iv: 1934, Letter to Li Jo-nung, 27 Apr. 1881.

[3] Marxist writers claim that the Ch'ing court secretly fostered the cleavage between the two groups in order to use the Hunan personnel to checkmate Li and his Huai army. See Liu K'un-i, i, 'Editorial Explanation'.

[4] Tso Tsung-t'ang, 'Memorials', 56: 6–11b; *WCSL*, 19: 9–13b, received at court 16 Apr. 1880.

show his determination to die for his country. He reached his destination on 15 June.[1] The court once again cautioned him not to begin hostilities, but it authorized him to resist Russian invasion the moment it began. Because of the vast size of Sinkiang, Tso set up a number of reconnaissance stations there to hasten communication and warning of attack. It was some comfort to him to learn that there were only a few thousand Russian soldiers in Ili.[2]

Tso was convinced that military preparedness and a resolute stand against Russian pressure could help Tseng's negotiations in St. Petersburg. He informed the Tsungli Yamen on 11 August 1880: 'If officers on the frontiers can hold firm, our envoy may have something to lean on and may thus be enabled to speak a few more strong words. Otherwise he will inevitably accommodate their [the Russians'] wishes.'[3] From a German visitor to his camp, Mr. Focke of Telge Company in Shanghai, came the information that the Russian national debt had reached fifty-two million taels; Tso therefore surmised that Russia would be financially unable to engage in a prolonged and large-scale war.[4] Also, taking into account the Russian defeat at the Congress of Berlin and the rivalry between Britain, Russia, and Germany, Tso concluded that Russia would not lightly begin a war against China.[5] He observed: 'Victory or defeat, good fortune or ill fortune—all these are hard to predict. Man does not know heaven's [disposition], but heaven does not intervene in human affairs either.'[6] He implied that his part of the 'human affairs' was in good order.

On 30 July the Tsungli Yamen informed the court that the Russian government had dispatched Admiral S. S. Lesovskii and twenty-three ships to China.[7] There was also a report of Russian reinforcements in Ili.[8] On 28 August Li Hung-chang learned from Commodore Shufelt of the United States Navy that a Russian fleet of two ironclads and thirteen fast ships was already in Nagasaki and had purchased five hundred thousand

[1] Tso Tsung-t'ang, 'Memorials', 56: 44b. [2] Ibid. 56: 55.
[3] Tso Tsung-t'ang, 'Letters', 24: 65b–66.
[4] Ibid. 24: 71b–72. Focke kept a record of his visit to Tso's headquarters. See Fu-k'o (Focke), 'Hsi-hsing so-lu' (Desultory notes on my Western trip), *Hsiao-fang-hu-chai yü-ti ts'ung-ch'ao*, 6: 4: 300–4.
[5] Tso Tsung-t'ang, 'Letters', 14: 4. [6] Ibid. 24: 6.
[7] *WCSL*, 21: 27–28. [8] Morse, ii. 333.

dollars' worth of fuel.[1] The Russians also had considered San Francisco as a supply base in the event of war.[2]

The court was frightened by the news of this Russian naval demonstration, but Tso was unruffled. He consoled the harassed court that the twenty-three Russian ships were fewer than those produced by the Foochow Dockyard alone; that, since each Russian ship could carry only a few hundred, or at most a few thousand, men, their power was limited. On the other hand, Chinese veterans of the Taiping, Nien, and Moslem campaigns were ten times as numerous as these Russians, and Chinese armaments had also been substantially improved since the days of the Self-Strengthening Movement. Tso reassured the court that the Russian naval demonstration was no cause for alarm. In an armed encounter, China might very well win, he said, because Russia had been exhausted by the Turkish war; she could not possibly make a deep and sustained thrust into Manchuria. In the unlikely event that the Russians did attack Manchuria, he could checkmate them by a counter-attack in the north-west. The frontier between Russia and China was equally long for both. If Russia could invade China at one point, China could also invade Russia at another.[3] In fact, Tso much preferred to fight in Russia to spare China any devastation, rather than wait for the Russians to invade Manchuria and so be forced to fight on Chinese soil.[4] To Admiral P'eng Yü-lin he boldly wrote: 'If war breaks out, I will blunt their edge here first.'[5] He was convinced that hard fighting would quickly expose Russian weakness in numbers as well as in equipment.[6]

The memorials of Tso Tsung-t'ang and Chang Chih-tung, which had been translated and printed in several English newspapers in Shanghai, created the impression that war was imminent.[7] It was true that activities linked with Chinese war preparations were proceeding rapidly; large amounts of guns

[1] Li Hung-chang, 'Letters to Tsungli Yamen', 11: 26–28b.
[2] R. R. Rosen, *Forty Years of Diplomacy* (New York, 1922), ii. 45.
[3] Tso Tsung-t'ang, 'Letters', 23: 55b–56.
[4] Ibid. 24: 17–17b.
[5] Ibid. 24: 19b.
[6] Ibid. 24: 44b.
[7] Li Hung-chang, 'Letters to Tsungli Yamen', 11: 6b–7, 2 June 1880; the *Shanghai Courier* of 15 May 1880 printed a translation of Chang's memorial in the form of a booklet, with the title: *China and Russia. Important Memorial to the Throne. Warlike Attitude of China.*

and munitions were acquired from the United States and European countries.[1] The German minister Max von Brandt estimated that as of November 1880 China had bought or ordered some 151 cannon of various calibres, and 51,500 hand weapons, apart from the 20,000 Remington rifles and 25,000 other older-style guns she already had.[2] Tso's purchasing agent in Shanghai, Hu Kuang-yung, alone bought 5,000 Remington guns, 7,500 breech-loading rifles, and some 24 cannon from Krupp, which had dispatched a special agent to China to make the sale.[3] To strengthen the coastal defences of Fukien and Chekiang, Tso, who had formerly been governor-general there, gave 200 mines and 20 torpedoes to the authorities of these provinces.[3] The Chinese navy, in addition to the two ironclads and six smaller warships newly purchased from Britain, consisted of 46 older gunboats and 41 steamers of varying sizes, ranging from 500 to 1,500 tons. The *Wan-nien-ch'ing* (Eternal Youth), for example, made in Foochow in 1869, had a tonnage of 1,450, a crew of 180, six 56-pound cannon, and one large cannon capable of a 150-pound thrust.[4]

If China was making intensive military preparations, Russia did not relax her vigilance either. In June 1880 General Kaufman, governor-general of Russian Turkestan, moved his headquarters to the advanced post of Vernyi.[5] His army was concentrated in the three areas of Tashkent, Samarkand, and Ili. At the height of the crisis, in August 1880, there were 14 battalions of troops in Ili, 4 in Tashkent, and 3 in Samarkand. There was no regular cavalry in Turkestan, but there were some 20 Cossack *sotnias* (centuries) in Ili, each with 6 to 10 rockets, and 5 *sotnias* each in Tashkent and Samarkand. In addition, 4 batteries of artillery were stationed in Ili, and 2 each in the other two centres. By Russian standards, each battery had 8 guns, each *sotnia* 150 sabres, and each battalion 1,000 bayonets. In the event of war, Kaufman planned to take a defensive stand in Ili while sending a striking force of 6 battalions, 3 batteries of

---

[1] *China: Dispatches*, 54: 683, Seward to Evarts, 8 May 1880.

[2] *China*, No. 1, Vol. 3, Conf. Vol. 4, A. No. 134, Brandt to German Foreign Office, Berlin, 11 Dec. 1880. (Politisches Archiv d. Auswärt. Amts, Bonn.)

[3] Tso Tsung-t'ang, 'Letters', 24: 52b–53.

[4] *China*, No. 2, Vol. 2, Conf. Vol. 3, A. No. 27, Brandt to German Foreign Office, 9 Feb. 1880; also Vol. 3, Conf. Vol. 4, same to same, 4 May 1880.

[5] F.O. 418/I/173, Dufferin to Granville, 2 Aug. 1880.

artillery, and 10 *sotnias* in a south-western direction toward Kashgar. Kaufman's arrangements did not seem to impress Lt.-Colonel George Villiers, the British military attaché in St. Petersburg, who reported confidentially to Ambassador Dufferin: 'Should the Chinese prove really in earnest, the Russian preparations in Central Asia may fairly be criticized as inadequate. The Russians appear to depend much on what they will be able to do with their fleet in Chinese waters.'[1]

The Russian fleet in the Pacific was more formidable. Captain Ernest Rice, British naval attaché in St. Petersburg, reported that it consisted of 26 ships: 2 armoured ships of 5,740 and 5,006 tons each, 2 ironclads of 4,603 and 4,602 tons each, 1 corvette of 2,245 tons, 4 cruisers, 9 clippers of slightly over 1,000 tons each, 4 gunboats, 3 schooners, and 1 armed transport.[2]

Because of these Russian and Chinese war preparations, the air was full of reports that hostilities were imminent. Foreign diplomats took the precaution of requesting naval protection from their governments.[3] In the Tientsin harbour British, American, French, and German gunboats lay ready to defend the interests of their countries.[4] The total numbers of foreign warships in China and other parts of the Far East in April 1880 were as follows: Britain, 23; the United States, 6; France and Germany, 4 each; and Italy, 1.[5]

2. LI'S VIEWS ON PEACE

Li Hung-chang, who would have to bear most of the burden of naval warfare if war broke out, repeatedly pleaded with the court against hasty action. He had been warned by Commodore Shufelt that the Russian fleet might harass Korea if it did not attack China directly. From interviews with British, French, and German consuls and officials, he collected the information that Russia might hurl 20,000 men into Manchuria and thrust overland to Newchwang, while their fleet might land 6,000 men

[1] F.O. 418/I/192, inclosure, Villiers to Dufferin, 12 Aug. 1880.

[2] F.O. 418/I/128, inclosures 1, 2, 3. Reports of Capt. Ernest Rice, R.N., naval attaché in the British embassy, St. Petersburg.

[3] *China: Dispatches*, 53: 619, Seward to Evarts, 9 Mar. 1880; also 53: 648, Seward to Adm. Patterson, 29 Mar. 1880. (National Archives, Washington, D.C.)

[4] Ibid. 56: 55, James B. Angell to William M. Evarts, 29 Nov. 1880.

[5] F.O. 418/I/70, Kennedy to Salisbury, 7 Apr. 1880.

in Liaotung, to drive towards Peking in a pincers movement.[1] The rivers would be frozen during the severe winter and the Russians could easily march over them and drive deep into Manchuria and North China.[2] For these reasons he urged the Tsungli Yamen to adopt a conciliatory policy toward Russia, and to allow Tseng greater discretionary powers in negotiation, so that a peaceful settlement might be reached.[3]

Li was of course very sensitive to the common criticism that large sums for defence had been invested in his fleet over the years and that it was high time to test its usefulness. In answer he declared that his fleet received only a meagre 300,000 to 400,000 taels a year, while the lion's share of the country's defence budget went to Tso's campaign in Sinkiang, which required six or seven million taels a year. He also pointed out that funds for the Huai army had been reduced by 40 per cent., and that as a result this army had been deprived of more than ten thousand soldiers in 1879. A sense of injustice made him indignant: 'Shoddy scholars who are unfamiliar with current affairs have insisted that since my command here used up huge sums every year in training troops and buying weapons, we have to advocate war. But let me ask the administration: what have they done in the way of real self-strengthening? To speak strong but empty language when one is in reality not strong is to invite immediate danger and extinction. There has as yet been no preparation in Manchuria; only a few meat-eating [useless] generals are there, but what can they accomplish? (People speak of) great columns of powerful troops, but where do the funds come from? The new recruits are too inexperienced to be useful, even if they are numerous.'[4] All in all, Li felt that his military strength was too insignificant to allow him to talk lightly of war.[5]

Financial exigencies and military unpreparedness were not his only arguments against war; the international situation was not favourable either. Li pointed out that too many Chinese were hopefully expecting British aid in a war with Russia. They were unaware that, despite the traditional Anglo-Russian

---

[1] Li Hung-chang, 'Letters to Tsungli Yamen', 11: 28–28b, 28 Aug. 1880; 11: 37–37b, 12 Oct. 1880.

[2] Li Hung-chang, 'Letters to friends and colleagues', 19: 33–33b, 5 Oct. 1880.

[3] Li Hung-chang, 'Letters to Tsungli Yamen', 11: 36b, 30 Sept. 1880.

[4] Li Hung-chang, 'Letters to friends and colleagues', 19: 33b–34b, 21 Oct. 1880.

[5] Ibid. 19: 7b.

rivalry, the British could offer China little more than moral
support, because the Russian sphere of activity was in frontier
areas like Sinkiang and Manchuria, far beyond the reach of
British influence. Not only would the British be unable to
counteract the Russians there but they would have no incentive
to do so; for they did not suffer from Russian gains in those areas.
In fact, the British might even gain new rights through application of the most-favoured-nation treatment, if the Russians
succeeded in exacting new concessions from China. How then
could China continue to rely on British aid?[1]

It was also apparent that France and Germany would not
go to war to defend China, and Japan, then actively engaged
in annexing the Liu-ch'iu islands, might even collude with
Russia to launch a joint attack on China. It may be recalled
that Liu-ch'iu had paid tribute to China since 1372 and to
Japan since 1609. Its double status was not contested until the
1870's, when Japan began to claim exclusive control. In 1879
Japan declared Liu-ch'iu a prefecture under the name of
Okinawa and prohibited the sending of tribute to China.[2]
Chinese protests and American mediation yielded no result.[3]
Li feared that once the Japanese started to make trouble, other
countries might follow suit. He impressed upon the court:
'The whole situation hinges on whether the Russian question
can be settled. If it can, Japan and all the other countries will be
hesitant (to move); if it cannot, they will plot (against us).
Rather than make concessions to the Japanese who cannot
help us resist Russia—thereby we lose to both Japan and
Russia—would it not be preferable to make some concessions
to Russia and secure her help in checking Japan? The strength
and weakness of Russia and Japan differ by a hundredfold.
Judging by the injustice of their claims, the Japanese also in-
sulted us far more (than the Russians).'[4] This analysis reveals

---

[1] Li Hung-chang, 'Letters to friends and colleagues', 19: 17–17b, 12 Apr. 1880;
19: 6b, 16 Jan. 1880.

[2] For details about the Liu-ch'iu issue, see Ueda Toshio, 'Ryūkyū no kizoku o
meguru Nisshin kōshō' (Sino-Japanese negotiations over the sovereignty of Ryūkyū),
Tōyō bunka kenkyūjo kiyō, ii: 151–201 (Sept. 1950); Mikuniya Hiroshi, 'Ryūkyū
kizoku ni kansuru Guranto no chōtei' (Grant's mediation of the Ryūkyū issue),
Tōhō gakuhō, 10: 3: 29–64 (Oct. 1939).

[3] *Nihon gaikō bunsho* (The diplomatic papers of Japan), 11: 271, document 125;
12: 176, documents 92, 95; 12: 178–81, documents 96, 99.

[4] Li Hung-chang, 'Memorials', 39: 3–4.

a basic principle of Li's foreign policy: peace with Russia and resistance against Japanese aggression. Settlement of the Ili dispute became, in his eyes, the key to peace. He chided the advocates of war:

> Since the discussion of the Russian affair last autumn, I have refrained from talking lightly about war, not with the aim of preserving myself and of keeping Tientsin and Taku intact, but with a view to our country's safety. Indiscriminate observers attacked me as the only one who did not advocate war, but they did not know that if we engaged in a decisive battle with a powerful enemy in the provinces, my troops, though somewhat thin, might yet carry on longer (than any other troops). It is small wonder that discussion of military affairs by those who know nothing about military affairs leads to a topsy-turvy view of what is right and wrong. . . . In times of peace the policy-makers made no efforts at (preparations for war); now they urge on us a reckless war with empty words. Are they not treating government affairs as something to toy with?[1]

It is natural that in all Li's criticisms of the exponents of war, Tso was uppermost in his mind. On 16 January 1880 he wrote to Marquis Tseng: 'Tso intends to fight it out. Apparently he does not know himself and his enemy. Neither does he care about future complications.'[2] In another letter to Tseng, dated 12 April, he wrote: 'Tso is senile and likes to boast. Actually his military performances and logistics have always been despised by the Russians. In the two provinces of Heilungkiang and Kirin, there is a dearth of officers and a shortage of strong forces and substantive funds. It is impossible to resist the Russians.'[3] His criticism of Tso was even more blunt in a letter to Ting Pao-chen, governor-general of Szechwan, dated 9 April 1880:

> Generalissimo Tso advocates war and leads a group of pedantic scholars and decadent officials to make high-sounding pronouncements to the detriment of our country's security. His performances in the Western Region were only mediocre. Where does his confidence come from? . . . The Russian situation has degenerated to a point where there seems to be no end to it. It will burden China until the whole country is exhausted, at which time internal rebellions will flare up and we shall be even less able to resist external troubles. The world is originally peaceful but stupid men create troubles for themselves. What can be done about it?[4]

---

[1] Li Hung-chang, 'Letters to friends and colleagues', 19: 33–33b.
[2] Ibid. 19: 6b.   [3] Ibid. 19: 17–17b.   [4] Ibid. 19: 14b.

Li attributed the worsening of relations with Russia to an outraged public opinion, which had been inflamed in the first
place by the high but impractical pronouncements of Chang
Chih-tung and Pao-t'ing under the secret patronage of Tso. He
pronounced the consequences of irresponsible *literati* opinion
[*ch'ing-i*] to be evil and detrimental to the state.[1]

Li's espousal of peace won him accusations of cowardice and
lack of interest in China's prestige. General Liu Ming-ch'uan
ridiculed him for having uttered the words 'unable to fight',
and suggested that he should emulate Tso in defending China's
honour. Li replied sarcastically:

His Excellency Tso commands a big army and huge funds in a place
like Sinkiang which nobody will contest for. Therefore he gives the
appearance of wanting war, but he does not care about the general
situation of the state. Those who are at all familiar with the affairs
of ancient and modern times can readily see through his falsehood.
Your letter asks me to imitate him, but this is against my established
principles. . . . With my high position and progressive ageing, I will
definitely not engage in such a shameless act. I admit to having
strongly urged peaceful negotiations, but I have never uttered these
three words: 'unable to fight'. Neither did I ever have any such
intention. Where did you hear this expression? Didn't you take it
from the hackneyed phrases of miserable metropolitan officials and
corrupt popular favourites in order to bait me?[2]

If Li was critical of Tso, there were others who also felt that
Tso had gone too far. Marquis Tseng, who had to negotiate
with the Russians, was troubled by Tso's over-confidence and
open advocacy of war, which he thought would hinder a peaceful settlement with Russia. In a letter dated 25 March 1880, he
noted: 'His Excellency Tso frivolously intends to start a war
just because he has been successful in his former campaigns.
But his is only a parochial view, which does not spring from a
comprehensive examination of the general situation!'[3] To the
Tsungli Yamen he wrote on the same day to say that Tso's army
might take Ili but that the defence of the long coast of China was

---

[1] Li Hung-chang, 'Letters to friends and colleagues', 19: 32–32b, 2 Oct. 1880.
For a study of *ch'ing-i*, see my *China's Entrance*, 200–4; Lloyd Eastman, 'Chinese
Officialdom's Reactions to Foreign Aggression: A Study of the Sino-French Controversy, 1880–1885', Ph.D. thesis, Harvard University (Feb. 1963).
[2] Li Hung-chang, 'Letters to friends and colleagues', 19: 34–34b, 21 Oct. 1880.
[3] Tseng Chi-tse, 'Literary collection', 3: 15b.

a totally different matter.[1] He chided Tso for giving the impression that Russia, because of her internal troubles, was not in a position to fight. He pointed out that, on the contrary, Russian rulers had often used foreign ventures to divert attention from domestic trouble.[2] Tso's militant attitude was deprecated as an overbearing act designed to provoke Russia.[3] He urged the Yamen to restrain Tso and his troops from goading the Russians into action.[4]

Kuo Sung-tao, the former minister to Britain and France, also reproved the advocates of war for their 'parochial views' and warned that 'once the war begins there will be no end to it'. He argued that in conducting foreign affairs one should aim at settling issues rather than provoking hostility; one should not advocate war to please court officials or to ride the tide of public opinion.[5]

Wu Ju-lun, acting prefect of Tientsin, spoke out even more sharply against war. First of all, he warned the court that China lacked the land forces and naval squadrons to conduct a successful war. Apart from Tso's army in the north-west, there were only twenty battalions of the Huai army, in the whole country, that were at all useful, and these alone could not be expected to defend both North and South China. Even if Tso should win in Sinkiang, Manchuria would be the target for a Russian invasion which would directly threaten Peking. The few ironclads China had were insufficient for naval battles or for defence of the coast; wooden vessels were useless in modern warfare. Moreover, China had been engaged in internal struggles for decades; the Taipings, the Niens, and the ten-year campaign under Tso in the north-west had literally exhausted her. There was little left with which to fight Russia. Also, China had begun to manufacture arms and to build ships only about a dozen years before, whereas Western nations had over one hundred years of experience in such techniques; Chinese weapons therefore were markedly inferior to those of the West. Wu took issue with Tso's assertion that the Chinese army was powerful and that Chinese guns and ships were at least equal to,

---

[1] Ibid. 3: 19–19b, 25 Mar. 1880.   [2] Ibid. 3: 15b.
[3] Tso Tsung-t'ang, 'Letters', 24: 54b.
[4] Tseng Chi-tse, 'Literary collection', 4: 2b, 25 June 1880.
[5] Kuo Sung-tao, 'Memorials', 12: 23 ff.

if not superior to, their Western counterparts. War, said Wu, could only bring disaster; even if China were victorious, there would be unending acts of revenge that would leave her no peace. 'To know (the truth) but not speak out is not loyal; not to know it and speak out recklessly is not wise.'[1]

3. AN INTERPRETATION OF THE CONTROVERSY

The views of Tso and Li reflected their different roles. Tso, supremely proud of his ten-year campaign in the north-west, did not intend to let Ili, a prize now so tantalizingly near, slip through his fingers. As a soldier, it was hardly appropriate for him to openly advocate peace, but his reasoning was not simply that of a foolhardy fighter. He was a strategist and a gambler. He knew perfectly well that China did not want war, but he guessed that Russia wanted it still less. He saw his own strength —perhaps overvaluing it—as he also saw Russian weakness— perhaps also overemphasizing that. He could not persuade himself that China would inevitably be the loser in a war with Russia. His pressure for military preparedness and his aggressive pronouncements were calculated to support Tseng in the Russian negotiations. His advice to the court had been diplomacy first and war only if that failed. In this sense he was not a warmonger or the head of a 'war party', as many people have said. He repeatedly warned his generals against goading the Russians, but if the Russians invaded China first, he was ready to strike back mercilessly. His fierce utterances, his military arrangements, and his aggressive posture helped rather than hindered Chinese diplomacy in St. Petersburg, as we shall see in later chapters.

Li, on the other hand, was a cautious politician, unwilling to take great risks. He saw the weakness of China, and saw it so clearly that he overestimated the strength of the enemy. He knew well that China's nascent navy was no match for the more experienced Russian fleet and that Chinese military organization would disintegrate in a modern war. Should war break out, he reasoned, Russia would most likely avoid fighting on the Sinkiang frontier and would instead attack directly the key

[1] Wu Ju-lun, *T'ung-ch'eng Wu-hsien-sheng jih-chih* (Diary of Mr. Wu of T'ung-ch'eng), 6: 14b–16.

points in Manchuria and on the coast. The major burden of the fighting would thus fall on his shoulders rather than on Tso's, and China's depleted finances, poor military training, and young navy offered no cause for optimism. If he fought and lost, he would be blamed for the failure, not Tso. His Huai army, his northern fleet, and his numerous modernization projects would be destroyed; once they were gone his power base in North China would be lost, and so would his exalted, predominant position in the Ch'ing hierarchy. He really could not see why China should risk her life and he his reputation, army, and navy for a place as insignificant and remote as Ili. The stakes were too great, and the prize too small, to warrant the risk.

As governor-general of Chihli and grand secretary, Li was virtually China's 'prime minister'. He was not a provincial official with a provincial viewpoint, but a national figure who had to weigh all internal and external variables in a national perspective. He had to be realistic to save his country and himself from ruin, but to be realistic in foreign affairs at this point was to offend *literati* opinion. He knew that genuine statesmanship, like almost everything else of value, exacted a heavy price, especially in times of crisis. For his open advocacy of peace, he was attacked, ridiculed, and condemned by his contemporaries, just as he had been censured by the court after Ch'unghou's reprieve. It was only because of his exalted position and unusual powers that he was not ignominiously relieved of his official functions. His warnings against a hasty war contained elements of truth and wisdom, although he perhaps erred by exaggerating the strength of Russia. Fortunately for China, the Russians in St. Petersburg, as we shall soon see, erred correspondingly by overestimating the strength of China. Li's conciliatory policy, in the short run, does not seem to have helped Chinese diplomacy in Russia. But he must be given credit for the courage to espouse an unpopular cause at a time and place when nobody else dared to do the same.

Under the constant attack of the *literati*, Li offered his resignation several times, but it was not accepted.[1] In depressed spirits he announced to his friends: 'My words are of no consequence. I definitely refrain from forcing my way into matters of high

[1] F.O. 418/I/118, Wade to Granville, *confidential*, 26 May 1880.

policy.'[1] In contrast, Tso's star was in the ascendant. On 7 August 1880 Pao-t'ing, supervisor of imperial instruction, requested that the court recall Tso from Sinkiang to serve in the central government in view of the threat of impending war.[2] Four days later an edict was issued: 'At present the situation is urgent and difficult. The Russians intend to start trouble, and we need an experienced high military officer to serve as adviser to the throne. Let Tso Tsung-t'ang come to the capital for an audience.'[3] Possibly, Tso's recall was an artful device of the court to reduce the possibility of conflict with Russia in Sinkiang.[4] But Tso himself took it as a mark of imperial favour designed to spare him the rigours of the frontier.[5] Li Hung-chang sarcastically remarked: 'His Excellency Tso has been recalled and I hear he will come for an audience shortly. A veteran in state affairs, he may have a special formula to beat off the enemy and win victory.'[6] Tso returned to Peking in the company of 1,400 *élite* foot soldiers and 500 cavalrymen, whom he hoped to use to strengthen the defence of the capital and Kalgan.[7]

China had done all she could to prepare for the ominous future, hoping all the while that Marquis Tseng would be able to secure peace in Russia.

[1] Li Hung-chang, 'Letters to friends and colleagues', 19: 35b.
[2] *WCSL*, 22: 1–3.   [3] *WCSL*, 22: 6b.
[4] Ch'in Han-ts'ai, 115.
[5] Tso Tsung-t'ang, 'Letters', 24: 56.
[6] Li Hung-chang, 'Letters to friends and colleagues', 19: 32.
[7] Tso Tsung-t'ang, 'Memorials', 57: 34–35b, 14 Nov. 1880.

CHAPTER V

Involvement of Foreign Ministers

Iɴ these critical days the Chinese government, following the tradition of playing off one barbarian against another (*i-i chih-i*), anxiously sought foreign support, and authorized Hart to engage foreign officers to help form a Chinese navy.[1] Sensing the Chinese need, the American legation proposed a relative of General Grant's for a high appointment in the Chinese army, and the German minister, Max von Brandt, pushed for the nomination of his brother-in-law as 'a sort of Director-Generalship [*sic*] of Organization'.[2] Wade, ever mindful of the preponderance of British interests in China, asked London: 'May it not be worthwhile to consider whether British officers could not be authorized to serve China in defensive war against any Power except England? The Chinese Government still holds Gordon Pasha in high honour.'[3]

Wade was fearful of the impact of war on British trade with China, which was estimated at more than £50 million a year. To maintain this trade it was necessary that Britain spare no effort to prevent the break-up of the Chinese empire.[4] 'Personally,' Wade informed London, 'I should advocate our helping them [the Chinese] . . . because I believe in their danger, and I have confidence in their improvement, if time be allowed them.'[4] He asked for instructions on the following points:

1. If the Chinese Government give me to understand that it desires our aid in the way of instruction by sea or land, am I to reply that officers of our army and navy cannot be authorized to do more than tender their services with the understanding that if war be declared between China and any power with which we are at peace, they must withdraw from the Chinese service? Or am I free to encourage a hope that our law affecting service with a foreign power will be relaxed, or that our officers will be enabled

[1] F.O. 17/829/4, Wade's telegram to Salisbury, *confidential*, 5 Jan. 1880.
[2] F.O. 418/I/29, Wade to Salisbury, *secret*, 27 Jan. 1880.
[3] F.O. 17/829/4, same to same, *confidential*, 5 Jan. 1880.
[4] F.O. 17/829/15, same to same, *most confidential*, 28 Jan. 1880.

by some other arrangement to remain in the service of China so long as she is acting on the defence [defensive]?

2. If an alliance with England be spoken of, are there any specific conditions under which alone the project of such an alliance will be considered by Her Majesty's Government?[1]

The War Office served notice on 4 February 1880 that although the question of employing British officers in China was more political than military, 'it would be very desirable that that officer [Gordon] should, if he is willing, be so employed'.[2] On the following day the Admiralty also announced that there were many retired naval officers who would be glad to serve China.[3] The Foreign Office, however, was not so ready to involve Britain in the Chinese crisis. Sir Julian Pauncefote, assistant under-secretary for Foreign Affairs, stressed the difference between allowing British subjects to serve in a Chinese civil war and allowing them to serve China in a war against Russia; the latter case would be a 'grave breach of neutrality' on the part of Britain. He remarked to Lord Salisbury, secretary for Foreign Affairs: 'The consequences would be more serious than those which Sir T. Wade fears from the employment of Germans or Americans instead of English officers. I doubt whether Germany or America would allow their officers to take part in such a conflict. Shall we inform Sir T. Wade that we had better not encourage the hope that H.M.G. will sanction the employment of British officers in their service for the purpose of carrying war against a Power at amity with the Queen?' Salisbury replied on 8 February: 'It seems to me out of the question that England can formally consent to officers, or indeed any of her subjects, taking part in a war against any power with which England is at peace. All idea, therefore, of a formal agreement must be put aside.' Salisbury, a firm believer of the 'Forward Policy', then went on to say, 'But I do not feel convinced that it is desirable to go any further than this; or to offer any discouragement. The class of men, both military and naval, that are formed by this sort of service are very useful, and it is valuable to have a greater hold

---

[1] F.O. 17/829/15, Wade to Salisbury, *most confidential*, 28 Jan. 1880.

[2] F.O. 17/845, War Office to Foreign Office, No. 083/2554, *confidential*, 4 Feb. 1880.

[3] Ibid., Admiralty to Foreign Office, No. 'M', *confidential*, 5 Feb. 1880.

on the Chinese maritime power, whatever it may be, than on that of any other nation.'[1] The War Office and Admiralty were informed that the Foreign Office would offer no discouragement to British subjects serving China in time of peace, but if war were to break out, they must be struck off 'the list'. Wade was told that Britain could not authorize her subjects to fight against friendly powers; that the question of British officers serving in the Chinese army or navy must be a matter of individual arrangement between the Chinese government and the officers whom it was proposed to engage; that the British government would offer no impediment to their serving in time of peace, but they could not remain officers of H.M. army or navy if they were serving China in time of war.[2]

Wade therefore advised foreigners in China to refrain from writing or talking about British participation in the Chinese army or navy in case of war, so as not to excite 'false hopes' on the one hand and produce 'a feeling of irritation' on the other.[3]

Wade personally was unsympathetic with China's angry reaction to the Treaty of Livadia and her war preparations. He had from the very beginning doubted her ability to recover Sinkiang. He was resigned to the fact that Russia would not return Ili to China; several times he even recommended the cession of Ili to Russia.[4] Tso's resounding victory in Sinkiang had proved him wrong, and his reputation as the foremost Western expert on China suffered somewhat. This may partially have accounted for his lack of enthusiasm for the militant Chinese stand on the treaty, but his chief concern was the effect of war on British trade as well as on the life of the Manchu dynasty. British trade constituted 77·5 per cent. of the total foreign trade of China. With such a large commercial interest at stake, Britain could not afford to see China drift into war.[5]

[1] F.O. 17/827, Sir Julian Pauncefote's memorandum for the Foreign Office, 7 Feb. 1880, and Lord Salisbury's remark on 8 Feb. 1880.

[2] F.O. 17/845, Foreign Office to War and Admiralty, *confidential*, 12 Feb. 1880; F.O. 17/827/23, Granville to Wade, 12 Feb. 1880.

[3] F.O. 17/833/146, Wade to Granville, 22 Aug. 1880.

[4] F.O. 17/825, Wade's memoranda to Foreign Office, 5 and 26 Mar. 1877.

[5] F.O. 17/857/8, Wade to Granville, 18 Feb. 1881, enclosing a trade report by T. Grosvenor dated 31 Dec. 1880, in which he estimated the total value of China's foreign trade for 1878 at £70,632,184 and for 1879 at £71,219,369. British trade accounted for 77·5% of total, U.S. for 7·5%, continental Europe 7·5%, and Japan, Russia, &c. the rest.

The question of possible Russian blockade of Chinese treaty ports and its effect on trade loomed large in Wade's mind, and he asked for advice from London. The Law Officers of the Crown offered their view that legally Russia had the right to blockade the treaty ports in case of war, 'notwithstanding the exterritoriality of foreigners in those ports'; hence it would be expedient for the treaty powers to come to an understanding with Russia as to the exercise of such a right.[1] The Foreign Office, however, did not find this strictly legal interpretation comforting. Pauncefote prepared a long memorandum in which he argued that, in view of the 'gigantic proportions' of British trade with China and the 'considerable injury' a Russian blockade would inevitably inflict on other powers, Russia should not 'reasonably expect that the Treaty Powers should calmly submit to the exercise by her of the right of blockade at the Treaty Ports'. Such a blockade would not only inhibit the free exercise of 'the power of egress or ingress' by foreigners in the ports, but also expose them to the danger of Chinese mob attacks. Because of the traditional 'solidarity' among the treaty powers in the establishment, maintenance, and development of the trade in China, 'its sudden disturbance by one Power to the detriment of all the others on account of a dispute . . . is of itself a ground of at least friendly remonstrance'.[2] He suggested joint mediation of the Sino-Russian dispute by Britain, France, Germany, and possibly the United States. France responded to the suggestion favourably, but Germany insisted that there should be prior acceptance of her good offices by Russia.[3] The project of collective mediation did not go far because Russia considered it 'premature'.[4]

The German minister, Max von Brandt, who was in close contact with the Russian legation, repeatedly assured Wade that Russia would 'keep clear of direct interference with foreign settlements at the ports' in case of war and that there should be

[1] F.O. 418/I/157, Pauncefote to the Law Officers of the Crown, 31 July 1880, and 418/I/181, the Law Officers to the Foreign Office, 11 Aug. 1880.

[2] F.O. 418/I/186, memo. by Pauncefote, 14 Aug. 1880, respecting blockade of the treaty ports of China.

[3] F.O. 17/831, memo. by Lord Tenterden, 5 July 1880; also F.O. 418/I/129, Lord Russell to Granville, *confidential*, 15 July 1880.

[4] F.O. 418/I/158, Lord Dufferin to Granville, 26 July 1880, reporting the views of Giers.

no 'evil consequences' to foreign interests 'from the terms that the Russian Government is likely to impose upon the Chinese'.[1] Wade, however, was unconvinced. He feared that the evil consequences would extend far beyond the realm of commerce. A war would inevitably lead to the Russian occupation of Peking, and that would indeed be a severe blow to the British position of leadership in China. The Manchu dynasty might even fall, or short of that, China would be crippled for years. The indemnity, which could only be met by appropriation of the customs revenue, would cause endless embarrassment to the Foreign Inspectorate, 'in the well-being of which we, the English, are specially concerned, not only for its regulation of trade, but as the one instrument by which progress is being introduced into China, as it were, unknown to herself, and therefore without provoking her suspicion; and lastly, unless I am greatly mistaken, for every measure of precaution possible against [China's] acquisition of a fleet or her organization of an army'.[2]

These political and commercial considerations convinced Wade that he ought to counsel the Chinese for peace. To the Tsungli Yamen he intimated that if Ch'ung-hou did have 'the large powers with which he was believed to have been entrusted, (China should) ratify this Treaty, be it good or bad'; but that if China felt that more was asked of her than it was just for her to yield, then she should stand up for her rights. However, since she was in no position to fight, she had better seek negotiations or foreign mediation.[3] He told Prince Kung: 'Were I a Chinese minister I should say, let the Russians keep Kuldja (Ili), which they have got, and which has been voted, ever since China annexed it last century, a burden to the state, and declare yourself ready to pay, if necessary, even a larger sum.'[4] The Chinese were singularly uninterested in this sort of advice. Feeling that foreigners were beclouded by misinformation on Ch'ung-hou's case, the Yamen, after long delay, finally prepared a circular in July, carefully setting forth how Ch'ung-hou had exceeded his authority in signing the treaty. This circular was originally intended for presentation to the legations in Peking,

[1] F.O. 418/I/239, Wade to Granville, *confidential*, 19 July 1880; also 418/I/242, same to same, *very confidential*, 25 July 1880.

[2] F.O. 418/I/242, Wade to Granville, *very confidential*, 25 July 1880.

[3] F.O. 418/I/111 and 112, Wade to Granville, *confidential*, 19 May 1880.

[4] F.O. 418/I/219, same to same, *confidential*, 29 June 1880.

but on Wade's confidential advice it was sent to Marquis Tseng in St. Petersburg for transmission to the Russian government first and then to the governments of the treaty powers.[1] After reading the *exposé*, Wade was convinced that it did 'make out a case' for China,[2] and Pauncefote also gained a new conception of the Chinese situation, as he wrote in a secret memorandum:

> This is the Chinese 'case' as laid before the Russian Government.
>
> It is a clear and interesting statement and if true Chung-hou behaved very badly and the concessions exacted from him by Russia most grasping and excessive.
>
> Under pretence of restoring Ili (according to promise) and in the face of their professions not to seek any encroachment or annexation, they retrocede Ili minus 7/10th of its territory.
>
> I annex a note of the principal concessions secured by Russia under the Treaty.
>
> If the statement is true, I wonder the Chinese don't give it the widest publication.[3]

Pauncefote suggested that copies of the circular should be sent to the British legations in St. Petersburg and Berlin, and Lord Granville, the new secretary for Foreign Affairs, remarked approvingly: 'Yes, and telegraph to Plunkett [first secretary at the British Embassy in St. Petersburg] that he is not to advise the Chinese Marquis to ratify.'[4] Thus China's clarification of the Ch'ung-hou case materially changed the British position from passive sympathy for China's plight to active support of her diplomatic campaign in Russia. Wade took the precaution to warn London that the greatest efforts should be made to open negotiations in St. Petersburg, so as to relieve Peking from the threat by the Russian fleet or other foreign interference and claims.[5]

The French were also interested in preventing a war between Russia and China, but for very different reasons. France had little trade in China to worry about and no tradition of rivalry with Russia to speak of. If anything, Russia was a potential ally against Germany. Fresh from Paris as chief of the Oriental

[1] F.O. 17/832/115, Wade to Granville, *confidential*, 23 July 1880.
[2] F.O. 418/I/148, Wade's telegram to Granville, 21 July 1880.
[3] F.O. 17/832, Pauncefote's memo. dated 18 Aug. 1880.
[4] Ibid. Granville's note on Pauncefote's memo.
[5] F.O. 418/I/72, Wade's telegram to Granville, *confidential*, 24 May 1880.

Department in the Quai d'Orsay, M. A. Bourée, the new French minister in China, examined the Ili crisis not from the standpoint of trade, as Wade did, but in the light of European international politics. From the French standpoint, Russia should not dissipate her strength in the Far East, because a strong and determined Russia was a check on Germany. If war broke out between China and Russia, the latter would have to divert some of her better troops and generals from Europe to Asia, thus relieving Germany of a threat and giving her the pleasure of a sense of security.[1] Bourée was convinced that 'war waged by Russia meant Germany's opportunity'.[2]

Bourée had visited Poland and Russia before coming to China. 'From what he saw and heard of the condition of the latter country (Russia), in particular its financial difficulties, and the discontent occasioned by the losses sustained in the late (Turkish) war, and the fruitlessness, from a Russian standpoint, of that war, M. Bourée is persuaded that nothing is less likely than that Russia should engage in a war with any power.'[3]

Consideration of these larger factors of European power politics was reinforced by a number of smaller but more immediate ones, such as the prospect of a Russian annexation of part or all of Korea, which France would have liked to see opened to European commerce; the possibility of Russia's securing some special arrangements from China as a result of war, to the detriment of other foreign interests; and the fear of Chinese mob attacks on French missionaries in times of general unrest.[4]

The inevitable result of these international and local considerations was the conviction that a peaceful settlement of the Sino-Russian dispute was in the best interest of France. Bourrée recommended to Paris that Marquis Tseng's peace mission in St. Petersburg should be supported by France, whose service as an 'honest broker' (*honnête courtage*) should be repaid in Tongking.[5]

[1] *Chine*, 58: 5, Bourée to Freycinet, 28 June 1880 (Archives des Affaires étrangères, Paris).

[2] F.O. 418/I/219, Wade to Granville, *confidential*, 29 June 1880, reporting a conversation with Bourée.

[3] F.O. 418/I/139, same to same, *confidential*, reporting a conversation with Bourée, 1 June 1880.

[4] F.O. 418/I/182, J. G. Kennedy to Granville, Yedo, 29 June 1880; 418/I/219, Wade to Granville, *confidential*, 29 June 1880.

[5] *Chine*, 58: 5, Bourée to Freycinet, 28 June 1880.

To representatives of other treaty powers he spared no effort in promoting the view that war, or even a Russian demonstration against China, would be disadvantageous to all foreign interests alike.[1] To the German minister, who worked exactly in the opposite direction, he said categorically: 'La France ne souffrira jamais que la Russie use ses forces dans l'extrême Orient.'[2]

Japan posed a serious problem to Peking during the Ili crisis. As noted before, the Japanese were actively engaged in detaching Liu-ch'iu from China, and the Chinese feared a possible collusion between Japan and Russia. Hart had information that if the war party in Japan prevailed, a striking force consisting of 40,000 foreign-drilled soldiers, 30 gunboats, and 68 steamers might descend on Amoy and another point more to the north. Li Hung-chang was highly apprehensive that China might face Russia and Japan simultaneously within six months from January 1880.[3] Since fighting on two fronts was suicidal, it was necessary to appease Japan, at least temporarily. Liu K'un-i, governor-general of Liang-Kiang, succinctly summarized the Chinese sentiment in a memorial to the throne: 'Japan is ultimately our problem and this we cannot forget whenever we eat. But at the present we should not rashly open hostilities with her so as not to be troubled by her.'[4]

Fortunately for China, the Japanese, prompted by a number of domestic and foreign considerations, had independently come to the conclusion that it was not in their interest to exploit China's trouble with Russia. Beset with popular demands for representative institutions, the Japanese government feared that a foreign war would give the agitators a chance to press their demands. Moreover, Japan was not only preoccupied with what seemed to be the perennial problem of treaty revision, but also alarmed by possible Russian designs on Korea, which Japan considered her sphere of activity. The Japanese foreign minister, Inoue Kaoru, believed that in the event of a Sino-Russian clash Russia would most likely seize a Korean port such as Pusan or Lazareff as a base of operations against China, and as a

[1] F.O. 17/831/81, Wade to Granville, 1 June 1880.
[2] *China*, No. 2, Vol. 3, confidential Vol. 4, A. 82, Brandt to Foreign Office in Berlin, 11 June 1880 (Politisches Archiv d. Auswärt. Amts, Bonn).
[3] F.O. 418/I/16, Wade to Salisbury, 5 Jan. 1880.
[4] *WCSL*, 20: 14–15b, 16 Apr. 1880.

condition of peace might even annex the whole of Korea. Such action would be a direct threat to the security of Japan. In fact, Russian selection of Nagasaki as a supply base for her fleet had already irritated Japanese sensibility.[1] Japan realized that her ultimate enemy was not China but Russia. For this reason, Japan decided to remain 'strictly neutral' and resist Russian attempts to 'induce her to interest herself in the quarrel' between China and Russia.[2] Inoue repeatedly assured John G. Kennedy, British minister in Tokyo, that 'no understanding existed between Japan and Russia with regard to China',[3] that 'Japan would remain neutral in the event of war between China and Russia', and that 'by no promise could Russia induce Japan to join her'.[4] The Japanese hoped that, by not profiting from China's trouble, they could obtain from her 'a favourable settlement of the Liu-ch'iu question, and an assurance of increased friendship for the future'.[4] The Tsungli Yamen was of course relieved by this attitude.

If the British and French ministers were for peace, the German minister worked to stir up war. Wherever he went—from Peking to Tientsin to Shanghai—he stimulated war sentiment in the belief that Germany, a late-comer in the market for colonies, stood to gain most from China in time of trouble. Personally he had no respect for China and Japan, both of which he considered not 'civilized',[5] and he had 'no more faith in the ultimate amelioration of the Chinese than in that of the Turks or the Persians'.[6] To Wade he once confided that 'he did not care a — for them' (the Chinese).[7]

Brandt spared no effort in promoting the idea that China's rejection of the treaty marked the beginning of a rising anti-foreign movement, for which the best answer was a foreign war to improve the position of foreigners in China.[8] Frequently

---

[1] F.O. 418/I/310, Kennedy to Granville, 3 Sept. 1880; also 418/I/348, same to same, *confidential*, 8 Nov. 1880.
[2] F.O. 418/I/308, F. R. Plunkett to Granville, 18 Oct. 1880, reporting a conversation with the Japanese minister in Russia.
[3] F.O. 418/I/60, Kennedy to Salisbury, 14 Mar. 1880.
[4] F.O. 418/I/67, same to same, *confidential*, 25 Mar. 1880.
[5] F.O. 418/I/239, Wade to Granville, *confidential*, 19 July 1880.
[6] F.O. 418/I/29, Wade to Salisbury, *secret*, 27 Jan. 1880.
[7] F.O. 418/I/238, Wade to Granville, *very confidential*, 16 July 1880.
[8] F.O. 418/I/150, Wade's telegram to Granville, 22 July 1880.

he accused China of ingratitude to Russia for the ten-year stewardship in Ili during a very difficult period. 'By the provision of supplies during the war of the last few years', he said, 'the Russian Government and people laid the Chinese under great obligations. The Chinese have, notwithstanding, withdrawn from Russian merchants in Kashgaria the trading privileges conceded by its late ruler, Yacub Emir.'[1] Repeatedly he declared his belief of an 'imminent' disruption of relations between China and Japan over the Liu-ch'iu issue.[2] To intensify the war atmosphere, he posed as China's friend by helping her to purchase large amounts of munitions from Germany, and in the spring of 1880 a special agent of Krupp's arrived in China to handle these lucrative transactions.[3]

Brandt's every move was calculated to bring war closer, and his manœuvres impelled Wade to inform London: 'Although M. von Brandt is always eager to disclaim a wish to see war break out, he none the less persistently maintains that unless China be once more worsted in foreign war, there will not only be no amelioration of the position of the foreigner in China, but an undoubted disimprovement.'[4] The British minister strongly suspected that Brandt intended to annex a piece of Chinese territory once Russia began annexation,[5] and this suspicion was supported by a conversation between the French and German ministers, in which the latter was quoted to have aid: 'Eh! Good Heavens, we'll always catch something in troubled waters.' (*Eh! Mon Dieu, nous pêcherons bien quelque chose dans l'eau trouble.*)[6]

On the assumption that China and Japan were not civilized states because they did not recognize all the obligations of international law and maintained no Prize Court, Brandt publicly declared that in the event of war between Russia and China, he would dispute China's right to interfere with German vessels carrying arms or provisions to China's enemy, and that if the Chinese should attempt intervention he would order a German man-of-war to seize or sink the offending Chinese vessels, even

---

[1] F.O. 418/I/48, Wade to Salisbury, *confidential*, 19 Feb. 1880.
[2] F.O. 418/I/29, same to same, *secret*, 27 Jan. 1880.
[3] Kiernan, 43, 124–5.
[4] F.O. 418/I/239, Wade to Granville, *confidential*, 19 July 1880.
[5] F.O. 418/I/150, Wade's telegram to Granville, 22 July 1880.
[6] *Chine*, 58: 6, Bourée to Freycinet, 29 June 1880.

if they were commanded by foreigners.[1] London was puzzled by this declaration. Pauncefote commented: 'This is a new idea which I should hardly think the German Government would endorse.'[2] Lord Odo Russell, British ambassador in Berlin, was instructed to ascertain whether the German government supported the views of its representative in China. The German Foreign Office disclaimed any knowledge of Brandt's declaration, and Russell informed London that 'Herr von Brandt's utterances and intentions are so completely at variance with those of Prince Bismarck, in the present instance, that he may have occasion to regret them if they should ever become known to His Serene Highness.'[3]

Brandt was in fact pursuing a secret personal policy quite independent of his government. In a *very confidential* report to London, Wade stated that he had learnt from the German minister that during the Sino-Japanese dispute of 1874, when war appeared imminent, Brandt, then minister in Japan, told the Chinese government that he would not recognize their right to issue letters of marque, as the seas would be filled with adventurers. 'He had not reported the decision in 1874 to his government,' Wade confided, 'being satisfied that, under the circumstances, his action would be approved. He based the right of dealing thus exceptionally by China or Japan, on the ground that neither of them is a civilised Power.'[4] Brandt believed that open wounds between China and Japan were of advantage to Western powers, and when he learnt that Wade had brought about a peaceful settlement of the Sino-Japanese dispute in 1874 'he could have cried with vexation'.[5]

Brandt continued to engage in war-stimulating activities, advocating that not only was it 'desirable' that Russian demands on China should be supported by force, but a combined foreign fleet of different nationalities should be assembled in Chefoo to exert an influence against the war party in Peking.[6] Wade again

---

[1] F.O. 418/I/130, Wade's telegram to Granville, 14 July 1880; 418/I/238, same to same, *very confidential*, 16 July 1880.

[2] F.O. 17/832/106, Pauncefote's memorandum, 20 July 1880.

[3] F.O. 418/I/176, Odo Russell to Granville, 2 Aug. 1880.

[4] F.O. 418/I/238, Wade to Granville, *very confidential*, 16 July 1880.

[5] F.O. 17/825, Wade's memo. to Foreign Office, *confidential*, 4 June 1877.

[6] F.O. 418/I/268, Wade's telegram to Granville, 20 Sept. 1880; also 418/I/290, same to same, *confidential*, 22 Aug. 1880.

reported these utterances to London, with the comment: 'Frankly, I mistrust my colleague.'[1] Inquiry was once again made of the German Foreign Office about Brandt's declarations, and the British ambassador in Berlin was able to report: 'I have good reason to believe that he [Brandt] has recently been strictly enjoined to desist from it in future, as it is entirely disapproved by the Chancellor. Prince Bismarck, I imagine, considers that in the present critical state of the finances in Russia, war for her with China or with any other Power would simply entail complete ruin, and I have little doubt that His Highness has not hesitated to express this opinion in quarters where it is calculated to produce the impression he desires.'[2]

The question of Brandt's unusual behaviour was analysed perceptively in an interesting account by Wade, who was a keen observer of human nature as well as of political situations:

M. von Brandt's policy is, I cannot doubt, in a large degree personal. He is a Prussian of considerable intelligence and education; but he commenced life as a military man, and, although he was very early in the consular service, he had been remarkable during a twenty years' career here and in Japan for a very uncompromising attitude in his dealings with the native authorities. I do not know that he has taken much by it; on the contrary, his *amour-propre* has been much piqued by his failure in diplomacy, and I fancy that I am correct in ascribing no small part of his advocacy of war to a desire to pay off old scores with his government. He has ambition, if not vanity, and he is jealous of all rivalry, whether in trade or otherwise. For this, if for no other reason, he is never sincerely friendly to the English. Exceptional circumstances have led to the maintenance of a great intimacy both in China and Japan between the Russian Representative and himself, and in the present conjunction, having little to risk, for German interests are small, he declares for war even more emphatically than his Russian colleague. My opinion is strong that if there is war the German fleet will render an assistance in these seas to the Russians, which would not be authorized in any other part of the world; that, on very slight grounds, Germany, or at least M. von Brandt, will authorize participation in hostilities, and that the annexation of territory which must unavoidably follow the invasion of China by a Russian force, once begun, some island or possession of China will pay the cost of German intervention in the quarrel.[3]

[1] F.O. 418/I/290.
[2] F.O. 418/I/319, Sir John Walsham to Granville, 5 Nov. 1880.
[3] F.O. 418/I/242, Wade to Granville, *very confidential*, 25 July 1880.

The most fantastic of Brandt's war-stimulating activities was the allegation, prevalent in the treaty ports at the time, that he urged Li Hung-chang to rebel against the Manchu government. The story and its credibility will be dealt with in the next chapter, but suffice it to say here that the German minister, when discussing with Wade the possible effect of war on the life of the Manchu dynasty, did state: 'There were plenty of Chinese who would make good emperors; why [should] not the Grand Secretary Li become Emperor?'[1] In another instance he told the British minister that 'the responsibility about to be cast on the Grand Secretary Li might prove the ruin of that statesman', but that the combined foreign fleet which he [Brandt] hoped to assemble in Chefoo would give Li all the support he [Li] needed to defend his perilous position *vis-à-vis* the Peking government.[1] It was known among foreign ministers in China that Brandt had urged Li to 'strike a blow for peace'.[1] It seems that, even if Brandt had not gone so far as to urge Li to rebel, he would have been glad to see China plunge into a civil or foreign war so that he could, as the French minister described it, 'catch something in the troubled waters'. This alleged plot of Brandt's was said to have something to do with the sudden appearance of Colonel Gordon in China.

[1] F.O. 17/832/124, same to same, *confidential*, 8 Aug. 1880.

CHAPTER VI

Gordon's Visit

COLONEL Charles 'Chinese' Gordon, leader of the 'Ever-Victorious Army' in the Taiping days and a legendary hero of Victorian England, visited China in the summer of 1880, during her most critical days. Since the spring of that year he had been private secretary to Lord Ripon, viceroy of India. For a man of action, the life of a desk officer in a colonial administration was 'a living crucifixion', as Gordon himself described it: 'I nearly burst with the trammels. £100,000 a year would not have kept me there.'[1] He resigned from Lord Ripon's service on 2 June 1880 with the intention of going to Zanzibar to help the Sultan suppress the slave trade.[2] At this point, a totally unexpected telegram dated 31 May from Robert Hart, inspector-general of Chinese Maritime Customs, reached him through J. D. Campbell, Hart's agent in London. It read: 'I am directed to invite you to China. Please come and see for yourself; this opportunity of doing really useful work on a large scale ought not to be lost. Work, position, conditions, can all be arranged with yourself here to your satisfaction. Do take six months' leave and come.'[3] Gordon, with his love for adventure, grasped the invitation without a moment's hesitation. To Campbell he telegraphed at once with characteristic impulsiveness: 'Inform Hart Gordon will leave for Shanghai first opportunity. As for conditions, Gordon indifferent.'[4]

I. GORDON'S INVITATION

Gordon set out for China immediately without knowing who directed Hart to invite him or for what purpose. A biographer of Gordon claimed that Gordon himself at first assumed that it

---

[1] D. C. Boulger, *The Life of Gordon* (London, 1896), 213. (Hereafter to be cited as *Gordon*.)

[2] Roger T. Anstey, *Britain and the Congo in the Nineteenth Century* (Oxford, 1962), 76–78.

[3] Stanley Wright, *Hart and Chinese Customs* (Belfast, 1950), 484.

[4] Boulger, *Gordon*, 214, Gordon's telegram to Campbell for transmission to Hart.

was his old comrade-in-arms, Li Hung-chang, who invited him, but he soon discovered that it was not Li but someone 'inimical' to Li who had asked Hart to extend the invitation; that the real purpose was to make him leader of the imperial forces to fight Li, should the latter decide to rebel under the influence of the German minister.[1] The German minister, however, denied the existence of any such plot, and stated that Gordon was called by Li.[2] An associate of Hart's believed that the invitation was 'suggested probably by Hart'.[3] On the other hand, another biographer of Gordon stated that 'it emanated from the imperial court'.[4] Henri Cordier, the French historian, ascribed the authorship of the invitation to Li.[5] The American consul-general in Shanghai, O. N. Denny, also stated in his report to Washington: 'Viceroy Li wrote to Colonel Gordon in India . . . to come to Tientsin to advise with him as to the best way out of China's present embarrassments.'[6] Wade, having been told by the Tsungli Yamen that it knew nothing of the origin of Gordon's visit, surmised that 'perhaps Grand Secretary at Tientsin had invited him'.[7] Which of these statements was true? Was Li the real author, and was the Yamen honest in disclaiming any knowledge of the invitation?

It must be remembered that Wade had asked London about the possibility of Chinese employment of British officers, and that the Foreign Office, the War Office, and the Admiralty in the Disraeli ministry agreed to allow British officers to enter the Chinese army before war broke out. Hart was certain that he could 'obtain the services of scores of competent men, men who would fight too, but he would put no faith in any nationality but our own'. Wade reported to London, 'Mr. Hart is satisfied that, if no legal impediment stood in the way, he would be authorized tomorrow to engage the services of 100 officers of our army, to begin the instruction of a corps of 10,000 Chinese— Mr. Hart argues, with perfect justice, that the introduction of

[1] See Note G, p. 200.
[2] Max von Brandt, *Dreiunddreißig Jahre in Ost-Asien; Erinnerungen eines deutschen Diplomaten* (Leipzig, 1901), iii. 157–8.   [3] Wright, 484.
[4] A. Forbes, *Chinese Gordon* (New York, 1884), 141–2.
[5] Henri Cordier, *Histoire des relations de la Chine avec les Puissances occidentales* (Paris, 1902), ii. 215.
[6] *Consular Reports*, Shanghai, Vol. 30, O. N. Denny to William M. Evarts, 21 July 1880 (Washington, D.C., National Archives).
[7] F.O. 418/I/105, Wade's telegram to Granville, 20 June 1880.

Germans or Americans in such capacities on a grand scale would be very seriously opposed to our interests in China.'[1]

If Hart was anxious to recruit British officers for China, it was only natural that the name of Gordon, who had so successfully helped China during the difficult days of the Taipings, should be considered. Wade had, in fact, mentioned Gordon's name to London in connexion with China's desire to recruit foreign officers—'The Chinese Government still holds Gordon Pasha in high honour.'[2] At any rate, the Tsungli Yamen did ask Li to assess Gordon's fitness. Li replied on 19 May 1880 that since China needed naval officers more urgently than army officers, Gordon was not the best choice; moreover, there was also the question whether the British government would permit him to serve with Chinese forces.[3] But apparently Li had a second thought. In his letter of 9 July he told the Yamen of his subsequent actions: 'Your previous letter asked me whether or not Gordon would come to help. I have since directed the German customs commissioner [Detring, a confidant of Li's] to write confidentially to Hart asking him to inquire for us. Hart therefore telegraphed him and Gordon resigned [from his Indian post] immediately to make the journey. The British War Office failed to prevent him and the various nations thereby were greatly aroused by the news.'[4]

In the light of this documentary evidence, one may conclude that Li was in fact instrumental in bringing Gordon to China, although it may have been the Yamen which originally suggested the name. Gordon was neither invited by those 'inimical' to Li to 'uphold the Dragon Throne', nor was he intended to be a pawn of the German minister to march Li's allegedly rebellious army against Peking. He had come on the invitation of the Chinese government through the service of Hart and with the full knowledge and approval of Li.[5]

2. GORDON'S RELATIONS WITH LONDON

Gordon's appearance in China gave rise to the general impression that he was sent by the British government to help

---

[1] F.O. 418/I/29, Wade to Salisbury, *secret*, 27 Jan.1880.
[2] F.O. 17/829/4, same to same, *confidential*, 5 Jan. 1880.
[3] Li Hung-chang, 'Letters to Tsungli Yamen', 11: 4.
[4] Ibid. 11: 8b–9.   [5] See Note H, pp. 200–1.

China organize defence against Russia, whereas in fact his visit was not made without some resistance from the new Liberal government in London which had come to power in April 1880.[1] Immediately after he had received Hart's invitation, Gordon telegraphed from Bombay on 6 June to Colonel Grant, deputy adjutant-general of the Royal Engineers at the Horse Guards: 'Obtain me leave till end of the year; never mind pay. Am invited to China; will not involve Government.'[2] The War Office replied two days later: 'Must state more specifically purpose and position you go China [*sic*]',[3] to which Gordon answered abruptly: 'Am ignorant. Will write from China before expiration of leave.'[4] An answer of this sort smacked of insubordination and London responded sharply: 'Reasons insufficient. Your going to China not approved.'[5] Gordon, smarting at what he felt was an insult, summarily wired back on 12 June: 'Arrange commuted retirement. If impossible, accept resignation (of) service. Ask Campbell, 8 Storey's Gate, London, reasons. If asked, will counsel peace, not war. Return by America.'[6] Without further ado, he left Bombay.

Highly displeased with Gordon's conduct, the Duke of Cambridge, the Commander-in-Chief of the British armed forces, sent Colonel Grant to ask Campbell what had prompted Gordon's action. Campbell pointed out that Hart's invitation had reached Gordon two days after his resignation from Lord Ripon's office and was therefore not the cause of his resignation; there was nothing extraordinary in his asking for six months' leave to return to England via China and the United States. If Gordon found work to his liking in China, then and only then would he file a formal application for permission to work there.[7] Campbell was astute enough to make it clear to Sir Charles Dilke, the parliamentary under-secretary for Foreign Affairs, that Gordon's presence in China would discourage foreign adventurers and would therefore be 'a step eminently calculated to prevent war and secure peace'.[8] This kind of statement appealed to the Gladstone government, which followed a policy of non-intervention and minimum responsibility abroad. London

---

[1] F.O. 418/II/26, Inclosure 10, report of Consul H. B. Bristow, Tientsin, 22 July 1880.   [2] F.O. 418/I/82, War Office to F.O., *confidential*, Inclosure 1.
[3] Ibid., Inclosure 2.   [4] Ibid., Inclosure 3.   [5] Ibid., Inclosure 4.
[6] Ibid., Inclosure 5.   [7] Ibid., Inclosure 8.   [8] Wright, 485–6.

pronounced itself satisfied and on 15 June informed Gordon, who had by then already reached Ceylon: 'Leave granted on your engaging to take no military service in China', to which Gordon yielded his ready consent: 'Will take no military service in China; would never embarrass British government. Tell Campbell.'[1]

3. GORDON IN TIENTSIN

Gordon arrived in Hongkong on 2 July and after a short stay went to Shanghai. O. N. Denny, the American consul-general in Shanghai, who obtained two interviews with him, found him inclined to advise the Chinese government to submit its case to arbitration by the United States. Gordon asked Denny: 'In such an event, what could China rely upon from the United States?' Denny answered: 'Everything that is just.' Gordon indicated that Sir Thomas Wade might be the medium through which the preliminaries of the arbitration might be arranged, 'as England and Russia are again on quite friendly terms'.[2]

Gordon proceeded north after a week in Shanghai. In Chefoo he received an urgent letter from Hart, dated 13 July, asking him to by-pass Tientsin, where Li Hung-chang was, and to come direct to Peking:

> Your telegram of the 16th of June from Galle ties your hands so completely that *it will be a good thing for you not to talk any kind of business to anyone until you have seen the British minister.* I don't see that you can avoid visiting *Li*, when passing through Tientsin; but it would be well to tell him, if he wants to talk business of any kind, that, with your *conditional leave* to consider, you must be silent—at least until you have seen the British minister. *Li* has interpreters at the Yamen; if you cannot get Bristow (British Consulate) to go with you to pay *a visit of ceremony*, you can talk through them. But considering the view Russia takes and the action our Government has taken, the *British Legation at Peking* is the only spot in China where your presence will not cause an immense amount of, for *China*, most embarrassing criticism. In fact, it would be well and BEST for you to come to *Peking first* and visit *Li* afterwards. Sir Thomas Wade is

---

[1] F.O. 418/I/82, Inclosures 6 and 7.
[2] *Consular Reports, Shanghai*, Vol. 30, O. N. Denny to William M. Evarts, 21 July 1880; *China: Instructions* 3: 37, W. Hunter to James B. Angell, 16 Sept. 1880.

sending an invitation. Please accept it. The advice I give you is most important at this critical juncture.[1]

The letter drove Gordon into a quandary. He nearly gave up the idea of going to Tientsin, but ultimately could not persuade himself that he could be in China and not visit his old comrade-in-arms. If a choice had to be made between Hart and Li, he would choose the latter. So he ignored Hart's advice and went to Tientsin directly, and there he enjoyed a warm and cordial reunion with his old friend. Li told him about the political climate and the war clamours in Peking. Gordon himself had also heard from other sources that Li's advocacy of peace had placed him in a dangerous position. He learned that Detring, the German Customs Commissioner in Tientsin, and von Hannecken, a young German officer in Li's employ, were both urging the grand secretary 'to strike a blow as much in defence of himself as of the Empire', and that the German minister von Brandt was also pushing Li 'to strike a blow for peace'.[2] Gordon sensed the delicacy of the situation, as he described his mind at that moment: 'The only thing that keeps me in China is Li Hung-chang's safety; if he were safe I would not care, but some people are egging him on to rebel, some to this, and some to that, and all appears in a helpless drift. There are parties at Peking who would drive the Chinese into war for their own ends.'[3] Gordon, feeling obliged to stand by a friend in need and a country in trouble, at once regretted his promise to London. On 21 July he told Li that, while he continued to hope the war with Russia could be avoided, he would nevertheless offer his services, should Russia attack Manchuria or Korea and penetrate into Peking. Li inquired about the attitude of the British government toward his action; Gordon offered to resign his British commission so as to be free to serve China.[4] Promptly he drew up a telegram for Colonel Grant in London: 'I am staying with Li Hung-chang, trying to keep peace between China and Russia to the utmost, because war would be disastrous to China, but will not desert China in trouble; therefore, with the object of being free

---

[1] F.O. 17/832/123, Wade to Granville, *confidential*, 7 Aug. 1880, inclosure, *italics* original.
[2] F.O. 17/832/124, same to same, *confidential*, 8 Aug. 1880.
[3] Boulger, *Gordon*, 219.
[4] Li Hung-chang, 'Letters to Tsungli Yamen', 11: 14b, 21 July 1880.

to act, resign commission.'¹ Li offered Gordon a monthly salary of three hundred dollars and an official residence.²

Wade, surprised by Gordon's conduct, told London that Gordon's decision to throw in his lot with the Chinese occasioned him no little trouble. 'Perfectly satisfied in my own mind of his sincerity,' Wade stated, 'I felt how difficult it would be to persuade other foreigners that he was not about to enter the military service of China. On the other hand, to have pressed him after the step he had taken to draw back could not have failed to occasion serious misgivings on the part of the Chinese.'³ Wade felt duty-bound to warn Gordon that if war broke out between China and Russia 'he must quit Chinese service or change nationality'.⁴ To London Wade suggested that if Gordon ignored the warning he 'should be prosecuted for a violation of the Foreign Enlistment Act'.⁵ But London was not inclined to discipline this famous Victorian hero. Pauncefote informed Granville that 'as long as Gordon is in the military service of China, he is under the protection of China in Chinese dominions'; hence 'the consular court *should not exercise* jurisdiction against him'.⁶ The Law Officers of the Crown also offered their opinion that, while it would be an offence for a British subject to take part in any operation of war without licence of Her Majesty in the service of China, 'the difficulty in the way of exercising the jurisdiction and the inconveniences which might arise from its exercise' convinced them that 'Sir Thomas Wade may properly be instructed that proceedings for offences of the nature referred to should not be taken without first communicating with the Home Government'.⁷

Wade was piqued by this rebuff. While protesting that 'nothing was further from my thoughts' than having Gordon prosecuted, Wade told the Foreign Office: 'If it be the desire of Her Majesty's Government that no British subject should be prosecuted under Article VI of the Order in Council until the

¹ F.O. 418/I/145; Chinese text in Li Hung-chang, 'Letters to Tsungli Yamen', 11: 14b.
² Li Hung-chang, 'Letters to Tsungli Yamen', 11: 14b.
³ F.O. 418/I/241, Wade to Granville, 25 July 1880.
⁴ F.O. 418/I/152, same to same, 23 July 1880.
⁵ F.O. 418/I/156, Pauncefote to the Law Officers of the Crown and Dr. Deane, 31 July 1880.
⁶ F.O. 17/832/114, Foreign Office memorandum, 23 July 1880. *Italics* original.
⁷ F.O. 418/I/193, Law Officers to Granville, 17 Aug. 1880.

Secretary of State shall have been first appealed to, amendment of the Article in question will be desirable.'[1] Pauncefote remarked: 'I certainly inferred from Sir T. Wade's telegram that he was prepared, in case of need, to instruct the Crown Advocate to prosecute Gordon—if not, why did he caution him? The subject, however, need not be pursued.' Granville agreed, and the question of Gordon's punishment was dropped.[2]

As to the technicality of nationality, Gordon was indifferent; in a letter to Wade he readily offered to renounce his British citizenship.[3] Deeply moved by Gordon's devotion and singleness of purpose, Li Hung-chang wrote to the ministers of the Tsungli Yamen: 'Since Gordon has stated that he is no longer a British officer, the British minister cannot control him. Nor is he worried about Russian jealousy. With a view to utilizing foreign talents, I ought to keep him here and discuss with him all relevant matters, so as to be benefited by his experience and knowledge. If Wade and Hart ask your Yamen about him, please answer in a non-committal way such as "Gordon and Li are old friends; the Chinese government will not interfere from a distance". Gordon is loyal and sincere at heart, unmoved by venal considerations. In times past he made illustrious records in Kiangsu and Egypt. In spite of his distinguished reputation, he is still frugal and diligent as before, and I find him most congenial. He will do his utmost to help us in case of an emergency. When the Russians hear about it, our position will doubtless be strengthened. This will not hurt the general situation. Hart is afraid of Russian anger, but I am sure that you realize that this is only his usual attitude of timidity and caution.'[4]

4. GORDON IN PEKING

Gordon felt impelled to warn the court at Peking of the inadvisability of war. Li informed the Tsungli Yamen on 25 July of Gordon's visit, and suggested that he be treated cordially

[1] F.O. 17/833/166, Wade to Granville, 1 Dec. 1880.
[2] Ibid. Attached notes by Pauncefote and Granville, unnumbered.
[3] Li Hung-chang, 'Letters to Tsungli Yamen', 11: 18, 25 July 1880; also F.O. 418/II/26, Inclosure 17, Gordon to Wade, 26 July 1880: 'As for naturalization, I must give, and, in fact, do give it up. Half measures are no good.'
[4] Li Hung-chang, 'Letters to Tsungli Yamen', 11: 14–14b, 21 July 1880.

as someone loyal to China and willing to give up his British citizenship. Stressing Gordon's estrangement from Hart and Wade, Li announced in advance that Gordon would not live with them in Peking, and urged the Yamen to keep Gordon's advice secret from them.[1] For Gordon's jouney to Peking, Li supplied him with an interpreter who was strictly ordered 'to translate every word, pleasant or unpleasant, according to the rules of propriety or otherwise'. Apparently Li intended to use Gordon's 'downright statement of the situation' to convince the war advocates of the futility of war.[2]

Gordon's state of mind can best be seen in a letter he wrote at this point:

> I am on my way to Peking. There are three parties—Li Hung-chang (1), the court (2), the literary class (3). The two first are for peace, but dare not say it for fear of the third party. I have told Li that he, in alliance with the court, must coerce the third party, and have written this to Li and to the court party. By so doing I put my head in jeopardy in going to Peking. I do not wish Li to act alone. It is not good he should do anything except support the court party morally. God will overrule for the best. If neither the court party nor Li can act, if these two remain and let things drift, then there will be a disastrous war, of which I shall not see the end. You know I do not mourn this. Having given up my commission, I have nothing to look for, and indeed I long for the quiet of the future. . . . If the third party hear of my recommendation before the court party acts, then I may be doomed to a quick exit at Peking.[3]

In Peking the high councils consented to give Gordon a full hearing, in deference to his military knowledge and Li's prior recommendation for polite treatment. Gordon enlarged on the wisdom of peace but offered his services in war if China agreed to move the court from vulnerable Peking to a safe and defensible place in the interior. He argued that the Taku Forts, though impregnable to a frontal attack, were inadequate to defend Tientsin and Peking because they could easily be taken from the rear. Prince Ch'un, father of the boy Emperor and leader of the war party, impressed upon him the need for upholding China's dignity by war. Gordon, impatient with the arguments, used terms so blunt that the interpreter, in spite of

[1] Li Hung-chang, 'Letters to Tsungli Yamen', 11: 18, 25 July 1880.
[2] F.O. 418/II/26, Inclosure 14, Consul Bristow to Wade, Tientsin, 25 July 1880.
[3] Boulger, *Gordon*, 220.

Li's strict order, was afraid to translate them. Gordon thereupon impulsively picked up an English–Chinese dictionary himself and placed his finger on the Chinese word for 'idiocy' before the members of the high councils.[1] He went so far as to suggest five conditions for peace, the last being a payment of indemnity to Russia for the occupation of Ili. This the Chinese councillors found too hard to accept.

Gordon pressed his argument with a memorandum in which he stated: 'China's power lies in her numbers, in the quick moving of her troops, in the little baggage they require, and in their few wants. It is known that men armed with swords and spear can overcome the best regular troops, if armed with the best breech-loading rifles and well instructed in every way, if the country is at all difficult and if the men with spears and swords outnumber their foe ten to one . . . (but) as long as Peking is the centre of the Government of China, China can never afford to go to war with any first-class power; it is too near the sea. The Emperor (Queen Bee) must be in the centre of the hive.'[2]

In another memorandum Gordon dwelt at length on the relationship between the Manchu court and the Chinese population:

So long as the Central Government of China isolates itself from the Chinese people by residing aloof at Peking, so long will the Chinese people have to remain passive under the humiliations which come upon them through the non-progressive and destructive disposition of their Government. These humiliations will be the chronic state of the Chinese people until the Central Government moves from Peking and reunites itself to its subjects. . . . There is, however, the probability that a proud people like the Chinese may sicken at the continual eating of humble pie, that the Peking Government at some time, by skirting too closely the precipice of war may fall into it, and then that sequence may be anarchy and rebellion throughout the Middle Kingdom which may last for years and cause endless misery. . . .'[3]

Gordon's blunt advice was not welcome. The ministers of the Yamen informed Wade that 'Gordon's visit had not been

[1] Ibid. 221.
[2] Gordon memorandum, first dated 7 July 1880 in Canton, revised 23 Aug. 1880 in Hongkong. See F.O. 418/II/26, Inclosure 15.
[3] Boulger, *Gordon*, 223–4.

altogether satisfactory. However great might be his military ability, his knowledge of the world seemed limited. His conduct had been strange.'[1] The high mandarins were said to be determined 'to have no more to say to him as a political adviser' and Wade was doubtful whether 'Gordon could do any good in China'.[1] To London he reported: 'I am concerned to say that neither at present nor in the future do I think much is to be hoped from his [Gordon's] presence here. His high-mindedness, perfect loyalty, and courage secure him the respect of everyone, but I doubt much that his judgment is any longer to be depended on.'[1] The Foreign Office, Wade suggested, should move the Commander-in-Chief to decline accepting Gordon's resignation of his commission, appeal to his original promise that was made when he got his leave, and order him home.[2] The Foreign and War Offices concurred.[3]

Throughout his stay in Peking, Gordon never saw Hart, who had extended the original invitation. Wade saw him only two or three times, but was kept ignorant of his residence, which was somewhere in the Chinese quarter outside the city wall.[4] Finding himself unwelcome to the Chinese as well as the British, Gordon left for Tientsin. *En route* he met the German minister, who had just returned from a visit to Li. From his own sources Brandt had learned that Russia dreaded war and was inclined to overestimate China's military strength.[5] He had therefore gone to Li in a new role as peacemaker, bearing a message of the Russian legation that the reopening of negotiations in St. Petersburg must be preceded by the settlement of the pending border trade issues. Having learnt from Detring that the German minister had lately been instructed by his government not to be partial to Russia,[6] Li urged the Yamen to give Brandt's suggestion serious consideration, and the Yamen accordingly recommended to the court a speedy settlement of five pending issues of border trade to show China's peaceful intentions.[7] The prospects for peace were thus slightly improved.

[1] F.O. 418/I/272, Wade to Granville, *confidential*, 7 Aug. 1880.
[2] F.O. 418/I/177, Wade's telegram to Granville, 3 Aug. 1880.
[3] F.O. 418/I/189 and 200, *confidential* notes exchanged between Foreign and War Offices.
[4] F.O. 418/I/271, Wade to Granville, 7 Aug. 1880.   [5] Brandt, 155.
[6] Li Hung-chang, 'Letters to Tsungli Yamen', 11: 20b–21.
[7] *WCSL*, 22: 5–6.

5. GORDON'S FAREWELL MESSAGE

In Tientsin Gordon worked hard on several memoranda for Li. Hart spoke of him as being 'very eccentric. Spending hours in prayer, and then acting on inspiration'.[1] In a letter to Campbell dated 11 August 1880 Hart wrote again: 'Much as I like and respect him, I must say he is "not all there". Whether it is religion or vanity, or softening of the brain—I don't know, but he seems to be alternately arrogant and slavish, vain and humble, in his senses and out of them. It's a great pity.'[2] Wade also repeatedly described Gordon's mind as 'thoroughly off its balance' and 'no longer perfectly sound'. He attempted an interpretation of Gordon's eccentricity: 'A long life of isolation, under circumstances well calculated to disturb coolness of head, has, I fear, told upon his reasoning powers. His nerve is perfectly unshaken, but his judgment is no longer in balance, and, if I am rightly informed, his very devoutness is dangerous; for he has taught himself to believe, more or less, that, in pursuing this course or that, he is but obeying inspiration.'[3] The German minister too spoke of traces of 'extreme fatalism' in Gordon.[4]

As Gordon prolonged his stay in Tientsin, rumours were rife in the treaty ports, especially in Shanghai, that he and the grand secretary were conspiring a civil war against the Manchu government in Peking.[5] The origin of the rumour might be traced to the Anglo-French suspicion of Brandt's activities as well as to a careless statement of Gordon's: 'As Li had told me that the court is *d'accord* with him as to making concessions to Russia, but is deterred by fear of the censors, I will persuade Li, if I can, to march on Peking, and assume charge as Guardian of the Emperor; of course, I do not know if Li will do it.'[6] An interesting description of the delicate situation appeared in a foreign newspaper:

Like everybody else the Viceroy [Li] is sensible of the diversity of views which separates foreigners influentially placed in China. Personal honour; the traditions of his class; content with a position which is impossible enough to satisfy any ordinary ambition, and

---

[1] Wright, 486.   [2] Ibid. 487.
[3] F.O. 418/I/294, Wade to Granville, *confidential*, 22 Aug. 1880; also 418/II/26, same to same, *confidential*, 29 Nov. 1880.
[4] Brandt, 157.   [5] *North China Daily News*, 10 Aug. 1880.
[6] F.O. 418/II/26, Inclosure 16, Gordon to Bristow, British consul in Tientsin.

which could be exchanged for one more brilliant only at vast individual risk, and with the certainty of desolation sweeping through the empire; humanity and love of established order, even though that order should be on a low plane—all these considerations are doubtless acting powerfully to keep the Viceroy in a state of equilibrium which visions of enhanced greatness, not discouraged by some whose encouragement is significant, tend to disturb. Just now the storm of conflicting wishes and emotions, the struggle between visions and principles, is encouraged and maintained by the Russian difficulty, which in fact is the occasion of the violent currents that at the present moment are soliciting the Viceroy in diverse directions. However imperfect and merely suggestive this sketch of Li's position is, it is sufficient to show that an honest and capable adviser, skilled in political history, uninfluenced by views of pressing personal interest, and independent of instructions based on a plan of policy framed to include Europe as well as Asia, is the most pressing need which, whether he fully realize the fact or not, the Viceroy is experiencing. And if he be in such want, the Peking Government, which may at any moment find itself conspired against and is always conspiring against itself, is in much direr want of a like adviser.[1]

Although the same paper a day later considered it 'a plain duty to protest against a perverse misconception of the question of revolution',[2] it was clear to many, including Wade, that Gordon's continued presence in Tientsin was not in the interest of Li or China. Gordon himself was annoyed by the rumours of his relations with Li, and he issued a statement: 'I do not consider that Li Hung-chang has the least idea of making any attempt to secure himself the control of the Emperor, though as a Chinaman, he may dislike the Manchu government. I do not believe he possesses the material physical forces to succeed. I believe, that, if he attempted it, and did succeed, that the whole of the country could be in disorder and chaos.'[3] The Peking government, Gordon felt, was hopeless and should be disposed of through a foreign war. But what would be the positions of Li and Gordon himself in such an eventuality? 'Supposing I stayed with Li Hung-chang and the march of a

---

[1] *North China Daily News*, 16 Aug. 1880.
[2] Ibid. 17 Aug. 1880.
[3] F.O. 418/I/276, Consul Clement F. R. Allen to Wade, Shanghai, 14 Aug. 1880, Inclosure 1, Gordon's memorandum, 13 Aug. 1880.

foreign power took place on Peking, I would be bound to push Li to attack them, which would immediately bring about Li's destruction by that foreign power; whereas if I was not with Li, I think Li would find excuses enough not to act, and then he would avoid annihilation . . . (but) what would be my position *vis-à-vis* that foreign power, when they called Li Hung-chang to Peking to preserve order?'[1] Gordon found the situation too 'mixed', and decided that the best thing for him was to leave. On 12 August Gordon left Tientsin and Wade telegraphed London: 'Pray try to save his commission.' Sir Charles Dilke, unimpressed with Wade's seeming hypocrisy, commented: 'This is really monstrous of Wade.'[2]

As he made his exit Gordon declared to the world: 'China needs no big officer from foreign powers. I say big officer because I am a big officer in China. If I stayed in China, it would be bad for China, because it would vex the American, French, and German governments, who would want to send their officers. Besides, I am not wanted. China can do what I recommend herself. If she cannot, I could do no good.'[3] His final recommendation consisted of twenty items, as follows:

1. Negotiations with foreign nations should always be conducted within China so that Chinese negotiators would not be deceived.

2. In negotiating treaties with foreign nations, China should use more written and fewer oral communications, so that she could show their contents to other foreign countries for their comments. Because of their mutual jealousies and rivalries, these foreign nations might well expose each other's hidden and ulterior motives in treaties injurious to China.

3. China should make good use of her own people who had learned foreign languages rather than use foreigners who had acquired only a smattering of Chinese.

4. If China invites foreigners to teach she must be humble and willing to learn; otherwise it is better not to invite them in the first place.

5. Unless China engages in a self-strengthening movement and starts a succession of projects, foreign assistance is of little use.

6. So long as Peking is her capital, China cannot fight foreign

[1] Ibid.
[2] F.O. 17/832/130, attachment.
[3] F.O. 418/II/26, Inclosure 25, Gordon memorandum, dated 23 Aug. 1880.

countries, because Peking is close to the sea whence foreign troops can easily come.

7. China should strengthen her army before her navy, because the latter must be supported by the former.

8. The purchase of gunboats is highly inadvisable. It would be better to sell these boats and use the funds to purchase breech-loading rifles. Ships can be bought after the army is trained.

9. More important than the creation of the navy is the establishment of telegraphic services all over China and the improvement of the Grand Canal. Those who advocate war when China is in no position to fight should be decapitated. Encouragement should be given Chinese merchants to go abroad to buy goods in person, so as to cut into foreign traders' profit, and China should give preferential customs rates to her own merchants.

10. A country without a telegraph service is like a man without hearing. Schools should be set up to train students in telegraphy so that China could control her own telegraph service.

11. The inspector-general of Chinese maritime customs should be stationed in Shanghai to take charge of customs duties only; he should not be permitted to meddle in other affairs. To begin negotiations with a foreign power, China need not ask for introduction from a third power.

12. Chinese diplomatic agents abroad should be instructed to purchase foreign armaments and to present China's position accurately to the accredited government, should foreign diplomats in China prove unreasonable.

13. China should make speedy settlement of all pending issues with foreign nations.

14. China should appoint two high officers to head the army and navy respectively, who should make tours to inspect the country's military outposts.

15. Railways and highways should be constructed between Peking and Tungchow to facilitate the transportation of rice. Any who oppose this should be punished by decapitation.

16. Dredging operations should be begun outside the mouth of Woosung.

17. Officials should be sent to Hongkong and Macao to investigate the smuggling of private stocks of salt.

18. Chinese consulates should be established in Hongkong and Macao.

19. Ships sailing from Hongkong and Macao should be required to present registers of all goods on board for inspection, with their destinations indicated. The smuggling of stocks of private

salt must be dealt with according to carefully prepared regulations.

20. Customs schools should be set up to train Chinese in customs operations, so that they may replace foreign customs officials. These Chinese officials should be well paid to prevent corruption. Any found guilty of irregularities should be punished by decapitation.[1]

Li Hung-chang was profoundly moved by Gordon's simple honesty that animated these direct and pointed suggestions. He wrote to the Tsungli Yamen: 'Gordon is a man of high rectitude and sterling character. . . . His loyalty and sincerity inspire respect.'[2] But some of Gordon's plans were highly impracticable. The first suggestion, recommending that all diplomatic negotiations be conducted in China, was exactly what Peking feared most in the Ili case. The sixth item recommending the shift of the capital from Peking; the seventh and eighth which underrated the importance of the navy; and the ninth, which prescribed decapitation of all advocates of war with Russia—all these were unrealistic. Furthermore, the importance of a telegraph service for China was exaggerated, and Gordon's view of the role of the customs inspector-general reflected his personal animosity towards Hart. Li felt, and rightly so, that because of his long absence from China, Gordon no longer had a clear and practical grasp of the country's conditions, and that he was too open to gossip and rumour.[3] Nevertheless, Li was very anxious for Gordon to stay in his service, but the proud soldier was determined to leave. Gordon was offered three thousand taels, but he would accept only a thousand for his return journey.[4] He gave assurance that if war broke out he could readily be called back to fight for China.[5]

In Shanghai a War Office telegram reached him through Clement Allen, the acting British consul: 'Leave cancelled, resignation not accepted; return England forthwith.'[6] This news came as a relief to Li and Hart who were responsible for his visit; they were happy to know that their action had not cost Gordon his

[1] Li Hung-chang, 'Letters to Tsungli Yamen', 11: 26–28.
[2] Ibid. 11: 24b.   [3] Ibid. 11: 23b, 24b.
[4] F.O. 418/I/276, Inclosure 1, Consul Clement F. R. Allen to Wade, *confidential*, Shanghai, 14 Aug. 1880.
[5] Li Hung-chang, 'Letters to Tsungli Yamen', 11: 25–25b.
[6] F.O. 418/I/276, Inclosure 5.

commission.[1] Gordon himself was indifferent to the telegram; he felt he should not obey the order to return to England. He had booked passage for Aden, hoping to enter the service of the Sultan of Zanzibar.[2] Hart wrote: 'I hope to goodness for his own sake, he'll change his mind and go home straight.'[1] Hart's hope was fulfilled when Gordon cabled to London from Aden: 'You might have trusted me. My passage from China was taken days before the arrival of your telegram which states "leave cancelled". Do you insist on rescinding the same?' The next day a reply came granting him nearly six months' leave to enable him to return to England.[3] Thus the Gordon episode ended on a comforting note; he lost neither his commission nor his citizenship.

Although his counsels were not welcomed in Peking at the time, Gordon nevertheless made a strong impression on the court as to the inadvisability of war. His presence in China at the height of the crisis was a warning to the Russians that China did not lack foreign support. All in all, Gordon was used by Li Hung-chang to serve the double purpose of discouraging Peking and St. Petersburg from a reckless war. Rather than a pawn of the German minister, as some suggested, Gordon was actually a stone used by Li to 'kill two birds' at the same time. In so doing the grand secretary succeeded in giving the age-old concept of *i-i chih-i* a new application: he used one barbarian to check another barbarian as well as his domestic opponents.

On balance Gordon's visit helped the cause of peace and facilitated the reopening of negotiations in Russia.

[1] Wright, 487.   [2] F.O. 418/I/276, Inclosure 4, Consul Allen to Wade.
[3] Boulger, *Gordon*, 224.

CHAPTER VII

Tseng in Europe: Preparations for His Russian Mission

TSENG CHI-TSE (1839–90) of Hsiang-hsiang, Hunan, was the elder son of the famous statesman Tseng Kuo-fan. Although physically fragile, he was firm in character and vigorous in spirit.[1] He received an excellent education in the Chinese classics, literature, history, art, and music, but made no effort to follow the accepted path to social position through the civil service examinations. Instead, he spent his youth in his father's headquarters during the Taiping campaigns and accompanied him on various tours of inspection. Many men of talent were then serving under his father, and young Tseng had an unusual opportunity to learn from them the secrets of political strategy, military operation, and administration. It was during this formative period that the foundations of his later statesmanship were laid.

In 1872, upon the death of his father, Tseng retired to his native place for a period of mourning in accordance with the conventions of the time. The period was prolonged by the death two years later of his mother. During this enforced absence from public affairs he resolved to study English and learn about the West, in accord with the spirit of the 'Self-Strengthening Movement' instituted by Prince Kung, Wen-hsiang, his father, and Li Hung-chang. He realized with them that China's survival depended on her facing squarely the expanding West with which she must learn to live, however unpleasant the learning process might be. Although thwarted by the lack of good teachers and good books, he was not discouraged—he studied on his own with the Bible and an English dictionary, occasionally receiving help from visiting foreigners, such as W. A. P. Martin, an American missionary who became president of the Tungwen College. In time Tseng acquired some understanding of Western affairs and a rudimentary knowledge of the English language,

[1] Martin, *Cycle*, 364.

as revealed in a doggerel poem he composed in his 'Bamboo English':

> To combine the reasons of Heaven, Earth, and Man,
>   Only the Sage's disciple, who is, can,
> Universe to be included in knowledge,
>   All men are, should,
> But only the wise man, who is, could.[1]

When the mourning period ended in 1877 he went to Peking to inherit the title *hou* or Marquis; henceforward he was commonly known among foreigners as Marquis Tseng. The following year he was appointed minister to England and France to succeed Kuo Sung-tao, the first Chinese minister in the West. While in London in 1880, Tseng received notice of his appointment to Russia, to revise the Treaty of Livadia. He was then forty-one, a diplomat of some experience, with the title of Marquis first class, and a civil service appointment as sub-director of the Court of Sacrificial Worship.[2]

1. TSENG'S APPOINTMENT

The new mission to Russia, it may be recalled, had its origin in the memorial of Prince Li dated 19 February 1880, cited in Chapter II (p. 76). After summing up the opinions of the leading officials on the Treaty of Livadia and on the question of war or peace, the prince went on to say: 'Since the treaty concluded lately by Ch'ung-hou . . . cannot be approved, can we not dispatch another emissary to explain, discreetly, reasonably and earnestly, to the Russian emperor and officials, how Ch'ung-hou had negotiated the treaty, the (trade) regulations, and the protocols in excess of his authority and in violation of his instructions, and how all the officials in China—high and low, inside and outside the capital—refused to accept them? . . . On our part (it shows) we have considered (the issue) from the standpoint of both reason and human feeling; on their part they may also utilize the occasion to make a graceful exit.'[3] The new emissary, Prince Li suggested, must be 'a high official thoroughly conversant with foreign affairs', and he must be provided with a new letter of credence.[3]

---

[1] Martin, *Cycle*, 364.   [2] *WCSL*, 19: 3.   [3] Ibid. 19: 1-3.

On the basis of this memorial, a court edict was issued on 19 February 1880: 'Ch'ung-hou negotiated a treaty, (trade) regulations, and protocols in violation of his instructions and in excess of his authority. The princes and the ministers, having deliberated (the issue), have now come to the unanimous conclusion that the memorials of all officials, high and low, uniformly consider this result highly objectionable and obstructive. Let Tseng Chi-tse proceed (to Russia) to reopen negotiations and manage everything safely and prudently.'[1]

On the same day another edict was issued: 'Tseng Chi-tse, Marquis first class, sub-director of the Court of Sacrificial Worship, is hereby appointed imperial commissioner and envoy plenipotentiary to Russia.'[1] Tseng, who had missed being appointed to the Russian mission the first time, now received the burden of negotiation, which in the interim had become much more difficult.

The decision to send a second mission to Russia, which was quite in keeping with Tso Tsung-t'ang's 'negotiation first, fighting next', had not been made without comments from several important persons. Chang Chih-tung suggested that the mission might better be postponed until Shao Yu-lien, Chinese chargé d'affaires in Russia, had sounded the Russian government.[2] Kuo Sung-tao, former minister to England and France, remarked that because Russia was suspicious of Britain it would be better for someone other than the Chinese minister in London to lead the mission. He first considered Li Tan-yai, Chinese minister in Berlin, the ideal man, but finally conceded that Tseng was also a good choice.[3] Tso Tsung-t'ang concurred in Tseng's selection, but suggested that he be assisted by an associate envoy.[4] Li Hung-chang considered the choice of Tseng ill advised: not only was Tseng's physical frailty a disadvantage in Russia's severe climate but also his close association with the British would arouse Russian suspicion in view of traditional Anglo-Russian rivalry.[5] Tseng's ministerial status, as compared with Ch'ung-hou's ambassadorial rank, would put him in an

---

[1] Ibid. 19: 3. [2] Ibid. 19: 1–3.

[3] Kuo Sung-tao, 'Memorials', 12: 23 ff.; 'Literary collections', 11: 22b–26, 11: 30b–31.

[4] Tso Tsung-t'ang, 'Letters', 24: 31.

[5] Li Hung-chang, 'Letters to friends and colleagues', 19: 18b–19, letter to Tseng Chi-tse, 25 Apr. 1880.

unfavourable light before the Russians at the very outset. Such a mission was therefore in Li's opinion unnecessary—it was like 'making a picture of a snake with feet'. Li believed that the mission could not 'benefit the affairs of the state but may even hurt it'.[1] Pao-t'ing, an imperial clansman, recommended that Tseng be recalled to China for instructions and consultations first.[2] All these suggestions and objections to Tseng's mission were overruled by Prince Li on 1 March 1880. Tseng was ordered to proceed direct from London to St. Petersburg, as soon as the letter of credence arrived.[3]

2. TSENG'S PLIGHT

Tseng, to be sure, was not enthusiastic about the appointment. He responded to the imperial call with a laconic but perfectly candid telegram: 'My ability is scant and my intelligence shallow; reading the telegram I tremble and quail.'[4] To the Tsungli Yamen he wrote on 4 March 1880: 'Upon opening and reading (the imperial edict of appointment) I was frightened out of my senses and was wholly at a loss (what to do). With all his modesty, peaceableness, tact, and power to please the host nation, Ch'ung-hou was still unable to conclude a just treaty. My ability is far inferior to his. . . . The difficulty of accomplishing the task can well be imagined.'[5] He described his mission metaphorically as one to 'block the current of a river and hold back the waves that have already gone', and also 'to look into a tiger's mouth to search for the food that has already been swallowed'.[5] Yearning to be released from a task that promised such difficulties, he pleaded with the Yamen that his ministerial work in London and Paris had already exhausted him, rendering him unequal to a new undertaking in Russia. His position in Britain, he said, also would incite Russian suspicion of British intrigues behind the scenes. He intimated that if it was difficult to cancel a commercial contract in a domestic market, how much more difficult it would be to

---

[1] Li Hung-chang, 'Letters to friends and colleagues', 19: 14–15, letter to Ting Pao-chen, 9 Apr. 1880.

[2] *WCSL*, 19: 4–4b. [3] Ibid. 19: 7–7b.

[4] W. A. P. Martin, *The Chinese, Their Education, Philosophy and Letters* (N.Y., 1881), 313. Martin mistranslated these lines as follows: 'My knowledge is scant and my powers are frail; at the voice of the thunder I tremble and quail.'

[5] Tseng Chi-tse, 'Literary collection', 3: 13.

make the great and powerful Russian nation give up the Treaty of Livadia.[1]

Tseng's views on China's rejection of the treaty were fully set forth in a letter to Ting Jih-ch'ang on 25 March 1880:

> To disavow a treaty that has been personally concluded by an envoy plenipotentiary (of a state) with the emperor of another is an act that even the smallest and weakest nation will not willingly accept. How much more so would it be with a great powerful nation like Russia, which can neither be enlightened by reason nor threatened by force? . . . What I fear is being humiliated when I enter their [Russian] borders. I should then be hard put to it to find a place for myself among the (foreign) ministers.
>
> There are different opinions on this issue everywhere. The Tsungli Yamen has its opinion; the metropolitan officials have theirs, Generalissimo Tso has his, and the Russians have theirs. Even if I succeed in finding a way out in this impossible chess game, yet because of the diverse opinions it is like building a house by the roadside, where few will help but many will destroy it.[2]

Li Hung-chang knew well Tseng's difficult position. To the latter he wrote on 25 April 1880: 'I am profoundly aware of your fear of cold weather and the inadvisability of your living in the North, but there is little I can help, much as I would like to. . . . Among the trials and difficulties of your life, this one may be the worst to face. Only by total disregard for yourself and your family may you gain some freedom of thought and action. I pray that you do not worry too much.'[3]

Tseng's plight was worsened when he was attacked, even before he went to Russia, for pro-Western views. Fan Tseng-hsiang, a bachelor in the Hanlin Academy, lashed out at him in a memorial that reached the court on 26 February:

> Tseng Chi-tse, though the son of Tseng Kuo-fan . . . has for some time whole-heartedly embraced the West and has renounced completely the basic teachings of the Duke of Chou and Confucius, relegating them to the dust-heap. That the court has now appointed him (to Russia) is merely its recognition of his rudimentary acquaintance with a Western language and his proximity to Russia as an envoy in Europe. But judging from the books he reads and his (lack of) interest in the ancients, is he not a voluntary traitor? It is exactly

---

[1] Ibid. 3: 13b–14.   [2] Ibid. 3: 15.
[3] Li Hung-chang, 'Letters to friends and colleagues', 19: 18b–19.

because he is filled with biased opinions that Western nations are one hundred times better than China, and that Western laws are far superior to Confucian teachings, that, even if foreign traders travelled all over the interior of China, and Russia took over the whole frontier, he would consider it a matter of course and would not quarrel with them. . . . If so, Russia wins a loyal minister and Ch'ung-hou gains an additional protector, but how does it help our country? Furthermore, after Ch'ung-hou's mismanagement, we are able to send Tseng Chi-tse. But if Tseng mismanages again, can we send another man to reopen the discussion once more?[1]

Tseng, fearful and angry, was disgusted with this kind of irresponsible attack. He had not sought the appointment; it was forced upon him by the court and there was no way of declining an imperial order. On 17 April 1880 the certificate of appointment reached him and on 23 April a remittance of 50,000 taels arrived from Robert Hart, inspector-general of the Chinese Maritime Customs, for the expenses of the mission.[2] He had to go to Russia regardless of his personal feelings. The prospects were ominous; the mission's failure not only would spell his political doom but also would expose him to public condemnation. As a last resort, he pleaded with the Yamen on 23 April that while he would do his utmost to change the terms of the treaty, it should be signed by someone else in China.[3] An imperial reply came on 4 May:

Tseng Chi-tse, after his arrival in Russia, should study the situation and send a memorial at once. On this occasion of proceeding to reopen negotiations, he should hold his own firmly and manage prudently. The Letter of Credence having now been prepared, the Tsungli Yamen will forward it. Let the Yamen in question deliberate carefully on the treaty provisions, the several (trade) regulations, and protocols, separating those items that are practicable from those that are not, and after receiving the imperial sanction notify the sub-director in question [Tseng] so that he may reopen negotiations with the Russians. If he cannot settle all the problems at once, he may take time to prepare safely and carefully for the negotiations. Under no circumstance should he be precipitous or complacent, so as to safeguard the general situation![4]

---

[1] *WCSL*, 19: 5–7.
[2] Tseng Chi-tse, 'Memorials', 2: 1–1b; 'Literary collection', 3: 20b.
[3] Idem, 'Literary collection', 3: 22.　　　　[4] Ibid. 2: 3–3b.

3. TSENG'S INSTRUCTIONS

It was, however, no simple matter for the Tsungli Yamen to execute this imperial order to prepare Tseng's instructions and to separate the impracticable from the practicable. Indeed, rejection of the treaty had not been the Yamen's original intention, but a decision enforced by fierce public opinion. The members of the Yamen felt the dilemma keenly. If their instructions to Tseng were too vigorous and limiting, the Russians would feel themselves hard-pressed and might resort to war. If the instructions were too flexible, the conservative and xenophobe officials in China would set up clamour of appeasement. Preparing the instructions, then, became a highly delicate task, and the Yamen made no haste in carrying it out. Meanwhile, Chang Chih-tung, the self-appointed spokesman of public sentiments, was steadily urging the court to command the Yamen to complete the instructions and to enlist the views of Li Hung-chang and Tso Tsung-t'ang on the strategy to be used in the forthcoming negotiations. The princes and the high state officials would then deliberate together on the views of these three authorities and work out some generally acceptable formulae for Tseng to follow. 'In this way', Chang said, 'we shall have a consensus of opinion from collective consultation so as to avoid further mistakes after the first one.'[1]

The Tsungli Yamen finally formulated seven guiding principles for Tseng:

1. It is advisable to negotiate the restitution of Ili along with all the other unsettled issues between China and Russia, in order to reap the benefits of bargaining.

2. It would be ideal if all of Ili could be recovered, but from reports of Hsi-lun, councillor at Chuguchak, it looks as if the Russians are not going to return Ili in its entirety. They have built a road twenty miles long outside the city of Ili and have enjoyed annual tax revenues of one million taels. If the restitution of Ili cannot be materialized, we must be extremely prudent about trade agreements.

3. Trade at Chia-yü-kuan, Hami, Barkul, Ku-ch'eng, and Kobdo, etc. should not be granted readily unless all of Ili is recovered.

4. We should stand firm on the boundaries of Ili, Tarbagatai,

---

[1] *WCSL*, 19: 21–22.

and Kashgaria. We shall not allow Russian navigation in the upper reaches of the Sungari River. Russia has a different relationship to China from that of the Western nations; Russia borders on her north-western, northern, and north-eastern frontiers, in sharp contrast to the maritime nations which for the most part maintain only commercial relations with China.

5. The revision of old treaties cannot be resisted for long. Small concessions such as the reduction of taxes and customs duties at Hankow may be made, but not great concessions.

6. The treaty or trade regulations should contain an injunction against sales in China of Chinese goods for export to Russia, or of Russian goods that are to be returned to Russia, in order to safeguard the livelihood of Chinese traders. But this is a minor point that is not worth too much argument.

7. To recover all of Ili is one way out of the present dilemma, but not to demand the restitution of Ili for the time being is another. As for Article 10 of the Treaty which stipulates the establishment of Russian consulates in several non-treaty ports, Article 11 which stipulates communication between Russian consuls and Chinese local officials, Article 12 which stipulates the exemption of Russian goods from customs duties, Article 13 which stipulates the establishment of a Russian consulate and a storehouse in Kalgan, and the agreement on Russian navigation in the Sungari up to Potuna—all these are highly objectionable and cannot be granted even if all of Ili is recovered.

To sum up its position, the Yamen stated that the best solution to the Ili crisis was of course the immediate return of the whole area. Failing that, China might drop the issue for a time, and plan for its recovery gradually, so as to avoid, for the present, unreasonable Russian demands. The Yamen sympathetically admitted that Tseng's mission was ten times more difficult than Ch'ung-hou's had been, and conceded that it would be inconceivable to send him to Russia without some sort of guidance. But such guidance, given several thousand miles from the scene of negotiations, could not anticipate all the difficulties that were bound to arise. Therefore it should take the form of 'suggestions' rather than instructions. The Yamen thus conceded that these points of guidance were not immutable.[1]

Li Hung-chang confirmed in a letter to Tseng that the court knew the impossibility of re-negotiating the treaty but was forced

[1] *WCSL*, 19: 50–50b.

by *literati* public opinion to take an unyielding stand.[1] He also stated that the Yamen had indicated that the seven suggestions were prepared 'on the basis of reasonable conjectures and are to be used only as aids in argument and can be modified on the spot according to the exigencies of the situation'. Li commented on the action of the Yamen: 'It knows full well that these instructions can never be carried out. It took this position in order to accommodate public opinion and to escape public condemnation.'[2] Thus Tseng was well aware of the Yamen's internal conflict and of his own predicament, as he wrote to his friend Ting Jih-ch'ang: 'All in all, rejection of the treaty was not the original idea of the Yamen, but it was forced upon the Yamen by public opinion. I happen to be the one who has to shoulder the burden.'[3]

4. TSENG'S PREPARATIONS

Tseng's lack of interest in the mission inspired him with a strong desire to dispense with the trip to Russia. Having some knowledge of international law and Western diplomacy, he hit upon the idea of arbitration as a way out of the predicament. On 15 March 1880, while still in Paris, he suggested to the Tsungli Yamen that a small nation having treaty relations with neither China nor Russia be invited to arbitrate the Ili case. The result of the arbitration might alter the terms of the Treaty of Livadia and restore Ili to China; even if it did not, China's acceptance of the verdict would be taken by the world as deference to objective justice rather than submission to Russian coercion. The sympathy of the world would thus be with her. Tseng cited Belgium's arbitration of the *Alabama* case for Britain and the United States as an example, in which Britain, the stronger party, had been made to pay £2 million sterling, or some $10 million, to the United States.[4]

Arbitration, however, did not appeal to the Tsungli Yamen, and Tseng on second thoughts also discarded it. He concluded that Western jurists were unreliable just as international law itself was still imperfectly developed. If China, which had laws and practices very different from the West, were to invoke

---

[1] Li Hung-chang, 'Letters to friends and colleagues', 19: 18b–19.
[2] Ibid. 19: 22b.
[3] Tseng Chi-tse, 'Literary collection', 3: 15b.   [4] Ibid. 3: 16–16b.

international law now, other countries in the future might force her to invoke it in situations that she found wholly unfavourable. Thus arbitration guaranteed no present benefit but might bring untold future complications. If the Russians had been amenable to reason and justice, Tseng reasoned, they would have accepted China's claim to Ili in the first place. Their disregard of China's position was clear proof of their rejection of reason and justice; they definitely would not accept the arguments of international jurists.[1]

To avoid his predecessor's mistakes, Tseng studied earnestly the geography of Ili. No effort was spared in comparing the several editions of the maps of Ili, prepared by the British, Germans, Austrians, and Russians.[2] He wrestled with all aspects of the case and spent days and nights formulating the strategy he would use in the forthcoming negotiations.

On 25 May a confidential telegram from the Yamen instructed Tseng to tell the Russians, as soon as he arrived, why China had not ratified the treaty. If they refused to return Ili, he was to drop the issue of the treaty, postponing it for future discussions. In this way the Yamen hoped to reach a temporary settlement.[3] Tseng himself reasoned that the more anxious he appeared to be to recover Ili, the more intransigent the Russians would become; therefore it might be well to delay its restitution, with a clear announcement that such delay was not outright cession. None the less he believed that this way was only temporarily satisfactory; a real solution could be found only in the complete restoration of Ili and the settlement of the trade problems. Fearing that such a stand might invite criticism from diehards, he explained to the court: 'Your minister, not yet having gone to the Russian capital, is not under Russian influence and is not promoting the absurd idea of compromise. Since he has weighed the forces of circumstance and has come to grips with the situation, he dares not refuse to speak out.'[4]

What worried Tseng most was the ominous possibility that the Russians might reject his mission outright. It was therefore a matter of first importance that he win their acceptance first and so establish a foothold in St. Petersburg. To this end, he adopted a conciliatory approach instead of following the

---

[1] Tseng Chi-tse, 'Literary collection', 4: 4–4b.   [2] Ibid. 3: 21; 'Diary', 2: 38b.
[3] Idem, 'Memorials', 2: 10–10b.   [4] Ibid. 2: 11–11b.

Yamen's suggestion of stating China's position on the treaty inexorably at the very outset. To the court he anxiously explained his tactics: 'When your minister arrives at the Russian capital, he will simply state that China and Russia, having had peaceful and friendly relations for many years, should naturally exchange envoys to communicate each other's feelings in sincerity, regardless of the Ili case; that he has come with an imperial appointment is proof of (China's) true intentions of peace and friendship. Discussions of official business and transmission of communications are the natural duties of a minister. When he has received official messages from his government, he will open discussions with them with a fair mind, etc. With this kind of opening statement he (hopes they will) not summarily reject him when he enters their boundary.'[1]

After careful deliberation on the issues at stake, Tseng reported his views to the court in a long memorial on 27 May 1880. He opened directly: 'The Ili case has three main issues: boundaries, trade, and pecuniary compensation. There are also three ways to approach it: war, defence, and peace.' Then he proceeded to grapple with the most important arguments of the war and peace advocates. The former, he said, had argued glibly that Tso's army could easily defeat the Russians and take Ili, but they did not know that Ili's topography favoured defence over offence. The Russians were not the same as the Moslem rebels; in a battle against the Russians, Tso might not win. Even if he took Ili the war would not be over, because the Russian navy could still harass the China coast at any time. China would have a hard time waging a war in Sinkiang and defending Manchuria and the coast at the same time; she should not do it before she had consolidated her maritime defence and recovered from the effects of internal rebellions. He ridiculed the war party's argument that China might find allies among the European states to checkmate Russia; he called this argument 'the application of the trite formula of the Warring States Period (403–221 B.C.) to the affairs of today'. Such alliances were impossible, he asserted, because European states were controlled by their parliaments and no amount of Chinese persuasion could convince any European parliament of the wisdom of such alliances. Moreover, foreign assistance usually

[1] Idem, 'Literary collection', 2: 9b.

had a price: Turkey had secured British support against Russia at the Congress of Berlin only at the high price of Cyprus.

Tseng also disputed the arguments of the peace advocates that Ili was only a waste land at the border and not worth the price of the commercial privileges and monetary compensation the Russians were demanding. He pointed out that former emperors had worked hard to conquer the Western Region because they knew that 'without pacifying the Western Region the state could not ultimately rest in peace'. Ili was not a barren land but a passage to the heart of the country. He called attention to the fact that the British and French military experts considered it a fortress for the defence of Sinkiang.

Tseng also took issue with the popular proposition that the restitution of Ili could be postponed. What then, he asked, would be the use of Tso and his huge army? Was he to be recalled, or allowed to stay in idleness on the frontiers? China's limited resources could not indefinitely support his troops and the coastal defences at the same time.

For these reasons, Tseng concluded that the restitution of Ili had to be faced as an immediate problem, not one that could be postponed. In short, he argued: 'The issues at stake do not exceed the three main categories of boundaries, trade, and compensation. Of the three, monetary compensation is the least important, and of boundaries and trade, the latter seems less important than the former.' It was clear to him that he should hold firm on the issue of boundaries, bargain with the Russians on trade issues, and be conciliatory on the question of monetary compensation for Russian expenses in occupying Ili. He knew that no state—not China, much less Russia—would give up a profitable treaty without proper compensation. Hence it was necessary to provide the Russians with a graceful exit on the boundary issue by granting them some trade privileges and liberal pecuniary compensation. 'The gains and losses may not be fair temporarily but it is important that both sides accommodate each other so that peace may be preserved and a sudden break averted.'[1]

As a deft court politician, Tseng knew that conciliatory language of this sort would not be welcomed at home. To forestall criticism he explained to the court:

[1] Tseng Chi-tse, 'Memorials', 2: 4–8.

Your minister has advanced the idea of mutual accommodation even before proceeding to the (Russian) capital, thereby giving the unavoidable impression of timidity, and provoking a barrage of enraged criticisms. In his humble opinion, (if he is only) to follow a fixed pattern (of action) with the (single) duty of transmitting the communications of the two governments, listing and arguing against those items that should be rejected with all his might—whether this will lead to success or failure he does not know—his obligations are truly much lighter than he had thought. If so, it is indeed easy . . . . But what worries him most is his fear that the court officials already have agreed upon an item-by-item rejection of all the articles on trade and boundary, with the single exception of the monetary compensation. They have certainly taken a high tone and made eloquent speeches, but they talk only about moral law and not the fact of power; they discuss reason but not force. The Russians definitely will not agree.[1]

Tseng foresaw only three possibilities if the Russians rejected Chinese demands: first, war, bringing with it wholesale destruction that the court could imagine for itself; second, giving up Ili for the time being; third, yielding what China now refused to yield. The issues were of such vital importance that he suggested a thorough examination of his memorial by all the important officials of the country.[1] He also attempted to palliate the effect of his memorial on the conservatives by explaining to the Tsungli Yamen on 27 May: 'My motive in presenting my views respectfully in a memorial was to seek confidential deliberation. My language may be rather blunt and direct, but because the issues involved concern the general situation, I cannot bear to keep silence. Naturally I know that those who are not connected (with the negotiations) will find much (reason) to quarrel with me, but I have no time to be distressed by it.'[2]

As he had expected, the court was not pleased with the memorial. Against his wishes, it was not referred to the high officials for comment. Instead, an edict was issued on 31 July, reminding him of China's just cause in demanding the restitution of Ili, and that the Russians never had claimed that Ili had been ceded to them; they had simply been keeping it for China during a period of disorder. Tseng was cautioned against being

[1] Ibid. 2: 8–9b.   [2] Idem, 'Literary collection', 4: 1b.

too conciliatory. He was told to negotiate with the Russians in strict accordance with his instructions and was allowed only to make minor changes after seeking the court's prior approval.[1]

Before he left London for Russia, Tseng was careful to request Lord Granville to instruct the British ambassador in St. Petersburg to give him 'unofficial assistance and advice' during his mission in Russia and to keep confidential all Chinese communications to Wade, whom he said the Chinese government had come to regard as a 'personal friend'.[2] John W. Forster, the newly appointed United States minister to Russia who visited London on his way to St. Petersburg, was also requested to aid and counsel Tseng during his stay in Russia.[3] After having received positive assurances from both statesmen, Tseng was fortified to set out on his new mission.

[1] Tseng Chi-tse, 'Memorials', 2: 12–12b.
[2] F.O. 418/I/74, Granville to Wade, *confidential*, 2 June 1880.
[3] John W. Foster, *Diplomatic Memoirs* (Boston, 1909), i. 155.

CHAPTER VIII

The Opening of Negotiations in St. Petersburg

MARQUIS TSENG left for Russia via Paris and Berlin, reaching St. Petersburg on 30 July 1880.[1] He was accompanied by Sir Halliday Macartney, his English adviser in the London legation; M. Prosper Giquel, the former French supervisor of the Foochow Dockyard; and several Chinese and Manchu interpreters and assistants.[2] Immediately after his arrival in the Russian capital, he assigned Macartney as his liaison man with the British embassy, and Lord Dufferin, British ambassador, reciprocated by placing his first secretary F. R. Plunkett in close touch with the Chinese mission.[3] Having made these arrangements, Tseng began a thorough examination of the conditions in Russia in accordance with the old Chinese adage: 'Know your enemy as well as yourself, a hundred victories out of a hundred battles.'

I. RUSSIA ON THE EVE OF THE NEGOTIATIONS

Russia in 1880 stood externally isolated and internally restive. Her international position was highly precarious. The spectre of Britain, her traditional rival, seemed to menace her designs everywhere. Ever since gaining control of India in 1763, Britain had made it a cardinal principle of her foreign policy to secure India against Russian advances, and especially to safeguard British communication routes to India. By a special provision of the Treaty of Paris in 1856 after the Crimean war, Britain succeeded in closing the Bosphorus and Dardanelles straits to Russian ships. Stung by their defeat and this subsequent penalty, Russian generals and politicians in the next two decades talked openly of invading India and made frequent assessments of the relative strengths of the Russian and British armies. Traditional Anglo-Russian rivalry gained a new edge.

---

[1] Tseng Chi-tse, 'Memorials', 2: 16–16b.
[2] D. C. Boulger, *The Life of Sir Halliday Macartney* (London, 1908), 342.
[3] F.O. 418/I/179, Dufferin to Granville, *confidential*, 6 Aug. 1880; 418/I/265, Plunkett to Granville, *secret*, 21 Sept. 1880.

In all fairness Russia did not really intend to attack India; she simply used the threat of war to bargain with Britain for the reopening of the Straits.[1] But Britain, fearing Russian penetration into India, and nourishing hopes of creating a buffer between Russia and her own colony, found Yakub Beg's empire-building in Kashgaria a fulfilment of her hopes and gave him her blessing. In retaliation, Russian generals on the Central Asian border marched into Ili in 1871.

Anglo-Russian rivalry in the Balkans was even more frustrating to St. Petersburg. In a fervour of Pan-Slavism Russia provoked a war with Turkey in 1877 and dictated the Treaty of San Stefano to a prostrate country the following year. Turkey had to cede the southern part of Bessarabia to Russia, recognize the independence of Serbia, Montenegro, and Rumania, and consent to the creation of the new princedom of Bulgaria. But the ink on the treaty was hardly dry when Britain intervened, Queen Victoria stating that it was not a question of upholding Turkey but of British or Russian supremacy in the world.[2] Bismarck offered to mediate as an 'honest broker', and the Congress of Berlin that was called in 1878 practically undid the Treaty of San Stefano. Bulgaria was reduced to half its size, Macedonia was left to Turkey, Bosnia and Herzegovina went to Austria, Britain won control of Cyprus, and France obtained Tunis. Alexander II's Balkan policy was a total fiasco. With Russia checked in the Near East, Britain again turned to Central Asia and in 1879 subjugated Afghanistan, thus weakening still more Russia's position in Central Asia.

Embittered by the outcome of the Congress, Alexander II accused Bismarck of favouritism toward Britain and Austria and ingratitude to Russia for her neutrality during the Franco-Prussian War. In the words of the Tsar, the Congress had been nothing but a 'European coalition against Russia under the leadership of Prince Bismarck'.[3] The Russian Foreign Office began a newspaper campaign against Germany, and Bismarck retaliated by increasing tariffs on Russian imports and proclaiming special quarantine measures against an outbreak of Russian

[1] James G. Allen, 'Anglo-Russian Rivalry in Central Asia, 1865–1885', Ph.D. thesis, University of California, Berkeley (1934), 66–69, 430.

[2] Carlton J. H. Hayes, *A Generation of Materialism* (New York, 1941), 28.

[3] Ibid. 34, quoting from *Die große Politik*, iii (1922), 3.

plague. When Russia moved her cavalry into Poland to put pressure on Germany, Bismarck signed a treaty of alliance with Austria against Russia.[1] There was a growing feeling that the mutual antipathy would inevitably lead to a war between Germany and Russia.[2]

Thus, as the decade of the 1870's drew to a close, Russia was deeply involved in European power politics and at the same time thoroughly isolated: Britain, Austria, Germany, and Turkey were all ranged against her, while France, traditionally the seat of liberalism and revolution, was not to the taste of Alexander II, troubled as he was by domestic revolutionary agitation. Russia's main concern after the Congress of Berlin was to put an end to this isolation and restore her lost prestige. Against this concern the Ili dispute paled into insignificance. In fact, the Russian Foreign Office had never taken kindly to the occupation of Ili by the border generals in the first place; it tolerated their action only so long as it did not embarrass the central government. But once international complications arose, together with the possibility of war, the Foreign Office withdrew its compliance and cast about for the means of making a graceful exit; it knew what Russia's international position was, if the generals on the border did not. It was constantly suspicious of British prompting behind the Chinese: Hart and Wade were after all advising the Chinese government, Gordon went to China, and Tseng was in close contact with the British legation in St. Petersburg. Miliutin was convinced that Britain yearned to stir up war between Russia and China to benefit herself.[3] Cardonne, the biographer of Alexander II, asserted that Russia's fear of British intervention had a decisive influence on her policy toward China.[4]

But Russia's internal troubles were far more decisive than her international predicament. Alexander II had inherited from Nicholas I a country of poverty, misery, and discord. Influenced by his preceptor, the poet Zhukovsky, the young Tsar carried out a number of far-reaching reforms: the abolition

---

[1] B. H. Sumner, *Russia and the Balkans, 1870–1880* (Oxford, 1937), 557–8. Bismarck also requested a new bill for military expansion, cf. Hayes, 36–37.

[2] F.O. 65/1083/595, Plunkett to Granville, *most confidential*, 8 Dec. 1880.

[3] Miliutin, iii. 276, 298. Russia had no doubt about Britain's secret role in China's war preparations. Cf. Terent'ev, iii. 253.

[4] Cardonne, 167–18.

of serfdom in 1861, the reform of the *zemstvo* system in 1864, the introduction of a new judicial system in the same year, and the initiation of universal military service in 1874. Contrary to all expectation, these reforms did not allay public discontent; instead they exposed Russia to new political instability and social unrest. The peasant reform of 1861, for instance, abolished the institution of serfdom but did not give land to the emancipated serfs—ownership of land now rested with the peasant communes (*mirs*) and not with the peasants individually. Such partial progress could not satisfy the peasants, but it was enough to goad the nobility into demanding new political rights to compensate them for the loss of economic and social privileges. The bureaucrats and the old guard also resented the sharing of power by a new class.[1] Public demands speedily outstripped the efforts of a reluctant government: the *raznochintsy*, the intelligentsia of no fixed social class, began to clamour for revolution and for reorganization of the country along democratic and constitutional lines. They won a large following among the half-starved university students, who now pressed for social as well as political revolution. When their initial demands for a democratic constitution with elective representatives in central as well as local government were not met, they called for terrorism and assassination of government leaders. Bakunin, urging the principle of populism (*narodnichestvo*) with great success, called for the destruction of state power by mass uprisings, and for the creation of peasant communes in its place. The government, torn by all these demands, could only respond with ceaseless arrests of the revolutionaries and nihilists. Russian society was convulsed and revolution was imminent.[2]

Financial difficulties also beset the state; the Turkish war had put a heavy strain on the treasury, and the government had to levy new taxes to meet its needs. The budget for 1879 was 661 million roubles, of which 228 million came from the new excise tax on spirits and 117 million from taxes on the peasantry and on land. The public debt that year increased by 267,951,859 roubles to a grand total of 2,783,281,720 roubles. Interest on the public debt alone was 172 million roubles, about one-fourth of the budget. John W. Foster, the American minister in Russia, said of this exigency: 'The actual expenditures for the year

[1] Sumner, op. cit. 5.   [2] Ibid. 10.

have exceeded the estimates by the large sum of 166 million roubles, of which excess about 34 million are chargeable to the regular wants of government and 132 million to extraordinary war expenses, mainly growing out of the Turkish war.'[1] Business circles in Russia entertained the worst possible apprehensions; stocks and exchange fell in value and government credit depreciated.[2]

The levying of new taxes added fuel to social and political unrest. Widespread lawlessness and disorder beset the provinces, as evidenced by the anti-Jewish riots. Crop failures in the winters of 1879 and 1880 caused additional suffering to large sections of the country, and rising unemployment swelled the ranks of the nihilists with hungry and idle men.[2] Financially and politically, therefore, Russia was in no position for another foreign venture. Jomini, senior counsellor in the Foreign Office, frankly admitted to Giers that although 'it is only a good beating that will make them [the Chinese] see reason, I confess that this necessity is rather hard on our poor finances'.[3]

Russia's military state was no more encouraging. The Siberian railway had not yet been constructed, and transportation of troops to Asia was slow and costly. Only 5,000 soldiers were dispatched to the Far East during the critical years of 1879–80, against China's reputed 180,000 under Tso Tsung-t'ang.[4] Such an exaggerated estimate of Chinese strength reflected the poor quality of Russian intelligence. In fact, the Chinese had always been something of an unknown quantity, and the Russian General Staff could not accurately evaluate their military capacity. Several authorities considered Tso's army the equal of Russia's and reckoned that at least 40,000 of his men possessed modern weapons. Uncertainty about Chinese forces and the long frontier between the two countries troubled the General Staff. Gordon's open advice to the Chinese about a long war of attrition elicited from a high-ranking Russian official the remark that here was 'an additional reason for us not to risk crushing the Chinese empire, which would put us face to face with a fearful unknown'.[5]

[1] *Russia: Dispatches*, 35: 70, Foster to Evarts, 24 Dec. 1880.
[2] Ibid. 35: 120, Foster to James G. Blaine, 23 May 1881.
[3] Jelavich, 118, Jomini to Giers, 3/15 Oct. 1880.
[4] Andrew Malozemoff, *Russian Far Eastern Policy, 1881–1904* (Berkeley, 1958), 20, 258, footnote 4.   [5] Jelavich, 121, Jomini to Giers, 12/24 Oct. 1880.

The Russian General Staff especially feared that, in case of a war, the Chinese might make a sharp thrust from Manchuria along the Amur River into Siberia. Since defence of that sparsely populated and remote area was impossible, the only alternative would be to launch an offensive against Manchuria first, but that could not be done for lack of soldiers.[1] Jomini admitted that 'on land we have not even the means of marching on Peking'.[2] Under such conditions, they knew, war with China would be prolonged and ruinous. Miliutin considered such a war 'a misfortune without any possible compensation', something to be 'absolutely avoided'.[3]

No keen observer of Russia could fail to notice all these internal and external difficulties. Foster made a summary of them in a succinct report to Washington:

> The government finances are in a very depressed condition; its foreign and bonded credit is low; its expenditures are now in time of peace greater than its receipts; and its forced paper currency is fifty percent below par. Commerce is without animation and the balance of trade is largely against the country, with slight prospect of an early improvement. The last year was one of general failure of crops in a large section of the richest agricultural part of the country; even in St. Petersburg and Moscow bread has advanced three and four hundred percent above ordinary prices; and whole provinces, embracing millions of people, are threatened with famine during the present winter. Added to this, there is a wide spread political discontent and a growing feeling that some important reforms in the government must be made. So that it would appear to be the part of prudent and patriotic statesmanship in Russia to seek for foreign peace, and to devote the energies and wisdom of political administration to the improvement of the internal affairs of the empire.[4]

It was this Russia, a state plagued with serious internal and external difficulties, that Marquis Tseng found when he arrived to reopen the negotiations. Whether Russian statesmen would devote their energies to social improvement as Foster hoped or to a foreign war which promised only misery and ruin was a matter which compelled the attention of the world.

---

[1] Malozemoff, 21.
[2] Jelavich, 121, Jomini to Giers, 12/24 Oct. 1880.
[3] Ibid. 128, same to same, 22 Oct./3 Nov. 1880.
[4] *Russia: Dispatches,* 34: 57, Foster to Evarts, 19 Nov. 1880.

2. THE OPENING OF THE NEGOTIATIONS

The Russian assistant foreign minister, Nikolai K. Giers, had discussed the Chinese matter with the British ambassador, Lord Dufferin. Giers had indicated that if Marquis Tseng began his mission with a 'monstrous' communication that Ch'ung-hou's ultimate fate depended on the outcome of the negotiations in St. Petersburg, he would decline discussion. The question of Ili, he intimated, was relatively unimportant, as compared with the issue of Chinese compensation for damages to Russian traders. Dufferin therefore secretly warned Tseng that he should not open negotiations in the manner Giers had anticipated and that a complete pardon of Ch'ung-hou was necessary in order to placate Russian irritability and sense of outrage.[1] Tseng accordingly sent a telegram to Peking requesting an immediate pardon of Ch'ung-hou, as noted previously. Dufferin indicated that Tseng's ministerial rank, as compared with Ch'ung-hou's ambassadorial, would not be a serious handicap.[2] He confided that 'the Russians professed to lay less stress on the territorial part of the Treaty than on the commercial concessions contained in it, and on the indemnities to be paid to certain Russians'.[3] Tseng was therefore not without an inkling of Russian intentions and tactics in the forthcoming negotiations. He was in fact prepared for a severe encounter with the Russians.

On 4 August 1880 Tseng met with Giers, Jomini, and Butzow.[4] Giers bluntly asked Tseng what had brought him to St. Petersburg. When the Chinese replied 'To negotiate', Giers interrupted abruptly: 'About what?' Tseng rejoined: 'Well, about the matters so clumsily dealt with by Ch'ung-hou at Livadia. . . .' Giers spoke out energetically: 'How is it possible to negotiate with a people who cut off the heads of their ambassadors? I may come to a settlement with you, and as soon as

---

[1] F.O. 418/I/158, Dufferin to Granville, 26 July 1880; 418/I/178, same to same, *confidential*, 2 Aug. 1880.

[2] Tseng Chi-tse, 'Literary collection', 4: 5–5b.

[3] F.O. 418/I/265, Plunkett to Granville, *secret*, 21 Sept. 1880.

[4] Giers, a Swedish Protestant by extraction, had served in Europe and the Middle East for 30 years, but had no knowledge of China. Jomini, also of Swedish extraction, knew well about European diplomacy but little about either Russia or China. 'He was ingenious, receptive, loquacious' but 'incapable of holding to any opinion or line of his own . . . his French style was excellent and he could turn out dispatches by the ream'. Cf. B. H. Sumner, 24–25. Butzow, minister to China since 1874, had been recalled to assist in the negotiations.

you reach Peking it is very possible that you may be condemned to death. The transaction of business under these circumstances is out of the question.'[1] Tseng replied apologetically that he too was sorry about Ch'ung-hou's punishment but explained that it resulted from violation of instructions, and was not intended in any way to offend Russia. Giers indicated that he was thoroughly aware of the domestic nature of the case and did not dispute China's prerogative of punishing her own nationals; however, since Ch'ung-hou had suffered for the results of his Russian mission, Russia was involved too. Tseng replied that the Emperor of China fortunately understood this view and therefore had pardoned Ch'ung-hou to protect Russian honour.

Giers then turned to the subject of China's war preparations. He condemned them as belligerent and branded them as the sole cause of Russia's increased military expenditure, for which he sought to hold China responsible. Tseng retorted that if Russia insisted on requiring China to pay her military expenditures, China could just as fairly ask Russia to shoulder hers. Such language, Tseng indicated, hurt the cause of peace and had best be avoided by both sides.[2] Then, in an earnest tone, he stated that he would try to settle all these unpleasant problems with 'finesse', a word which was probably an incorrect rendering by the interpreter but which amused Giers.[3] The tense atmosphere grew more peaceful, and Giers in the end agreed to set a date for Tseng's presentation of his Emperor's letter to the Tsar. Dufferin, having learnt the details of this initial meeting from Giers himself, sent Plunkett to see Macartney for a Chinese version of the interview, which turned out to be similar. Dufferin believed that Giers would be more courteous in the ensuing meetings with Tseng.[3]

The Russians wavered in their attitude toward Tseng. Ostensibly he had come simply as a new minister but his real mission, they knew, was to change the contents of the Treaty of Livadia. Should he be allowed to reopen the negotiations, and if so, was Peking not preferable to St. Petersburg as the site of

---

[1] F.O. 418/I/179, Dufferin to Granville, *confidential*, 6 Aug. 1880, reporting Tseng's initial meeting with Russian negotiators, as told by Giers.

[2] Tseng Chi-tse, 'Diary', 2: 37b; also *ILTY*, 87–91, first meeting, 4 Aug. 1880.

[3] F.O. 418/I/179, Dufferin to Granville, *confidential*, 6 Aug. 1880.

negotiations? Giers found the Russian translation of the Chinese Emperor's letter 'moderate and friendly', even though it stated clearly China's decision not to ratify the treaty. He asked the Tsar for permission to reopen negotiations with China, but specified Peking as the place for them, as a punishment for China. Count Miliutin, minister of War, asked that the negotiations not be permitted to continue indefinitely, since he feared that Russia might exhaust herself even before war began.[1]

On 9/21 August the St. Petersburg government learned from Koiander, their chargé d'affaires in Peking, that Ch'ung-hou had been pardoned and released. Taking this as a significant turn of events in their favour, the high Russian officials met at Tsarskoe Selo and recommended that Tseng, along with the new Japanese minister, be accorded an audience with the Tsar on the following day, at which time Tseng would be commanded to explain non-ratification of the treaty. After the audience, the Russians would meet at Miliutin's office to deliberate on Tseng's explanation.[2] On 10/22 August Tseng presented his Emperor's letter to the Tsar:

The Great Emperor of the Great Ch'ing Empire greets the Great Emperor of the Great Russian Empire. Having received the Mandate of Heaven and inherited the throne, I now, in solicitous regard for your friendly nation, speak to renew our amicable relations. Some time ago I specially dispatched Ch'ung-hou, senior vice-president of the Board of Civil Offices, as ambassador plenipotentiary to your country, with personal instructions for conducting the matters relating to the negotiations. But the treaty, regulations, and protocol concluded by him in your country—which I have personally examined—contain much that violates his instructions and exceeds his powers. All the officials of our state, high and low, have deliberated on them endlessly and have come to the unanimous conclusion that there is much in them that is objectionable and impracticable. I deeply regret it. Mindful of the peaceful and friendly relations between our two states over the past two hundred-odd years, I fear that you, the Great Emperor, might suspect that China's intention is to impair peace. For this reason I again specially dispatch Tseng Chi-tse, Marquis first class and subdirector of the Court of Sacrificial Worship, as imperial commissioner and minister plenipotentiary to your country. He bears with him a Letter of Credence

---

[1] Miliutin, iii. 263, 22 July/4 Aug. 1880.   [2] Ibid. 264.

to express my innermost feelings as proof of our true intention of peace and friendship. He will explain in detail our entire position on the various issues of the last negotiations—item by item why they are objectionable and impracticable. I therefore hope that you, the Great Emperor, will appoint an official to negotiate in earnest with my high emissary. I know that Tseng Chi-tse is peaceful, fair-minded, understanding, and thoroughly conversant with the issues pertaining to Chinese foreign relations. I earnestly hope that you will trust him sincerely so that he may fulfil his duty, that we may have lasting friendly relations and enjoy together a rising peace. This happy state, I trust, is what we all look forward to with deep satisfaction.[1]

The next day Tseng visited the Russian Foreign Office. He was told by Giers that since he, Giers, was to accompany the Tsar on a journey to the Crimea within a week, Tseng should state his position as soon as possible. Tseng promised to prepare a formal memorandum within a few days, but he volunteered this advance statement of his main ideas:

1. China is determined not to cede any territory. If Russia has the kind intention of returning Ili, she should return all of it.

2. The old boundaries of Kashgaria and Tarbagatai remain as they are. Minor changes may be made, but only after examination on the spot by Chinese and Russian special commissioners. Tseng himself, not having been there, cannot discuss this issue.

3. Russian requests for trade in Chia-yü-kuan and for trade routes through Nerchinsk and Kobdo may be granted if Russia agrees to the first item mentioned above.

4. Russian requests for establishing consulates in several Chinese cities cannot be granted except in Chia-yü-kuan.

5. Russian traders may establish a storehouse in one, but not all, of the following places: Hami, Ku-ch'eng, Barkul, etc.

6. The present exemption of Russian traders from commercial taxes and customs duties in Sinkiang needs re-examination because it is detrimental to China.

Giers, caught unprepared by Tseng's torrential declaration, burst out: 'In this way you have rejected everything in the last treaty'; to which Tseng replied: 'For all practical purposes the Russians have already gained a great deal from trade in Chia-yü-kuan and the trade routes through Nerchinsk and Kobdo.' Giers then said bluntly: 'Frankly I am quite dissatisfied with

[1] *WCSL*, 19: 3–3b.

Your Excellency's statement today'; but Tseng glibly returned: 'Because our two countries have different views, we need discussion. If we agree, what is the use of discussion?' On leaving the conference, Giers sarcastically muttered that he could not imagine how many years it would take to conclude such negotiations.[1]

When reading Tseng's formal memorandum, which set forth China's position on the Treaty of Livadia, Jomini remarked: 'It is very adroit. They reason very tightly.'[2] He hoped, however, that since the Chinese placed high strategic value on the Tekes Valley and the Muzart Pass, Russia could play on this Chinese predilection and use it to win all the other points.[2] But it was not easy for the Russians to work out a definite policy toward China; there were conflicting opinions from the Foreign Office, the War Ministry, the Naval Ministry, the Finance Ministry, and the border generals such as Kaufman. But the immediate questions still to be answered were whether the reopening of the negotiations should be allowed to take place at all, and if so, where and on what conditions.

3. THE PLACE OF THE NEGOTIATIONS

On 13/25 August a grand conference of high Russian officials from the Foreign Office, War, and Navy was held in the office of Miliutin. After lengthy and heated debate, it was decided that in view of the peaceful intentions of the Chinese government, as shown by the pardon and release of Ch'ung-hou, Russia would reopen negotiations to discuss the modification of minor points in the Treaty of Livadia, but the substance of the treaty was to be kept intact. The negotiations, Giers insisted, were to be held in Peking and not in St. Petersburg, as a reproof to the Chinese government, and Butzow was ordered to Peking to conduct the negotiations. The conference adopted three principles:

1. Russia will not insist on keeping the Tekes Valley, as stipulated in the Treaty of Livadia, if China agrees to increase her indemnity and compensate her with boundary adjustment in other places.

[1] *ILTY*, 93–94.
[2] Jelavich, 102, Jomini to Giers, 20 Aug./2 Sept. 1880.

2. Russia will allow only those changes in the treaty that will not appear to be concessions that injure her dignity and prestige.

3. Any protracted misunderstanding with China is unprofitable; hence Russia will demand the quickest conclusion of the negotiations, under threat of military demonstration.[1]

On 28 August Tseng was notified by Giers that, because of China's rejection of the treaty, he had sent Butzow to Peking to settle differences between the two countries.[2] Admiral S. S. Lesovskii was also dispatched with a fleet to the Far East, to exert pressure on China.[3] Interpreting the Russian moves as tests of his firmness, Tseng felt compelled to adopt a conciliatory tactic at this point. He suppressed his intention of rejecting the whole treaty in order to avoid an open break, since he believed that the Russians were caught between their reluctance to start a war on small provocation and reluctance to abandon the treaty.[2] He suggested to Peking that, because of the transfer of negotiations to China, it might be advisable to send Shao Yu-lien, chargé d'affaires in the St. Petersburg legation, back to Peking to assist in the negotiations with Butzow.[2]

Highly displeased with Tseng's failure to keep the negotiations in Russia, Peking reprimanded him for evading his responsibility and the normal difficulties of arguing with the Russians. 'To negotiate the treaty and the trade regulations is the sole responsibility of Tseng Chi-tse'; an edict stated, 'we have pardoned Ch'ung-hou at his request so as to pave the way for the re-negotiation of the treaty. Now, as soon as some initial disagreements with their Foreign Office arise, Tseng Chi-tse does not even attempt to placate them and discuss the matter with them at leisure. Was our pardon (of Ch'ung-hou) useful only for settling the issue of presenting the Letter of Credence?' A stern warning was administered to Tseng that he should not leave Russia without imperial permission and that he should redouble his efforts to keep the negotiations in St. Petersburg. His recommendation that Shao Yu-lien be sent home was refused and Shao was ordered to stay in Russia to help Tseng in the negotiations.[4]

[1] Miliutin, iii. 267, 13/25 Aug. 1880.
[2] Tseng Chi-tse, 'Memorials', 2: 25–25b, 2 Sept. 1880.
[3] *WCSL*, 22: 15–16b, memorial by the Tsungli Yamen, 4 Sept. 1880.
[4] *WCSL*, 22: 22b.

Peking was thoroughly alarmed by the Russian move to transfer negotiations to China under the threat of Admiral Lesovskii and his fleet. Memories of the Tientsin and Peking negotiations in 1858 and 1860 under the shadow of the Anglo-French army were still vivid in the minds of the mandarins, and they dreaded any recurrence of such a scene. The coming of Butzow and Lesovskii was certain to create intense psychological pressures and an atmosphere of crisis in China. The court was desperately hoping to keep the negotiations, and the inevitable foreign pressure, as far as possible from Peking. Furthermore, a treaty negotiated in St. Petersburg could be rejected by China; one negotiated in Peking could not easily be disowned.

The troubled court asked the princes and high officials to re-examine the whole situation in the light of these new developments. Prince Ch'un warned of the impossibility of defending the 10,000 *li* of frontier between China and Russia, and Prince Tun worried about Russian attacks in Manchuria and Tientsin. The whole tenor of their memorials bespoke anxiety and fear, and the prevailing atmosphere at the court was filled with a sense of portentous calamity that was about to descend.[1]

Wade and Bourée took notice of the Chinese alarm and urged Peking to ratify the treaty immediately to forestall Butzow's return.[2] London was surprised by Wade's precipitous advice to the Chinese government. Pauncefote remarked in a Foreign Office memorandum:

I was certainly startled by this announcement. That the *French* minister, under the pretext of friendly advice to China, should endeavour to secure a triumph for Russia would not surprise me. But why *we* should advise China to succumb at once, without at least ascertaining the views of Germany seems to me premature and somewhat rash. If the Germans are bent on opposing the action of Russia and in protesting with us against a Blockade of the Treaty Ports, it would render mediation not impossible and that would be far better for China than surrendering at discretion.[3]

Granville then instructed Wade by telegram on 21 September 1880: 'I approve your proceedings so far as they regard advice given by you to the Chinese to be very conciliatory, but Her

[1] Weng T'ung-ho, 19: 56–56b.
[2] F.O. 17/833/155, Wade's telegram to Granville, 10 Sept. 1880.
[3] Ibid. Pauncefote's memorandum, attached to the above telegram from Wade.

Majesty's Government are not prepared to recommend without more consideration the immediate ratification of the existing Treaty.'[1] Wade, therefore, had to make an about-face and he informed the Chinese government that Britain could not 'take the responsibility of recommending ratification of the treaty'.[2]

Under the new pressures from Russia, Li Hung-chang urged the Tsungli Yamen to instruct Tseng to be more flexible in his approch to treaty revision and to relax his stand on such issues as Russian trade in Han-chung and Sian, and Russian shipping in the Sungari.[3] Tso Tsung-t'ang, on the other hand, asked the government to stand firm, as we have noted earlier: Lesovskii and his twenty-three ships were nothing to be afraid of; the Foochow Dockyard alone had turned out more ships than he commanded. Tso also pointed out that the Russians were reported to have incurred a national debt of some fifty-two million taels, a sign of their financial straits and of their inability to wage a war against China.[4]

Chang Chih-tung, now senior deputy supervisor of Imperial Instruction, soothed the terrified court by saying that the transfer of negotiations to Peking might be a blessing in disguise. When Butzow saw China's war preparations and her determination to fight, he might be sufficiently impressed to take a more conciliatory stand. What Tseng Chi-tse could do in Russia was only to plead and argue. Since time immemorial it had been far more effective to show one's teeth than to beg. Thus negotiations in St. Petersburg might fail, while negotiations in China might succeed.[5] But the high circles in Peking were not impressed with this 'bookish view' of the emergency. They wanted to keep the negotiations in St. Petersburg at all costs.

Peking's anxiety was easily detected by the Russian legation. Koiander reported that the Chinese government was willing to offer an additional ten to twelve million roubles in exchange for the Tekes Valley and the Muzart Pass. Jomini was so elated by the good news that he exclaimed: *'Dai Bog!'* (May God grant it!)[6] But on second thoughts he and Butzow both felt that Russian acceptance of such a large sum was undignified, and

[1] F.O. 418/I/252, Granville to Wade, telegram, 21 Sept. 1880.
[2] F.O. 418/I/159, Wade to Granville, telegram, 2 Oct. 1880.
[3] Li Hung-chang, 'Letters to the Tsungli Yamen', 11: 28–28b, 28 Aug. 1880; 11: 33–33b, 13 Sept. 1880.   [4] *WCSL*, 24: 19b–22.   [5] Ibid. 22: 27b–29b.
[6] Jelavich, 102, Jomini to Giers, 24 Aug./5 Sept. 1880.

that it would be of more lasting value to secure commercial advantages.[1] The Finance Ministry agreed that commercial advantages deserved priority over all other considerations.[2]

Butzow left for China by way of Germany and Western Europe with no instructions. The Russian Foreign Office had been unable to prepare them without first consulting the Ministries of Finance and War on Russian commercial and territorial concessions to China. Nor was the Foreign Office able to decide when Butzow should deliver the ultimatum, if necessary, because the Army and Navy disagreed on the best time for war: the former preferred quick action in November or December, while the latter considered operations impossible until the following spring. The Foreign Office was therefore in no position to tell Butzow just how long he should extend the negotiations. Jomini hoped to forward definite instructions to Butzow in Marseilles.[3]

On 5/17 September the Russian Foreign Office learned from Koiander that the Chinese government was insisting on keeping the negotiations in St. Petersburg. Jomini, who was now in charge of the Foreign Office, as Giers had left with the Tsar on the annual journey to the Crimea, was unable to understand China's reasons. While admitting that Giers's demand to negotiate in Peking was prompted by the desire to penalize the Chinese government for the rejection of the treaty and the punishment of Ch'ung-hou, he himself felt that St. Petersburg was a better place for negotiations. To Giers he wrote:

It seems to me that, after having rejected what we have negotiated here, it would satisfy their pride to bring us to negotiate in Peking. There, they are the masters of postponing, accelerating, or breaking the negotiations at their convenience. . . . I have no clear idea as to what we should ask as a place for negotiations. . . . But, after all, since Butzow is still immediately available, it would be more advantageous for us to negotiate here, where we should have the advantage of being able to co-ordinate the negotiations with our military conveniences. Moreover, if we do not reach an agreement, we should avoid accentuating the break by Butzow's departure from Peking.[4]

[1] Ibid. 102–103, Jomini to Giers, 27 Aug./8 Sept. 1880.
[2] Ibid. 103, same to same, 29 Aug./10 Sept. 1880.
[3] Ibid. 99, same to same, 20 Aug./2 Sept. 1880.
[4] Ibid. 104–5, same to same, 5/17 Sept. 1880.

On 18 September Tseng received an urgent order from Peking: 'The Russian affair has become increasingly urgent. If you can follow the previous edicts and resist [conceding anything] on important issues while making concessions on the lesser ones, it would of course be ideal. Otherwise you should make them agree not to force China to promise anything; according to this principle you should fight for a few items and find room for a graceful exit. The important thing is to settle the matter in Russia.'[1] Tseng was asked 'to counter them with reason in a firm yet conciliatory spirit. To win back one part is to suffer one part less.'[2] Meanwhile, new orders were issued by the court to strengthen coastal defences against possible Russian attack.[3]

Witnessing the urgency of the situation, Plunkett on 19 September suggested to Tseng that the ratification of the Treaty of Livadia was perhaps 'the best course' under the circumstances.[4] Immediately he was rebuked by Granville: 'You should not give the Chinese Envoy advice in favour of the ratification of the Treaty with Russia, but should confine yourself to recommending a conciliatory course.'[5] To make it doubly clear, a second telegram was sent on the following day: 'Your language to Chinese Envoy should be in conformity with my telegram of this day to Sir T. Wade.'[6] Plunkett then impressed upon Tseng the importance of a conciliatory stand in the delicate situation without urging the ratification of the treaty. Plunkett stressed the dangers that might befall the Manchu government under the threat of Lesovskii's fleet, and pointed out: 'Here greater concessions could be made with safety than could even be dreamt of if negotiations were transferred to Peking.'[7]

Tseng hastened to the Russian Foreign Office and earnestly requested that the negotiations be kept in St. Petersburg. He assured Jomini repeatedly of his full powers to negotiate to a conclusion, and stated that what he could not sign away in Russia would not be signed away in Peking either. To Jomini's argument that Russia feared a second rejection by China of her

[1] Tseng Chi-tse, 'Memorials', 2: 28–28b.
[2] Ibid. 2: 28b.   [3] *WCSL*, 22: 27–27b.
[4] F.O. 418/I/248, Plunkett to Granville, telegram, *very confidential*, 19 Sept. 1880.
[5] F.O. 418/I/251, Granville to Plunkett, telegram, 20 Sept. 1880.
[6] F.O. 418/I/253, same to same, 21 Sept. 1880.
[7] F.O. 418/I/266, Plunkett to Granville, *secret*, 22 Sept. 1880.

representative's commitments, Tseng replied that such a possibility did not exist because he had been provided with detailed instructions on all points of importance, and that his position was totally different from Ch'ung-hou's. In an earnest and conciliatory manner he pleaded with Jomini to recall Butzow. Jomini, who had secretly doubted the wisdom of negotiations in Peking all along, promised now to do his best.[1]

The following day, 7/19, Jomini wrote to Giers that he had found in Tseng and his government a new conciliatory spirit. He mentioned again that he saw no reason for declining negotiations in Russia. Morally, he said, the Chinese government had apologized for its bad international conduct and had promised no recurrence; therefore, to consent to its request to reopen negotiations in St. Petersburg would not hurt Russian dignity. Materially, such consent, which was quite different from concession, would bring many advantages. 'We shall be able to direct it [the negotiation], to prolong it, to accelerate it or to break it at will. It will avoid the difficulties which would attach to Butzow's departure from Peking in case of a break. It will always be easy for us to close it by the first of November, or to prolong it until the spring according to our military and naval conveniences. If we decide to cede the Tekes Valley, it will be possible to give to this occasion the value of an expression of friendship emanating from the Tsar.'[2] Jomini recommended that the negotiations should be 'most mild' but 'most firm', and such negotiations could only be directed in St. Petersburg.[2]

Giers insisted, however, on moving the negotiations to Peking, and Jomini had to continue his persuasion. On 10/22 September he again wrote Giers: 'The Chinese really desire to terminate this absurd quarrel.' He argued exhaustively the advantages of negotiations in St. Petersburg:

We have insisted on negotiating in Peking simply because we do not want to expose ourselves to a new disappointment. I doubt if they will repeat it. We can ask for guarantees. The essential question is that we should not lend ourselves to their possible intention of gaining time and dragging on, so that they may complete their armaments. Note that negotiations in St. Petersburg can proceed much faster than in Peking. The two months needed for Butzow to go to China will suffice to see clearly their intentions here. True, in case

---

[1] *ILTY*, 94–96.   [2] Jelavich, 105, Jomini to Giers, 7/19 Sept. 1880.

we should not come to an agreement here, Butzow's departure to China would have to be delayed until spring. The time would be lost to us. But if we could not agree *here*, probably we would not agree any better in Peking. If we have negotiations here, we can always break it *at our convenience*, either in March or in May, according to our judgement of what is most advantageous. I doubt if we shall have the same latitude in Peking.[1]

Giers finally gave in to Jomini's exhortations and authorized him to recall Butzow to St. Petersburg.[2] So the negotiations in Russia were saved, and Tseng won a chance to demonstrate his diplomatic talents.

[1] Jelavich, 106–7, Jomini to Giers, 10/22 Sept. 1880.
[2] Ibid. 107, Giers to Jomini, telegram, 9/21 Sept. 1880.

CHAPTER IX

The Treaty of St. Petersburg

T HE recall of Butzow and the reopening of the negotiations in St. Petersburg pleased Tseng immensely, and he expressed his gratification to Jomini on 27 September.[1] After reassuring the Russian of his full powers to conclude an agreement, and of the ascendancy of the moderate party in Peking, he declared that 'his government does not reject the Treaty of Livadia completely but is only asking for some modifications, after which it will be ready to ratify it'.[2] Jomini was elated to report to Giers: 'I can't tell you how friendly this interview was. The good Zeng [Tseng] has a radiant face. I am not sparing the honey either. God willing, let it lead us to a worthy port.'[2] Tseng was told by Jomini that the Tsar did not insist on a 'pure and simple ratification of the Treaty of Livadia' either.[3] Thus the original deadlock was broken.

I. THE RUSSIAN LACK OF POLICY

The Russians had great difficulty in formulating a definite policy on the Ili question, and nobody knew the government's stand. Giers was away with the Tsar in Livadia, and Jomini knew nothing about China. Butzow, though an old China hand, had insufficient rank to decide policy; he could only make suggestions to Jomini, who in turn had to report to Giers for instructions. Giers would have to consult the ministers of War, the Navy, and Finance, who would then discuss the issues extensively from different points of view and would finally come to no conclusion. The whole procedure was tedious and ineffective; there was a conspicuous lack of co-ordination. These high ministers were of course preoccupied with more pressing domestic problems and Russia's European involvements. They knew that Russia had gained more from the Treaty of Livadia than she would risk a war to retain, but the question was how to

---

[1] *ILTY*, 96–97; Jelavich, 108, Jomini to Giers, 16/28 Sept. 1880.
[2] Ibid. 110, same to same, 19 Sept./1 Oct. 1880.
[3] *ILTY*, 98.

retreat gracefully. They continued to waver between the magnanimous gesture of renouncing Ili and the fear of losing face before the Russian public and the world at large, and this procrastination, depriving their negotiators at St. Petersburg of any definite guidance, placed them in a very difficult position. It became necessary for Jomini to improvise temporary measures in the negotiations until his government developed a policy. It appeared that while the Russian high circles were unanimous in their desire for a speedy conclusion of the negotiations, every step they took only served to prolong them.

Jomini adopted the ingenious device of sending Butzow to contact Tseng privately, testing the limits of the concessions the Chinese would make without giving him any written, formal memorandum. Butzow was instructed to declare that his authority was restricted to hearing China's offers and reporting them to the Tsar, who would then decide 'whether there is any basis for possible negotiations'.[1]

The Russian high officials asked General Kaufman for recommendations. Kaufman suggested restitution of the Tekes Valley at the enormous price of 100 million roubles or else the cession of an equally large area north of Ili. These recommendations were found unrealistic, as Jomini told Giers: 'Butzow finds General Kaufman's opinion impossible as a basis of negotiations. The proposed border strikes him as impracticable, for it would still remove half the province of Ili from China, as well as a route indispensable to her, without giving us a secure natural border. As for the pecuniary transaction, he finds it not very dignified.'[1] Jomini doubted whether China would accept Kaufman's idea of territorial readjustment, for it was 'like taking away from her on the right what we would be giving back on the left'. In view of Kaufman's confidential remarks that the new territory north of Ili that was to be annexed had no strategic value and little economic value to Russia, Jomini asked Giers some pointed questions: 'Must we insist on a compensation which is without value for us but which will probably meet with rejection by the Chinese government? . . . What is the final goal pursued by the Imperial Cabinet? Does it want to bring the Chinese government to

---

[1] Jelavich, 109, Jomini to Giers, 19 Sept./1 Oct. 1880.

reason even at the risk of war? Or does it want to avoid a war, which offers only liabilities without compensations?'[1]

If the Russian government was prepared to go to war, Jomini continued, he would adopt the tactics of forcing the Chinese either to ratify the treaty or to break with Russia. He doubted if China would fight Russia; more likely, she would let Russia keep Ili under protest and reserve the right to demand its return later. On the other hand, if the Russian government wanted to avoid war, it should return the Tekes Valley to China at the good price of new commercial privileges, new navigation rights on the Sungari River, and a new frontier in the Ussuri area. In addition, an indemnity should be demanded —as a lesson to China—to compensate Russia for military expenses incurred as a result of Chinese war preparations. Jomini begged Giers to clarify two essential points: the ultimate goal of the government, and the maximum and minimum gains, concessions, and demands in view of that ultimate goal.[2] Jomini believed that Russia should not involve herself in a war with China but should extricate herself from her present predicament as soon as possible. Uppermost in his mind were the two considerations of reducing military expenses and maintaining decent relations with China.[3] While waiting for instructions from Giers, Jomini postponed the deadline for the ratification of the treaty a month so that the negotiations could continue.

Giers, apparently unable to see the really crucial issue, told Jomini that the goal of the Russian government was to have the Treaty of Livadia 'ratified with slight modifications'. Jomini reminded him that the prime issue—the restitution of the Tekes Valley and the Muzart Pass—constituted a fundamental alteration of the treaty and was quite different from 'slight modifications'.[3] On 23 September/5 October Giers adopted the idea of seeking territorial compensation along the Ussuri River near Eastern Siberia; Kaufman's recommendations were discarded. 'But', Giers warned, 'the most important thing in our opinion is to conduct the negotiations as fast as possible so that we may recall the fleet, and return our troops on the Chinese frontiers to a peaceful state.' He was afraid of a new war with

---

[1] Ibid. 112, Jomini to Giers, 22 Sept./4 Oct. 1880.
[2] Ibid. 112–13, same to same, 22 Sept./4 Oct. 1880.
[3] Ibid. 111, same to same, 22 Sept./4 Oct. 1880.

Turkey, in which case the Russian Far Eastern fleet would have to be recalled to reinforce the European fleet. It was therefore doubly necessary to reach a speedy settlement with China.[1] He repeated the same opinion to Jomini two days later: 'More than ever before we must desire that they [the negotiations] reach a good solution as soon as possible.'[2]

However, Giers never made clear the maximum and minimum demands and concessions Russia would make. Butzow, ignorant of the intentions of his superiors, had to make his way in the dark until the high officials in Livadia made up their minds. He played a brilliant delaying game with Tseng. On 1, 2, 6, and 9 October, he charged China repeatedly with bad faith in rejecting the treaty and with violation of the usual standards of international conduct by punishing Ch'ung-hou. When reminded by Tseng that non-ratification of treaties was accepted practice in Western diplomacy, Butzow retorted sarcastically that he knew of no case in which rejection of the treaty was followed by war preparations on the one hand, and the dispatch of a new negotiator to change the treaty on the other. He intimated that unacceptable treaty arrangements might indeed be re-negotiated through confidential, friendly requests from China but never by the threat of war. To give in to China's demands now would expose Russia to the ridicule of her people and the whole world. He kept reiterating that Russia could not be sure that China would not reject the re-negotiated treaty again.[3]

Anxious to keep the negotiations alive, Tseng could not afford to employ, at this point, equally sharp language. He apologized for China's treatment of Ch'ung-hou, blaming it on her lack of experience in modern international affairs. But he was adamant in affirming that China was guilty of nothing else. Reassuring Butzow of his full powers to negotiate, he pledged that there was no possibility of a second rejection by Peking. China did not want to dismiss the whole Treaty of Livadia but only to revise some difficult items, he declared. The Tsar, he intimated, by not insisting on 'pure and simple' ratification of the treaty, certainly could provide a satisfactory basis for successful negotiations.[4]

[1] Jelavich, 150, Giers to Jomini, 23 Sept./5 Oct. 1880.
[2] Ibid., 150, same to same, 25 Sept./7 Oct. 1880.   [3] *ILTY*, 100–1, 105–6.
[4] Ibid. 100–1, 105, 114.

Butzow asked for Tseng's formal representations, and Tseng repeated the six points he had stated to Giers on 23 August. He agreed to the Russian demands for financial compensation and pardon of those inhabitants of Ili who had collaborated with the Russians. For the restoration of the Tekes Valley, he indicated that China was willing to assign Russia an equally large area west of Ili for settlement of the Tungan refugees who wanted to leave Ili. But he demanded in return that Russia quarantine Pai Yen-hu, the Moslem rebel who had fled to Russia, and restrain him from any clandestine return to China to stir up trouble.[1] Butzow argued that, since the area west of Ili already had been ceded by the Treaty of Livadia, it could not compensate for the restitution of the Tekes Valley. He asked for some territory along the China coast, but Tseng positively refused to discuss cession of new territory.[2] Butzow then threatened to move negotiations to Peking. The Chinese remained unimpressed, indicating that what he could not accept in St. Petersburg would not be accepted in Peking.[3]

Having no definite instructions from Giers, Butzow was unable to be positive about his demands. He repeated again and again the old accusations of China's bad faith and Tseng's attempt to change the whole treaty. After several lengthy meetings of repetitions of former diatribes, words lost their meaning and the negotiations stalled. On 9 October Butzow declared: 'China regards the late treaty as if it were non-existent but my country wants to use it as a basis (for negotiations). The views of our two countries being so divergent, how can we negotiate?'[4]

The negotiations were heading toward collapse, and the one-month extension of the date of ratification was fast running out. The weather was turning cold, and the best season for naval operations was passing. The ominous prospect of war was averted until at least the following spring, and the time gained worked in China's favour. Tseng saw this very clearly. He did not act as if he were anxious to force the Russians to make up their minds. He had probably grasped the hollowness of Russian threats by observing their social and financial problems. Plunkett

---

[1] Ibid. 101–5, 115. [2] Ibid. 112, 120.
[3] Jelavich, 114–15, Jomini to Giers, 27 Sept./9 Oct. 1880.
[4] *ILTY*, 116.

described the situation to London: 'Chinese Envoy is in no hurry, and will wait until Russians make their meaning clear.' Tseng was convinced that 'Russia is as anxious for peace as China'.[1] His tactics were to force the Russians to formulate their demands so that he could know the worst and then judge how far he could go to meet them.[2]

Jomini was disgusted with the fruitlessness of the negotiations, remarking that 'this cursed affair is giving us insomnia!'[3] He alerted Giers: 'Tseng plays dead! —we are imitating him. It's a bad sign—since he is not impressed with Butzow's allusion to the impossibility of continuing the negotiations here. Has he been reassured by discovering the internal and external difficulties here that we must handle?'[4] News also came from the Russian minister in Japan, K. V. Struve, of China's purchase of a large number of mines in Germany, and of her dilatory tactics designed to gain time for war preparations. Jomini regretfully exclaimed: 'They have already succeeded in gaining the winter, which puts them out of danger from our fleet for six months!'[4]

2. JOMINI'S PLIGHT

Jomini began to have serious second thoughts about the whole Ili issue and became quite critical of the Russian position. On 1/13 October he wrote at great length to Giers about the need for a new policy:

The more I think about this unfortunate affair, the more I am convinced that a *fair and moderate* attitude supported by *inflexible decision* is the only way to get out of this blind alley. We can admit it to ourselves: our present embarrassment comes from the fact that we have deviated from the start from this triple principle.

Our conditions for the restitution of Kuldja [Ili] have been neither fair nor moderate. We have just made a searching but painful study, comparing the protocol of the committee held last year with that of this year. The contradiction is complete!

We have sustained, without *rights* or sufficient motives, a bad thesis. To sustain it we have made an *apparent demonstration* without

---

[1] F.O. 418/I/299 and 300, Granville's telegrams to Wade, 18, 19 Oct. 1880, transmitting Plunkett's reports.
[2] F.O. 418/I/334, Plunkett to Granville, *very confidential*, 10 Nov. 1880.
[3] Jelavich, 114, Jomini to Giers, 27 Sept./9 Oct. 1880.
[4] Ibid. 115, same to same, 1/13 Oct. 1880.

the greatest desire of putting it into execution. From this follows the fact that the Chinese have been exasperated by our demands without being frightened by our demonstration!

To get out of this blind alley, it is necessary to go back to true principles. I persist in believing that we will reach the goal by a fair and moderate ultimatum, i.e., the ratification of the Treaty of Livadia with additional protocols providing for a generous restitution of the Tekes Valley to the Chinese Emperor and reimbursement by him of the expenses to which he has forced us. But this ultimatum must be presented by the hand on the hilt of our sword, *ready and decided to come out of its scabbard!*

If this kind of solution is adopted, there remains to be decided *the moment when we would be in a position to act by land and sea,* for it is essential that the ultimatum coincide with *that* moment. *I beseech you to give us precise instructions on that point.*[1]

From Giers came the answer: 'We want to get out of this detestable affair with dignity. That's why, besides the concessions we are disposed to make, we ask for some compensations which it is impossible for us to renounce without offending public opinion. If the Chinese do not want to understand that, and—as a consequence—if they take our good will for weakness, then we shall have to show them our fist. It will be wretched but inevitable.'[2]

Jomini did not see eye to eye with Giers, reminding him that if he were presented with the actual difficulties of the negotiations he might change his mind about 'the fist'. 'It is not a question of limiting oneself to showing the fist, but of being *ready and determined* to use it.' Jomini also demurred on the role of public opinion: 'Be assured that whatever we do, public opinion will accuse us. If we make war to save our dignity, it will reproach us for leading the state into a ruinous war at a time when, without that, our financial and commercial affairs are already in a bad state. If, on the other hand, we show conciliation so as to have peace, it will accuse us of giving away the dignity and interests of the state. To blame the government *in everything*, to criticize its acts without rhyme or reason so as to discredit it—such is the mission which it [public opinion] has assigned to itself. To take into consideration such a public opinion appears to me to be impossible.'[3]

[1] Ibid. *Italics* original.   [2] Ibid. 151, Giers to Jomini, 27 Sept./9 Oct. 1880.
[3] Ibid. 117, Jomini to Giers, 1/13 Oct. 1880. *Italics* original.

In Jomini's view, a war with China would be 'ruinous, end-less, and without advantages'. Neither Russia nor China was likely to declare war in the event of a diplomatic impasse. More likely than not, China would reject the treaty and leave Ili in Russian hands for the time being under protest. China, Jomini feared, then would arm herself with more foreign weapons and force Russia into a prolonged military build-up until exhaustion. It would be better to strike 'quickly' and 'strongly' now, while Russia was still in a position to do so. Giers was told that the situation was 'far more serious than you judge it from a distance'.[1] Jomini blamed the military for having plunged Russia into the 'insoluble dilemma' of 'this cursed Chinese affair'. He poured his heart out to Giers: 'I do not forgive those who plunged us into it last year by protesting against pure and simple restitution of the territories which we had occupied temporarily with the promise of giving them back!' And he added philosophically: 'A new proof that straightforwardness and honesty are the best policies!'[2]

Giers met with Miliutin on 4/16 October to discuss the China affair again. They decided that the Treaty of Livadia had to be ratified by China, but that Russia would promise in a separate protocol to abandon the Tekes Valley at the price of Chinese payment of all Russian military expenses caused by the Ili dispute. If Tseng refused to accept these terms, then Jomini and Butzow should threaten to transfer negotiation to Peking, under the direction of Admiral Lesovskii.[3] Jomini thought that a piece of Chinese territory along the Ussuri River might be accepted in place of a large indemnity, if China was not in a position to pay.[4]

Miliutin and Giers, in Livadia, began to feel that Tseng no longer possessed any 'lively desire' to end the negotiations, a change of attitude which they attributed to some 'ill-disposed adversaries', meaning the British.[3] Giers told Jomini on 7/19 October: 'We must suppose that he [Tseng] wants to keep us in suspense in order to gain time. . . . We want to be moderate but firm. . . . In the sad eventuality of a military action against

---

[1] Jelavich, 118, Jomini to Giers, 4/16 Oct. 1880.
[2] Ibid. 118, same to same, 3/15 Oct. 1880.
[3] Miliutin, iii. 276.
[4] Jelavich, 119–20, Jomini to Giers, 5/17 Oct. 1880.

the Chinese, you would like to know just when and where we should act by sea and land. In effect, this question is of great importance, but nobody can decide it better than Admiral Lesovskii himself.'[1]

Meanwhile, more news came from China of preparations for war and the concentration of troops at key points, as well as the dispatch of two German ships, loaded with gunpowder, from Hamburg to China. Reports came also, belatedly, of Gordon's activities in China and of his advice to remove the Chinese court to the interior, for a long war with Russia. Jomini was certain that this was 'an additional reason for us not to risk (trying) to crush the Chinese empire, which would bring us face to face with a fearful unknown (future)'. Both he and Butzow felt that Russia had to choose between a 'risky, dangerous, and onerous war, and a bad, dubious, and precarious peace'.[2] The more he contemplated the prospects, the more was Jomini convinced that Russia should entertain no more illusions or wishful thinking. He told Giers:

They [the Chinese] are very proud and very well informed on the general situation. Our demonstrations have not frightened them. . . . To be sure they do not want war and they are afraid of it. But they are convinced that we do not want it any more than they do, and that we are not in a position to wage it. They certainly are not ignorant of the fact that Lesovskii, obliged as he is to respect foreign trade, cannot do anything very serious with his fleet, and that on land we have not even the means of marching on Peking. If they have not guessed it themselves, they do not lack good friends here who have shown them the light. Let us therefore face things as they are. Let us accept the status quo in spite of its disadvantages.[3]

Tseng had clearly observed the Russian indecision, vacillation, and lack of co-ordination. He now boldly pressed Jomini and Butzow for a written reply to his memorandum. While Jomini agreed to obtain it from Livadia, he warned that China must pay the twelve million roubles for Russian military expenses, and that if Tseng procrastinated further, the indemnity would increase. Jomini wanted to hold Tseng responsible for the delay in negotiations, but Tseng insisted that

[1] Jelavich, 152–3, Giers to Jomini, 7/19 Oct. 1880.
[2] Ibid. 121, Jomini to Giers, 10/22 Oct. 1880.
[3] Ibid. 121–22, same to same, 12/24 Oct. 1880.

this delay was the result of Russian failure to respond to his memorandum. The Chinese negotiator offered to do one of two things to untie the knot: either negotiate for the restitution of Ili, or reject the Treaty of Livadia for the present and demand the return of Ili later.[1] Jomini would not accept a 'delay' in the restitution of Ili except in the sense that Ili would be transferred permanently to Russia on receipt of a formal note from Tseng. This, of course, Tseng refused to do.[2] The one-month extension of the ratification date was fast expiring, and Russia agreed to extend it two more months.[3] The negotiations, so far, had been inconclusive.

3. THE PROTRACTED NEGOTIATIONS

In Livadia the high government officials continued to debate the China issue. Miliutin had received secret information about China's war preparations and her purchase from Europe and America of large quantities of arms, gunpowder, and torpedoes, enough to make Russian preparations look insignificant. Russian defences in the Orient had not been consolidated during the winter because of severe weather and lack of funds.[4] Miliutin noticed that Tseng had become 'uncommunicative' and 'even abrupt' in the negotiations, as he pressed for a written reply to his memorandum. Giers ordered Jomini to draft a memorandum for the Chinese in such a way as to show that it was not the last word of the Tsar, in order to leave the door open for further negotiations.[5] A. A. Mel'nikov, vice-director of the Asiatic Department of the Foreign Office, was dispatched as a courier of new instructions to St. Petersburg. Butzow informed Tseng that a written reply would be ready as soon as Mel'nikov arrived from Livadia.[6]

Mel'nikov arrived in St. Petersburg—but with no specific new instructions except the report that Miliutin wanted very much to avoid war, although he did not favour a patched-up peace, because it would place a heavy defence burden on Russia indefinitely.[7] Jomini, disappointed by the lack of new instruc-

---

[1] *ILTY*, 128–9.   [2] Ibid. 121–6 *passim*.
[3] Ibid. 134.   [4] Miliutin, iii. 278–80.
[5] Jelavich, 155, Giers to Jomini, 21 Oct./2 Nov. 1880.
[6] *ILTY*, 136.
[7] Jelavich, 128–9, Jomini to Giers, 22 Oct./3 Nov. 1880.

tions, was now more than ever convinced that 'it would have been wiser to give them back Kuldja honestly as we had promised. . . . We have made the mistake of absorbing immense territories with an appetite which bears little relation to our digestive capacity.'[1] But an indemnity should be demanded of China, he insisted, although the amount should be moderate and the instalment payments widely spaced.[2] Giers, anxious as he was for peace, approved this idea, and suggested in addition that the indemnity might be diminished if Tseng proved intransigent.[3] Giers still refused to state categorically whether the ultimate goal of Russia was war or peace. Jomini had grown weary of waiting for a definite answer; he pressed Giers for clarification. On 25 October/6 November Giers finally replied that it was obviously for the purpose of avoiding war that Russia had consented to open negotiations with Tseng, but she did not want to concede so much as to hurt her dignity. For this reason, he said, it was hard to fix either war or peace as a final goal.[4]

The long-awaited Russian memorandum finally reached Tseng on 8 November, the Russians agreeing to return the Tekes Valley but to keep the western portion of Ili for the settlement of the Tungan refugees. The Russians also demanded an indemnity and the right of navigation in the Sungari River. On 10 November the Chinese and Russian negotiators met again. They debated about the western border of Ili, but decided that Russian navigation in the Sungari would be curtailed to a certain point, to be recorded in a special protocol.

The really inflammatory issue was that of the indemnity, which the Russians fixed at eleven million roubles. Plunkett told Jomini that he knew of no 'precedent of an "indemnité de guerre" being demanded when there had been no war'.[5] Tseng also argued along the same lines and indicated that China might be willing to increase the compensation for Russian occupation expenses, but would never pay an indemnity. Jomini was quick to intimate that he was more interested in the

[1] Ibid. 130–1, Jomini to Giers, 25 Oct./6 Nov. 1880.
[2] Ibid. 128–9, same to same, 22 Oct./3 Nov. 1880.
[3] Ibid. 155, Giers to Jomini, 28 Oct./9 Nov. 1880.
[4] Ibid. 155, same to same, 25 Oct./6 Nov. 1880.
[5] F.O. 418/I/283, Plunkett to Granville, 6 Oct. 1880.

sum than in its name.[1] To Giers he confided that it looked as if Tseng were willing to pay an additional one or two million roubles, besides the original five million stipulated in the Treaty of Livadia. Jomini was eager to make China pay as much as possible, both to help defray Russian military expenses and to teach the Chinese that they could not provoke Russia without incurring a financial penalty.[2] Butzow, who knew China's financial straits, thought it best to keep the indemnity small, but still maintain the *principle* of payment, on moral grounds.

Tseng fought a brilliant diplomatic battle. His mental agility, perspicacity, and quick reasoning were sufficiently demonstrated in the conference room. When Jomini attempted to hold China responsible for Russian military expenses, Tseng stated that if China paid Russia for a naval demonstration directed against herself, she would be the laughing-stock of the world. Jomini replied that Russia would also look foolish if she spent eleven or twelve million roubles for the pleasure of giving up Ili.[3] Tseng pointed out that it was Russian ships that had entered Chinese waters and not vice versa; the identity of the aggressor was clear. If Russia asked China for an indemnity, China could as well ask Russia for the same. Jomini answered that Russian ships had not invaded Chinese waters but had stayed in international waters. Tseng quickly asked: 'If Russian ships did not reach Chinese waters, why do you ask for Chinese compensation?'[4] Jomini was unable to answer. Sharp exchanges such as these took place often, but no real progress was made in the negotiations.

Tseng was of course in contact all this time with the British legation in St. Petersburg. At his request, Plunkett asked Jomini not to press too hard on China lest the Peking government collapse, an eventuality which would not be in the interest of either Russia or Europe. Jomini assured him that Russia had no intention of pushing things to extremes and had no desire to press unduly hard on China.[5] Tseng was also in touch with the American minister, John W. Foster. On 19 November

---

[1] *ILTY*, 136–51 *passim*.
[2] Jelavich, 131–5, Jomini to Giers, 29 Oct./10 Nov. 1880.
[3] Ibid. 135–6, same to same, 5/17 Nov. 1880.
[4] *ILTY*, 149, 153, 155, 160.
[5] F.O. 418/I/313, Granville to Wade, 3 Nov. 1880, transmitting Plunkett's report.

1880 he informed Foster that the Russians were unreasonably taking the rejected Treaty of Livadia as 'an accomplished fact, fully ratified and binding upon the parties thereto'. Regarding the Russian demand for an indemnity, Tseng stated that China 'would forfeit the respect of the other nations of the earth by yielding to a demand so humiliating to her honour and independence'. He asserted that she was willing to reimburse the Russians for their occupation expenses in Ili 'cheerfully and liberally', but she would not give a single rouble for 'a hostile and menacing naval demonstration in its [her] own waters in time of peace'. To Tseng's request for mediation in the dispute, Foster responded with a promise to do what he could to promote a peaceful settlement.[1]

Giers had also come to the conclusion that Jomini should not quarrel about the character of the payment—whether 'indemnity' or 'compensation'—and that two or three million roubles in addition to the original five million should be considered satisfactory.[2] Jomini, still aiming at what he called 'the most possible', asked for a total of ten million roubles under the name of 'compensation for military expenses in Ili'. Tseng accepted his description of the payment, and indicated that the Chinese government would not quibble about the sum if it was reasonable.[3] Thus the two parties were coming closer.

4. THE TURNING-POINT

Lack of progress in the negotiations, while largely the result of indecision and hesitation in high Russian circles, was also partially a result of the absence of the Tsar and the assistant foreign minister from the scene of the conference. Correspondence between Jomini in St. Petersburg and Giers in Livadia took at least four days.[4] But negotiations took a rapid turn after the first week of December, when the Tsar and his suite returned to St. Petersburg and Giers himself replaced Jomini as the leading negotiator for Russia. He was impatient to finish with the negotiations.

[1] *Russia: Dispatches*, 34: 57, John W. Foster to William M. Evarts, 19 Nov. 1880 (National Archives, Washington, D.C.).
[2] Jelavich, 156, Giers to Jomini, 4/16 Nov., 11/23 Nov. 1880.
[3] Ibid. 137–8, Jomini to Giers, 12/24 Nov. 1880.
[4] Ibid. 100.

Tseng, on his part, was also anxious to complete his mission, lest the delay give the war party in Peking an excuse to obstruct the progress he had already made. With a view to making the most of British and American support, he asked Plunkett to use his good offices 'to induce the Russian government to be as lenient as possible towards China' since he, Tseng, had already reached the limit of the concessions he was allowed to make. Plunkett, while declining to take 'any active part whatever in the negotiations', agreed to urge conciliation upon the Russians.[1] He told Giers that if Russia could be more yielding on the pecuniary issue and reduce her demands to what she intended to accept, 'it would hasten matters'.[2] Tseng also turned to Foster again to request his good offices. Foster considered mediation 'a very delicate task to undertake' but agreed to do what he could on the proper occasions. When he later visited Giers to discuss the problem of the Jews in Russia, and the pro-scriptive law against them, Giers reminded him of the poor treatment of the Chinese in the United States. Foster seized the opportunity to express the hope that the negotiations be-tween Russia and China would come to a 'peaceful and satis-factory conclusion'. Foster reported to the Secretary of State: 'Mr. Giers listened to me with much interest and expressed him-self as highly gratified to have an opportunity to talk with me on the subject. He assured me that the Russian government was desirous of coming to an amicable arrangement with China and had no disposition to be harsh or to exact inconvenient conditions. . . . (He) expressed strong hopes that a mutually satisfactory result would be reached.'[3]

Giers was now more anxious than ever to rid himself of the 'cursed' Chinese affair. When he heard from Koiander in Peking that General Tso had been recalled to Peking, he suspected a resurgence of war sentiment in the Chinese govern-ment. Fearing that the peace talks in St. Petersburg might be wrecked by Tso, Giers several times solicitously inquired of Tseng the purpose of Tso's recall, and the Chinese diplomat spared no effort to reassure him that Tso's mission was an entirely peaceful one.[4] But Giers apparently decided on his own

[1] F.O. 418/I/342, Plunkett to Granville, *most confidential*, 30 Nov. 1880.
[2] F.O. 418/I/341, same to same, telegram, *confidential*, 4 Dec. 1880.
[3] *Russia: Dispatches*, 35: 77, Foster to Evarts, 1 Jan. 1881.   [4] *ILTY*, 207, 215.

that he had to race against Tso or there would be no peace at all. With this impetus the negotiations in St. Petersburg progressed rapidly.

In his meeting with Tseng on 11 December Giers agreed to prepare a formal memorandum stating Russia's final position on all the issues at stake and to conclude the negotiations in a few meetings.[1] A grand conference was called by him at the Foreign Office to discuss the China problem, attended by Miliutin, Jomini, Butzow, and the new finance minister, Abaza. The prevailing temper favoured avoiding war at all costs. The conference adopted Giers's recommendation that Russia make more concessions to Tseng in new terms instead of insisting on ratification of the old treaty, and that the changes be recorded in separate protocols. Butzow, though unsympathetic with the decision, volunteered to prepare a formal memorandum for Tseng, and Jomini agreed to put the necessary literary touches to it.[2]

In the category of territorial adjustment, Giers formally proposed to return the Tekes Valley but retain the land west of Ili for the settlement of the Tungan refugees. He agreed to accept the existing Sino-Russian border in south-western Ili set by General Ming-i in 1864. The boundaries of Kashgaria and Tarbagatai as stipulated in the Treaty of Livadia were to be ignored, and new Russo-Chinese commissions were to be set up to settle boundary problems on the spot.

As for trade provisions, Tseng succeeded in committing Giers to giving up the demand for new routes to Hankow via Sian and Han-chung. The Russians, however, were permitted to trade in Chia-yü-kuan in the same manner as in Tientsin. The number of new Russian consulates was reduced to two, in Suchow and Turfan, but as trade increased in the future Russia might negotiate for the establishment of five more in Kobdo, Uliasutai, Hami, Urumchi, and Ku-chʻeng. Russian traders in Mongolia were allowed tax exemption, but those in Sinkiang were given only temporary exemption until such time as increased trade called for new arrangements. The old protocol on Russian navigation in the Sungari was dropped for good. Thus most of the points of contention in the Treaty of Livadia were resolved.[3]

[1] Ibid. 165–8.   [2] Miliutin, iii. 283.   [3] Tseng Chi-tse, 'Memorials', 2: 28–36.

The remaining irritant was the issue of monetary compensation. Jomini had previously asked for eleven to twelve million roubles but he now indicated his willingness to accept four million roubles for extended occupation expenses in Ili, without asking China to bear the expense of the Russian naval demonstration. This four million roubles, together with the original five million

Territory Ceded to Russia by the Treaty of St. Petersburg

stipulated in the Treaty of Livadia, made an acceptable sum of nine million roubles, the equivalent of five million taels which Tseng was authorized to offer.[1] So the monetary issue too was finally settled to mutual satisfaction.

The Russians were overjoyed by the terms of the settlement, for they had been resigned to a far less profitable outcome. Giers lost no time in passing the good news to Miliutin and he asked

---

[1] At the suggestion of his secretary, Macartney, Tseng insisted that Russia pay the remittance charge, thus he succeeded in saving China some 280,000 roubles. See Boulger, *Macartney*, 351–5.

the Tsar to approve all the conditions.[1] Request was also made of the British government that Peking be urged to accept the settlement, and Granville was pleased to comply with it. Wade was instructed by telegram: 'Do your best to promote arrangement.'[2] The Tsungli Yamen was more than satisfied with the results of the negotiations, which had restored to China some seventy or eighty per cent. of the rights lost in the Treaty of Livadia.[3] When Tseng informed the Russians, on 17 January 1881, of Peking's approval,[4] Miliutin was so overcome by the good news that he exclaimed: 'Now we can count on the peaceful end of our misunderstanding with China!' He hastened to order the border generals to relax their military preparations.[5]

The Ili settlement, though generally considered a Chinese victory, nevertheless awarded Russia considerable advantages. The territory west of Ili went to her and became part of the Alma-Ata province. Russian properties in Ili were retained and the right to establish consulates in Suchow and Turfan secured. Russian trade with Sinkiang remained duty-free, even though only temporarily. These new privileges materially strengthened Russia's position in Central Asia, and with the demise of the Yakub Beg empire the northward extension of British influence from India was checked. The nine million roubles of compensation was a welcome relief to her hard-pressed finances; it gave a new impetus to the development of the Trans-Siberian Railway, without which, the Russians learned, they could not wage an effective war in the East. Thus, all in all, Russia was quite handsomely compensated for her return of Ili.

Since the Treaty of Livadia had been virtually emptied of its contents, Giers suggested that it be discarded altogether and that a new document be drafted. Tseng could not have been more willing. The Treaty of St. Petersburg was signed on 24 February 1881, and it was formally approved by the Chinese government on 15 May of the same year. The exchange of the ratifications took place in St. Petersburg on 19 August, and in February 1882 Ili was transferred to China.[6]

---

[1] Miliutin, iii. 285–6.
[2] F.O. 418/II/3, Granville to Wade, telegram, 3 Jan. 1881.
[3] *WCSL*, 25: 16.   [4] *ILTY*, 206.   [5] Miliutin, iv. 13–14.
[6] *ILTY*, 211, 213; Tseng Chi-tse, 'Memorials', 3: 11b, 16–16b. It may be noted here that although the Treaty of St. Petersburg restored Ili to China, Russia still managed to gain more than 15,000 square miles in the boundary agreements that

Tseng's remarkable performance won him the praise from Giers that in all his forty-two years of diplomatic life he had seldom seen anyone from Europe, America, or Asia who was Tseng's equal.[1] Lord Dufferin also complimented Tseng by saying, 'China has compelled Russia to do what she had never done before: disgorging territory she had once absorbed.'[2] The grateful court at Peking rewarded Tseng with a concurrent appointment as senior vice-president of the Censorate and a year later, on 7 February 1882, raised his salary to that of a first-class imperial commissioner, i.e. ambassador, although his official rank was still second-class commissioner, or minister. On 20 November 1884 he was given the title of junior vice-president of the Board of War.[3] After nine years of diplomatic life he returned home in 1886 as the most successful diplomat of modern China.

followed—regarding the southern boundary of Ili concluded in Aug. 1882, regarding Kashgar in Nov. 1882, regarding Kobdo and Tarbagatai in July 1883, and regarding Kashgar again in 1885. See W. A. Douglas Jackson, *The Russo-Chinese Borderlands* (Princeton, 1962), 117.

[1] *ILTY*, 213, 225.   [2] Boulger, *Macartney*, 351.
[3] Tseng Chi-tse, 'Memorials', 6: 12.

CHAPTER X

The Legacy of the Ili Crisis

I. CHINA: THE PRICE OF VICTORY

Neither Russia nor China was in a position to wage war, but the prevailing moods of the two countries were very different. Russia was hampered by internal unrest and external isolation, while China had gained new vigour from the Self-Strengthening Movement. Having suppressed three great rebellions in succession—the Taiping, the Nien, and the Moslem—the Ch'ing dynasty had gained a new lease on life, and the re-establishment of imperial authority in Sinkiang gave rise to new confidence. In spite of Li Hung-chang's warning of the dangers of war with Russia, the majority of Chinese officials and scholars felt that China was not invading Russia but was merely defending her territory against an aggressor, and that where the cause was just the army would prevail. Their spirited pronouncements stimulated sentiments of war and inspired confidence of victory, even though the material basis for such a victory was lacking. In their outcry for war and eagerness to defend China's honour, the painful memories of past defeats in the Opium and Arrow Wars became dimmed. There seemed to be a feeling that China's position was now totally different. She had lost the earlier wars because her enemies, Britain and France, were a new type of seafaring invader with unpredictable striking-power, for which China was ill prepared. But Russia was something of a known quantity. China had dealt with her for nearly two hundred years: fought her at Albazin (Ya-k'e-sa) in the 1680's, negotiated with her at Nerchinsk and Kiakhta in 1689 and 1727, and sent diplomatic missions to her under Tulisen in 1714 and under T'o-shih in 1731 and 1732. There was also a number of Chinese writings on Russia. Confrontation with her was therefore not a rendezvous with the unknown. Consequently, the mandarins of 1880 seemed less fearful of Russia than of the maritime countries of Western Europe. There was even some wishful thinking that if China did successfully repel Russia at Albazin before, she might well repeat the performance now. The more venturesome Chinese talked about war with Russia as an occasion to test the result of China's twenty-year Self-Strengthening Movement. Li Hung-chang was constantly reminded that he should prove his usefulness in times of crisis, since the country had invested heavily in his fleet and army.

The spirited pronouncements of the Chinese war advocates and the confidence they manifested created the unmistakable picture of a country determined to defend its territory and honour. Such an image could not have failed to make an impression on the Russian legation in Peking and the government in St. Petersburg. A war with China, the Russians reasoned, would perforce be long, costly, and inconclusive. Victory would be uncertain and the risks too great to justify fighting over Ili.

The Chinese war advocates were of course playing with fire. They pushed their country so close to the brink of war that they might easily have precipitated it into a disaster of major proportions. Fortunately for China the present enemy was not Britain, the mistress of the seas, but Russia, a nation beset with foreign and domestic difficulties. By playing the dangerous game of brinkmanship, the Chinese forced their enemy to fight or retreat, allowing no chance of victory by mere threat of war. In the end Russia chose peace.

The decision for war or peace is perhaps always something of a gamble, and this time China luckily won. Chinese readiness to fight revealed the hollowness of the Russian threat. If Li Hung-chang and his peace party had been dominant at the time, China would in all likelihood have succumbed to that hollow threat, and Russia would have been spared the painful decision of war or peace; her weakness would not have been revealed. China was able to extricate herself from the predicament not so much by her own strength as by forcing the enemy to recognize his weakness. In this respect the *ch'ing-i* outcry for war, which had many times led the country into ruinous wars, unexpectedly turned out to be a blessing in disguise.

Knowing Chinese officialdom as he did, Tseng Chi-tse, the victor of the diplomatic battle in Russia, felt impelled to warn his countrymen against easy pride and over-confidence. He feared that the victory might encourage Chinese courtiers and scholars, especially the *ch'ing-i* group, to believe that if China could deal successfully with a country as powerful as Russia, there could be nothing in foreign relations that she could not cope with. The natural outcome would be over-confidence, undue optimism, and arrogance, which would seriously damage China's relations with other countries. To forestall such an unwarranted attitude, he submitted a long memorial to Peking on 26 February 1881, only two days after the signing of the Treaty of St. Petersburg, stressing the difficulties he had encountered in the negotiations. He pointed out China's good fortune in having confronted Russia at a time when she was troubled by great internal and external difficulties, and implied strongly that such a favourable combination of circumstances was not likely to recur.[1]

But Tseng's restraint in victory, statesmanlike as it was, did not prevent a domestic surge of elation at the thought of a victory won from a powerful country. Chinese conservatism and complacency received a new impetus, and the *ch'ing-i* group, gratified at the result of what they thought was their endeavour, became ever more vociferous in the ensuing years. This was clearly demonstrated during the Sino-French controversy over Annam a year later. In April 1882 the Ch'ing government dispatched troops to Tongking to check French aggressive designs, even though it was totally unprepared to meet the challenge.[2] The *ch'ing-i* phenomenon rose to a new height. Chang Chih-tung and Chang P'ei-lun took the lead in clamouring for war with France, a nation they disparagingly described as a 'spent arrow', on the brink of bankruptcy. They argued confidently: 'If we are desirous of peace, then France will wage war; but if we are capable of conducting a war, the French will be peaceable.'[3] The weapon with which they wished to combat the enemy was 'the love of the people and high morale', and the resolute will of courageous men and women.[4] They attacked Li Hung-chang for his appeasement policy, calling it 'an illusory and unreliable palliative', and they compared him with Ch'in Kuei, the arch-traitor of the Sung

---

[1] Tseng Chi-tse, 'Memorials', 3: 6–9b.

[2] Lloyd Eastman, 'Chinese Officialdom's Reactions to Foreign Aggression: A Study of the Sino-French Controversy, 1880–1885', Ph.D. thesis, Harvard University (Feb. 1963), draft, 35.   [3] Ibid. 12ᵛ   [4] Ibid. 123–4.

period. He was ridiculed for his gullibility before the unscru-
pulous French. A sub-chancellor of the Grand Secretariat
announced: 'The wily plans of the French were known to boys
and servants. The only person that believes in them without
suspicion is Li Hung-chang.'[1] Another senior metropolitan
censor admonished the court: 'I am afraid that Li Hung-chang
has been deceived by the French and that the court has in turn
been deceived by Li Hung-chang.'[2] Li was of course disgusted
with these irresponsible attacks, as he told a friend: 'I am troubled by the idle talk of people not in positions of authority. . . .
They discussed events first and then they discussed men. Most
of them engage in sharp bullying. My loyalty and rectitude
are only clear to myself.'[3]

The *ch'ing-i* pronouncements reached such fierce proportions
and the outcry for war so filled the air that the court was harried
by them into a course of greater belligerency than it had
intended. Milder elements were forced out of the government,
and Prince Kung, head of the Tsungli Yamen, was replaced
by Prince Ch'un, father of the boy Emperor and a diehard
conservative. The Grand Council was also reorganized in
favour of the war party. The government was led step by step
to the brink of war. The result was not victory over France but
destruction of the Foochow Dockyard by enemy bombardment.
The France of 1884–5 was not the Russia of 1880. The price of
Chinese over-confidence and bellicosity was defeat and loss of
suzerainty over the tributary state of Annam, and this over-
confidence and pride could be traced to the Ili victory.

The French war dealt a severe blow to Chinese pride, and
a sense of dejection and resignation developed as an aftermath.
Rapidly approaching what might be called its 'pre-ordained
finale' (*ch'i-shu i-chin*), the Ch'ing dynasty complacently allowed
itself to drift into a state of unrealistic quietude. There was a
general decline of government morality, as manifested in the
rebuilding of the Summer Palace with naval funds[4]—an act

---

[1] *Kuang-hsü chao Chung-Fa chiao-she shih-liao* (Historical materials on Sino-French
negotiations during the Kuang-hsü period), 18: 24, document 682.

[2] Ibid. 14: 12, document 485.

[3] Shao Hsün-cheng *et al.* (ed.), *Chung-Fa chan-cheng* (The Sino-French war)
(Shanghai, 1955), 4: 8.

[4] Li Chien-nung, *The Political History of China, 1840–1928*, edited and translated
by S. Y. Teng and J. Ingalls (New York, 1956), 98, 128.

that definitely contributed to the defeat by Japan in 1895. To guard against future Japanese aggression, the court rediscovered the importance of Russia as a northern neighbour who had been 'good' to China during the Ili settlement. The upshot was the conclusion of a secret alliance in 1896. But the Ch'ing pursuit of security proved illusory: barely a year had passed when Russia cast her covetous eye on Port Arthur, thereby touching off the partition of China by foreign powers. What followed was the outbreak of a violent anti-foreign movement, the Boxer Rebellion, which precipitated an eight-power expedition to China and the subsequent occupation of Peking. Thus, insofar as the Ili victory had any significance in the historical sense, it is that it confirmed the tradition of anti-foreign conservatism, fostered the spirit of complacency, and prepared the way for the ultimate disaster of the dynasty.

Nonetheless, the Ili settlement was China's first diplomatic victory in modern times and it made possible the establishment of a province in Sinkiang.

2. SINKIANG: CHANGE BEYOND TRADITION

The settlement of the Ili crisis created a major impact on the institutional status of Sinkiang. Chinese relations with the *Hsi-yü*, ever since the Han period, had revolved around the three phases of conquest, appeasement, and relinquishment, as reflected in the three historical concepts of Grand Unification, Minor Unification, and Precarious Security. The Western Region was never an integral part of China proper, but a frontier area. During the Ch'ing period Sinkiang was in essence a military colony of the Manchus. But after the Treaty of St. Petersburg the Ch'ing government took the unprecedented step of raising its status to that of a regular province. Thus, for the first time in history Sinkiang was on a par with the rest of the empire. It was indeed a landmark in Chinese frontier history.[1]

The guiding spirit of this epochal undertaking was Tso Tsung-t'ang, though he was not the first to espouse the idea. Kung Tzu-chen (1792–1841), a famous scholar of the late Ch'ing period, made 'A Proposal for turning *Hsi-yü* into a Regular Province' in his *Literary Collection*, which was printed

[1] Ch'in Han-ts'ai, 220–1, 226–7.

posthumously in 1868. In it he advocated that the land west of Barkul to Urumchi should be detached from Kansu province for incorporation into Sinkiang, the eastern boundary of which should be just west of Anhsi. The new province should be made up of eleven prefectures (*fu*), three independent departments (*chih-li chou*), two departments (*chou*), and forty-six counties (*hsien*). There should be a governor-general in Ili and a governor in Urumchi. A financial and a judicial commissioner should be appointed under them, just as in the other provinces. The provincial commander-in-chief (*t'i-tu*) should be stationed in Urumchi, and three brigade-generals and three intendants of military circuits should be placed in the several key places. Moslem *begs* should be made subdistrict magistrates.[1]

In time these ideas became the nucleus of a proposal submitted to the throne by Tso Tsung-t'ang. Five times—once in 1877, twice in 1878, and once each in 1880 and 1882—he urged the court to make Sinkiang a province so as to ensure lasting peace and order.[2] His ideas were most explicitly elucidated in a letter to his leading general and later successor, Liu Chin-t'ang, in 1878:

> Whether court opinions can agree or not, there is no better way to lasting peace and order in Sinkiang than to make it a province. Soon I plan to memorialize my general views [on the subject] and request the appointment of a governor-general and a governor first, leaving the details for later expatiations, so as to achieve quick result. . . . The governor-general should be stationed in Urumchi, and the governor in Aksu. Ili should be the seat of the military-governor and commander-in-chief, and Chuguchak that of a brigade-general. All the traditional posts of assistant military-governors and imperial agents can be abolished. A provincial commander-in-chief should be stationed in Kashgar. The old commandants of the forces in the several places should be replaced by brigade-generals and intendants. All vacancies in the offices of the governor-general, governor, circuit intendants, prefects, sub-prefects, and county magistrates should be filled by Manchus and Chinese without distinction. . . . The garrison forces that are transferred periodically may be recruited selectively from the natives, but for the time being the visiting [i.e. Manchu-Chinese] army should not be withdrawn too readily . . . [The land] west of Hami should be governed by

[1] Kung Tzu-chen, *Ting-an wen-chi* (Literary collection of Kung Tzu-chen), 1868, ii: 4b–11.   [2] Ch'in Han-ts'ai, 117–19.

Sinkiang and that east of Anhsi and Tun-huang by Kansu. When the boundary line is clear, the task of government is rendered easy. . . . The old set-up of Moslem *begs* and *t'ai-chi* may be allowed to continue, but those who are unfit for duties should be dismissed and replaced forthwith.[1]

A formal proposal containing these ideas was dispatched to the court in 1878, but the government would not approve these measures before the recovery of Ili. However, Peking encouraged him to continue his planning for the eventual establishment of a province in Sinkiang. On 26 May 1880, at the height of the Ili crisis, Tso again presented the plan, requesting that a governor-general of Sinkiang be appointed first at Urumchi and a governor at Aksu. The court was unwilling to make these far-reaching commitments at such an unsettled time, and Tso was told that his plan would entail many difficulties before the actual recovery of Ili.[2] After the final settlement of the crisis by the Treaty of St. Petersburg, the persistent Old Soldier renewed his request in a memorial dated 18 October 1882.[3] The court could no longer use the same pretext, and the Board of Civil Offices, with lingering doubts as to the ability of Sinkiang's small population to support a provincial system, reluctantly approved Tso's recommendation in principle. After further delay and debate, the court finally sanctioned the establishment of the Sinkiang province on 16 November 1884, with General Liu Chin-t'ang as the first governor. All the old positions of military-governor, assistant military-governors, commandants of the forces, imperial agents, and assistant imperial agents were abolished. Sinkiang at long last emerged from the status of a colony and territory. Tso did not live to see his dream realized, for he had died half a year earlier.[4]

Although Sinkiang had become a province of the empire, the Ch'ing dynasty, its life-span nearly over, was unable to keep a firm hold on it. The Nationalist government that came into power after the Manchus also exercised only a nominal control over it. But today the Communist government in Peking has successfully asserted its control of Sinkiang, moving

---

[1] Tso Tsung-t'ang, 'Letters', 21: 8–8b.
[2] Idem, 'Memorials', 52: 3–5, 56: 34–37b.
[3] Ibid., 59: 57.
[4] Wen-djang Chu, *Policy*, 304–6.

large columns of immigrants into it and making it a vital and active part of the state, tied indissolubly to the rest of China by the strongest of all bonds, those of blood and ideology. Chinese influence in Sinkiang now is probably stronger than ever before. The old imperial dream of Grand Unification through domination of the Western Region has been unexpectedly fulfilled by the Marxist converts in China under the red banners.

Notes

A. The Russian expert on Central Asia, Lieutenant-General M. A. Terent'ev, in his *Istoriia zavoevaniia* . . . gave what he termed an 'inaccurate' estimate of the population of Ili in the 1860's as follows: Taranchi, 38,211; Tungan, 5,130; Kirghiz, 22,344; Sibo, 15,484; Mongol, 17,954; Chinese, 3,373; and Manchu, 450. Of the total 102,910, the author claimed that 65,685 were Moslems. Cf. Terent'ev, ii. 56.

Baron Kaulbars of the Russian General Staff, who visited Ili in 1870, put the population of Ili at 130,000, as follows: Taranchi, 40,000; Tungan, 10,000; Kirghiz, 35,000; Mongol (Kalmuk), 30,000; Turγūd, 10,000; Chinese and Sibo, 5,000. These figures are quoted in Eugene Schuyler, *Turkistan: Notes of a Journey in Russian Turkistan, Khokand, Bukhara, and Kuldja* (New York, 1877), ii. 197. On the same page Schuyler suggested the figure of 350,000 as the probable census of Ili before the rebellion in the 1860's. W. L. Bales gave the same figure of 350,000 in his *Tso Tsungt'ang, Soldier and Statesman of Old China* (Shanghai, 1937), 311.

B. Anonymous, 'P'ing-hui chi-lüeh' (A brief account of the pacification of the Moslems), in Pai Shou-i (ed.), *Hui-min ch'i-i* (The righteous uprising of the Moslem people) (Shanghai, 1953), iii. 9; see also Wen-djang Chu, *Policy*, 251. Western research on the New Sect has been inconclusive and disappointing. H. M. D'Ollone in his *Recherches sur les Musulmans chinois* (Paris, 1911) simply stated that the New Sect taught the worship of the tombs of saints (p. 216). Marshall Broomhall in his *Islam in China* (London, 1910) made a passing remark that 'the New School or *Sin Kiao* are more liberal in their religious views and practices' (p. 253). This view is in obvious conflict with later research by Saguchi and Chu, quoted above. Mary Wright made a good summary of Western research on the New Sect in her *The Last Stand of Chinese Conservatism, The T'ung-chih Restoration, 1862–1874* (Stanford, 1957), 107–8. The Chinese scholar, Wen-djang Chu, has written a comprehensive essay on the New Sect in his *Policy*, Appendix IV.

C. An old version of the outbreak of the Tungan Rebellion based on the studies of Broomhall and Andrew had been accepted for years until the recent publication of *Hui-min ch'i-i* (The righteous uprising of the Moslem people) (Shanghai, 1953), and the scholarly research based on it by Wen-djang Chu, quoted above. The old version ran as follows:

In 1861 the Chinese and Moslem population of Shensi organized separate militia against the invading Taipings. The Moslem militia drove the Taipings out of Huachow and took possession of sizable treasures. Refused any share of the spoils, the Chinese militia became angry and resentful. Antagonism between the two ethnic groups was brought to a high pitch several months later when eighteen Moslems were arrested by Chinese authorities for robbing a customs house. Their summary execution without consultation with Moslem officials generated a strong feeling of injustice in the Moslem population.

The sparks that set off the rebellion were kindled the following year, 1862, during a quarrel between a group of Moslems and Chinese. The Moslems were alleged to have cut bamboo to make lances in a Chinese village near Huachow without first securing permission from the Chinese owner. Upon receiving the complaint, the Chinese magistrate ordered the death of all Moslems in the village near the scene of the incident. The Moslems responded by indiscriminately killing all Chinese and Manchus in a bloody uprising that continued three days and nights. Government troops were sent to fight them, but being largely Moslem themselves, they soon defected to the rebels. The court in Peking, thoroughly alarmed, ordered the extermination of all Moslems in Shensi, but the tide of rebellion could not be stemmed. By the end of 1863 the entire province had fallen to the rebels (see Broomhall, 152–3; Andrew, 79–80).

D. Tso Tsung-t'ang (1812–85) was born into a family of moderate means in Hsiang-yin, Hunan. He was a very promising scholar in his early years and achieved the *chu-jen* degree at the age of nineteen. Then his fortune declined and three times—in 1833, 1835, and 1838—he failed the metropolitan examinations for the *chin-shih* degree. His attention was drawn to an official work on the Chinese conquest of Sinkiang called the *Ch'in-ting huang-yü Hsi-yü t'u-chih*, which proved to be of great value years later. His knowledge of Sinkiang was further extended in 1849 when he learnt about the conditions of Ili from the famous statesman Lin Tse-hsü, who had been exiled there after his 'mismanagement' of the opium problem in 1840.

Although Tso was considered by Lin to have a 'most unusual talent' (*ch'i-ts'ai*), his life before forty was rather uneventful. But in 1852, on the recommendation of an influential friend, Hu Lin-i, he joined the staff of Chang Liang-chi, the governor of Hunan, and was charged with military action against the Taipings. His success in the campaign won him fame and imperial attention and his fortunes soared thereafter. In 1862 he became governor of Chekiang and in the following year governor-general of Fukien and Chekiang. Then followed a succession of honours, among them the title of junior guardian of the Heir Apparent, with the coveted Yellow Jacket, and an earldom of the first class. After the Taipings had been suppressed, Tso did much to rehabilitate Chekiang and Fukien provinces. Among the many projects he originated was the famous Foochow Dockyard. In 1866 the court made him governor-general of Shensi and Kansu, with the special assignment of suppressing the Moslem rebellion.

As a man, Tso was proud, brusque, argumentative, and outspoken, regardless of time, place, or circumstance. He liked to compare himself with the wise scholar-strategist Chu-ko Liang of the Three Kingdom Period (A.D. 221–65). Supremely confident, he carried himself with an air of will and determination, and never wavered under the severest test. His pronouncements, though egotistical, were couched in a terse, classical style that make good reading. 'Men admired his achievements and respected his ability but they did not warm up to him personally', wrote his biographer

Bales. Indeed, many feared him. Physically, he was short and stout, with barely 'three hairs' on his chin and a somewhat thicker moustache. His eyes were small, bright, and crafty. The Russian traveller Dr. P. Piassetsky (Piasetskiĭ), who saw him in 1875, said he looked rather like Bismarck, except that Tso's face was darker.

For a biography of Tso, see Arthur W. Hummel, *Eminent Chinese of the Ch'ing Period* (Washington, 1944), ii. 762–7; Gideon Ch'en, *Tso Tsung-t'ang, Pioneer Promoter of the Modern Dockyard and the Woolen Mill in China* (Peiping, 1938); see also W. L. Bales, *Tso Tsungt'ang, Soldier and Statesman of Old China* (Shanghai, 1937), 407; and P. Piassetsky, *Russian Travellers in Mongolia and China* (London, 1884), ii. 118.

E. The Ch'ing recovery of Sinkiang was such a remarkable event that even Marxist writers today see merit in it. Although Yakub Beg's movement looked like a minority uprising against the oppressive Manchu rule, they say, it was in essence nothing more than a feudalistic contest with the Manchus for the monopolistic right of exploiting the peoples of Sinkiang. Yakub Beg, once in power, was even worse than the Manchus he replaced. Cruelty, fear, secret police, and irregular taxation characterized his corrupt administration, which was supported by the British and Turkish imperialists. Such a reactionary and tyrannical puppet régime naturally had no basis for a lasting existence. Chinese victory came not so much because of Tso's personal ability as because of the powerful 'social forces' behind his campaign, for in destroying Yakub Beg, Tso reflected the 'general will' of the Chinese people. The Sinkiang campaign might even be considered 'progressive' because it shattered the imperialist scheme of splitting up the Chinese family and liberated the Moslem people from colonial servitude. One should not deny the 'positive' nature of Tso's work simply because of his earlier reactionary campaign against the Taipings. See Hung Yüan, 'A-ku-po cheng-ch'üan te pen-chih ho Ch'ing-ping hsi-cheng te i-i' (The very nature of Yakub Beg's régime and the meaning of the western expedition of the Ch'ing army), *Hsin-hua yüeh-pao*, 65: 207–8; Fan Hsiao, 'Tui-yü A-ku-po che i-jen-wu p'ing-chia te shang-ch'üeh' (An appraisal of the man Yakub Beg), *Hsin-hua yüeh-pao*, 65: 208–9.

F. The Turγūd tribe formerly lived in the Tarbagatai area but had migrated to Russia in 1630. By 1654 they had become Russian vassals, although their chieftains continued to send periodical tribute to China. In 1712 K'ang-hsi sent Tulisen, an assistant reader of the Grand Secretariat, to the Turγūd tribe in Russia with the twofold objective of improving China's relations with the Turγūd and forestalling any possibility of alliance between them and the Ölod. Cf. *Ku-kung O-wen shih-liao* (Documents in Russian preserved in the National Palace Museum of Peiping), edited by Wang Chih-hsiang and Liu Tse-jung (Peiping, 1936), 12–13. (Cited as *OWSL*).

Tulisen reached the Volga in June 1714 and met the Turγūd chief, Ayüki, on Lake Manuto. He returned to China with an account of his travels entitled *I-yü lu* (Description of a foreign land), which was probably the first authentic Chinese work on Russia in the Ch'ing period.

Emperor Yung-cheng sent T'o-shih to Russia in 1731 and 1732 with the proposal that, during the Ch'ing campaign against the Ŏlod leader Galden Cereng, if he and his men took refuge in Russia, the Russian government should extradite the Ŏlod leaders and noblemen to China but keep their tribesmen under strict control so that they would not make trouble for China in the future. For this co-operation, China was willing to compensate Russia with part of the land seized from the Ŏlod. The Russian government expressed willingness to discuss the question of extradition in a friendly manner when it arose but refused to make other commitments. Cf. *OWSL*, 13, 307, 312; see also Mark Mancall, 'China's First Missions to Russia, 1729–1731', *Papers on China* (East Asia Regional Studies Seminar, Harvard University), 9: 93 (1955); Immanuel C. Y. Hsü, 'Russia's Special Position in China during the Early Ch'ing Period', *Slavic Review*, 23:4:688–700 (Dec. 1964).

G. Boulger's story unfolds as follows:

'His [von Brandt's] plan was startlingly simple and bold. Li Hung-chang, the only prominent advocate of peace, was to rebel, march on Peking with his Black Flag army, and establish a government of his own. . . . Gordon went to China in the full belief that, whatever names were used, it was his old colleague Li Hung-chang who sent for him, and the very first definite information he received on approaching the Chinese capital was that not Li, but persons whom by inference were inimical to Li, had sent for him. The first question that arises then was who was the real author of the invitation to Gordon that bore the name of Hart. It cannot be answered, for Gordon assured me that he himself did not know; but there is no doubt that it formed part of the plot and counter-plot originated by the German minister, and responded to by those who were resolved, in the event of Li's rebellion, to uphold the Dragon Throne. . . . Sir Robert Hart knew exactly what was being done by the German minister. . . . The German minister, thinking that he had obtained an ally who would render the success of his own plan certain, proposed that Gordon should put himself at the head of Li's army, march on Peking, and depose the Emperor. Gordon's droll comment on this is: "I told him I was equal to a good deal of filibustering, but that this was beyond me, and that I did not think there was the slightest chance of such a project succeeding, as Li had not a sufficient following to give it any chance of success!" ' (Boulger, *Gordon*, 218–19).

H. Boulger's story is unbelievable, even without documentary evidence to the contrary. It is most unlikely, not to say ridiculous, that a man of Li's stature and position should be supposed to have thought of rebellion. If he had been a failure in politics, or a frustrated scholar like the Taiping leader Hung Hsiu-ch'üan, he might have had a grudge against the existing system that might have provided an incentive for revolt. He was, in fact, a great success, holding those positions and honours that were the dream of every Confucian scholar-official. There was no reason for him to want to overthrow a government that offered him power, prestige, wealth, and security. Why should he have risked all this to satisfy the whims of the

German minister? If the court had had the merest suspicion of disloyalty, it could have removed him instantly by decree; there would have been no need to call Gordon from India to fight against him. Moreover, Li did not have enough of a following to start a successful uprising. The country's best troops were in Sinkiang; Tso and others could easily have crushed Li in a military encounter. Common sense alone makes Boulger's statements incredible.

Bibliography

ALLEN, JAMES GARLAND, 'Anglo-Russian Rivalry in Central Asia, 1865–1885'. Ph.D. thesis, University of California, Berkeley, 1934; 481 pp.

ANDREW, G. FINDLAY, *The Crescent in North-west China*. London, 1921; 113 pp.

ANSTEY, ROGER I., *Britain and the Congo in the Nineteenth Century*. Oxford, 1962; 261 pp.

BADDELEY, JOHN F., *Russia, Mongolia, China*, 2 vols. London, 1919.

BALES, W. L., *Tso Tsungt'ang, Soldier and Statesman of Old China*. Shanghai, 1937; 436 pp.

BARTHOLD, V. V., *La découverte de l'Asie: Histoire de l'orientalisme en Europe et en Russie*. Trans. from Russian, with notes by B. Nikitine. Paris, 1947; 367 pp.

—— *Histoire des Turcs d'Asie centrale*. Adaptation française par Mme M. Donskis. Paris, 1945; 202 pp.

—— *Turkestan down to the Mongol Invasion*. English translation, second edition. London, 1958; 513 pp.

—— *Four Studies on the History of Central Asia*. English translation by V. and T. Minorsky. 2 vols. Leiden, 1956.

BELL, Colonel MARK, 'The Dungan Rebellion and Hankow', *The Imperial and Asiatic Quarterly Review*, 3rd series, vol. i, nos. 1 and 2 (Jan.–April 1896), pp. 55–64.

BELLEW, H. W., *Kashmir and Kashghar: A Narrative of the Journey of the Embassy to Kashghar in 1873–74*. London, 1875; 419 pp.

BOULGER, DEMETRIUS C., *The Life of Sir Halliday Macartney, K.C.M.G.* London and New York, 1908; 505 pp.

—— *Central Asian Portraits; The Celebrities of the Khanates and the Neighbouring States*. London, 1880; 310 pp.

—— *The Life of Gordon*. London, 1896; 337 pp.

—— *The Life of Yakoob Beg*. London, 1878; 344 pp.

BRANDT, MAX VON, *Dreiunddreißig Jahre in Ost-Asien: Erinnerungen eines deutschen Diplomaten* (Thirty-three years in East Asia: the memoirs of a German diplomat), vol. iii, Leipzig, 1901; 333 pp.

British diplomatic papers, Public Record Office (London):

    Foreign Office:

        List of Confidential Prints. Search Dept., 1959.

        Lists and Indexes, no. L 11: List of Foreign Office Records to 1878. London, 1929; 431 pp.

        List of Records of the Foreign Office: 1879–1885. Typed and bound, 1930; 311 pp.

        Embassy and Consular Archives, no. 41 U; 394 pp.

        China: Papers in the Chinese Language. 1961; 109 pp.

    F.O. 418, *Confidential* (4521). Correspondence respecting the Russo-Chinese Treaty (Kuldja Territory). 2 vols. 1878–80.

F.O. 17 (China):

Vol. 547: From Sir R. Alcock and Mr. Wade, nos. 1–44. Jan. to March 1870.

Vol. 548: From Mr. Wade and Sir R. Alcock, nos. 45–66. April 1870.

Vol. 549: From Mr. Wade and Sir R. Alcock, nos. 67–122. May and June 1870.

Vol. 588: From Mr. Wade, nos. 191–224. Aug. to Oct. 1871.

Vol. 589: From Mr. Wade, nos. 225–67. Nov. 1871.

Vol. 590: From Mr. Wade, nos. 268–84. Dec. 1871.

Vol. 626: From Mr. Wade, nos. 1–27. Jan. to Feb. 1872.

Vol. 627: From Mr. Wade, nos. 28–49. March 1872.

Vol. 825: Operations against Kashgar, &c. 1876–7.

Vol. 826: Operations against Kashgar, &c. 1878–9.

Vol. 827: To Sir T. Wade. Jan. to Jun. 1880.

Vol. 828: To Sir T. Wade. 2 July 1880 to 30 Dec. 1880.

Vol. 829: From Sir T. Wade. Jan. 1880.

Vol. 830: From Sir T. Wade. Feb. to April 1880.

Vol. 831: From Sir T. Wade. May to 10 July 1880.

Vol. 832: From Sir T. Wade. July to Aug. 1880.

Vol. 833: From Sir T. Wade. Aug. to Dec. 1880.

Vol. 857: From Sir T. Wade. Jan. to May 1881.

Vol. 845: Domestic Various. Jan. to April 1880.

Vol. 846: Domestic Various. May to July 1880.

Vol. 847: Domestic Various. Aug. to Dec. 1880.

F.O. 65 (Russia):

Vol. 822: From Sir A. Buchanan, nos. 142–232. July to Sept. 1871.

Vol. 1082: From Mr. F. R. Plunkett, nos. 422–528. Sept. to Nov. 1880.

Vol. 1083: From Mr. Plunkett and Earl Dufferin, nos. 529–630. Nov. to Dec. 1880.

Vol. 1086: From Earl Dufferin, telegrams, nos. 1–118. Jan. to July 1880.

Vol. 1087: From Earl Dufferin and Mr. Plunkett, telegrams. nos. 119–251. Aug. to Dec. 1880.

Vol. 1110: From Lord Dufferin, nos. 1–110. Jan. to March 1881.

F.O. 233 (Chinese Secretary's Office, Legation File):

Vol. 76: The Russo-Chinese Question. (Translation of seven Chinese documents.)

F.O. 682 (In Chinese):

No. 23. Decree regarding Yakub Beg's children.

No. 29. Russo-Chinese Question.

No. 348. Confidential: five documents in Chinese relating to the organization of the Turkestan government.

No. 398. Six documents re finance and military operations in North-West. Feb.–Aug. 1876.

No. 401. Two memorials by Board of Revenue, re army expenditure in Djungaria. 1877.

British Museum, Department of Oriental Printed Books and Manuscripts: Chinese Accessions. 2 vols. 1931.

BROOMHALL, MARSHALL, *Islam in China*. London, 1910; 332 pp.

BRUNNERT, H. S., and V. V. HAGELSTROM, *Present Day Political Organization of China*. Shanghai, 1912; 572 pp.

BURHAN, SHAKHIDI. *See* PAO ERH-HAN.

CAHEN, GASTON, *Histoire des relations de la Russie avec la Chine, 1689–1730*. Paris, 1912; 274 pp. + appendixes.

—— *Some Early Russo-Chinese Relations*, trans. and ed. by W. Sheldon Ridge. Shanghai, 1914; 128 pp.

CARDONNE, C. DE, *L'Empereur Alexandre II: vingt-six ans de règne (1855–1881)*. Paris, 1883; 868 pp.

A Catalogue of Files and Microfilms of the German Foreign Ministry Archives, 1867–1920. Prepared by the Committee for the Study of War Documents, American Historical Association. Oxford, 1959; 1290 pp.

CHANG, CH'AO 張潮 (ed.), *Chao-tai ts'ung-shu* 昭代叢書 (Collection of the shining dynasty). 172 chüan. First appeared in 1697, later enlarged and published in 1833.

CHANG, CHI-HSIN 張集馨, 'Lin-t'ung chi-shih' 臨潼紀事 (Events in Lin-t'ung), in *Hui-min ch'i-i* 囘民起義 (The righteous uprising of the Moslem people), compiled by Pai Shou-i 白壽彝. 4 vols. Shanghai, 1953.

CHANG, CHIH-TUNG 張之洞, *Chang-wen-hsiang-kung ch'üan-chi* 張文襄公全集 (Complete works of Chang Chih-tung). Series I: Memorials. 100 chüan. 1928.

CHANG, HSING-LANG 張星烺, 'O-kuo ti-i-tz'u t'ung-shih Chung-kuo chi' 俄國第一次通使中國記 (The first Russian mission to China), *Ti-hsüeh tsa-chih* (The Geographical Journal, Peking), no. 2 (Dec. 1928), pp. 197–215.

CHANG, P'EI-LUN 張佩綸, *Chien-yü chi* 澗于集 (Works of Chang P'ei-lun). 6 chüan. 1918.

CHANG, WEI-HUA 張維華, 'T'u-erh-hu-t'e hsi-hsi yü T'u-li-ch'en chih ch'u-shih' 土爾扈特西徙與圖理琛之出使 (The westward migration of the Toryūd and the mission of Tulisen), *Pien-cheng kung-lun* (Frontier Affairs), vol. ii, nos. 3, 4, 5 (June 1943), pp. 26–35.

CHANG, YÜ-SHU 張玉書, 'Wai-kuo chi' 外國紀 (Descriptions of foreign countries), *Chao-tai ts'ung-shu* 昭代叢書, edited by Chang Ch'ao 張潮, supplementary chüan 6, *hsin* 辛 section; reprinted in 1833.

CHANG-CHÜN 長君, 'Hsin-chiang chuang-k'uang chi-yao' 新疆狀況紀要 (An outline of conditions in Sinkiang), *Hsi-pei yen-chiu* 西北研究, no. 5 (March 1932), pp. 11–28.

CH'EN, AGNES FANG-CHIH, 'Chinese Frontier Diplomacy: the Coming of the Russians and the Treaty of Nerchinsk', *The Yenching Journal of Social Studies*, vol. 4, no. 2 (Feb. 1949), pp. 99–149.

—— 'Chinese Frontier Diplomacy: Kiakhta Boundary Treaties and Agreements', *The Yenching Journal of Social Studies*, vol. 4, no. 2 (Feb. 1949), pp. 151–205.

—— 'China's Northern Frontiers: Historical Background', *The Yenching Journal of Social Studies*, vol. 4, no. 1 (Aug. 1948), pp. 15–87.

CH'EN, FANG-CHIH 陳 芳芝, 'Ch'ing-tai pien-chih shu-lüeh' 清代邊制述略 (A brief account of the frontier system in the Ch'ing period), *Yenching Journal of Chinese Studies*, no. 34 (June 1948), pp. 133–64.

CH'EN, FU-KUANG 陳 復 光, *Yu-Ch'ing i-tai chih Chung-O kuan-hsi* 有清一代之中俄關係 (Sino-Russian relations during the Ch'ing period exclusively). Kunming, 1947; 464 pp.

CH'EN, GIDEON, *Tso Tsung T'ang, Pioneer Promoter of the Modern Dockyard and the Woolen Mill in China*. Peiping, 1938; 93 pp.

—— 'Tso Tsung-t'ang: the Farmer of Hsiangshang', *The Yenching Journal of Social Studies*, vol. 1, no. 2 (Jan. 1939), pp. 211-25.

CH'EN, PING-KUANG 陳 炳 光, *Ch'ing-tai pien-cheng t'ung-k'ao* 清代邊政通考 (A general study of the Ch'ing border systems). Nanking?, 1934; 416 pp.

CH'EN, PO-WEN 陳 博 文, *Chung-O wai-chiao shih* 中俄外交史 (A history of Sino-Russian diplomacy). Shanghai, 1928; 159 pp.

CH'EN, TENG-YÜAN 陳 登 元, *Chung-O kuan-hsi shu-lüeh* 中俄關係述略 (An outline of Sino-Russian relations). Shanghai, 1929; 186 pp.

CHENG, HO-SHENG 鄭 鶴 聲, *Chin-shih Chung-Hsi shih-jih tui-chao-piao* 近世中西史日對照表 (Comparative tables of Sino-Western historical dates in modern times). Shanghai, 1936; 880 pp.

CHENG, TIEN-FONG, *A History of Sino-Russian Relations*. Washington, D.C., 1957; 389 pp.

CHESHIRE, HAROLD T., 'The Expansion of Imperial Russia to the Indian Border', *The Slavonic and East European Review*, vol. 13, no. 37 (July 1934), pp. 85-97.

CH'I, YÜN-SHIH 祁 韻 士, 'Hsin-chiang yao-lüeh' 新 疆 要 略 (An essential outline of Sinkiang), *Huang-ch'ao fan-shu yü-ti ts'ung-shu* 皇 朝 藩 屬 輿 地 叢 書 (Collection of geographical works on the outer tribes and dependencies of our reigning dynasty), ts'e 24. 1903.

—— *Hsi-ch'ui yao-lüeh* 西 陲 要 略 (An essential outline of the Western frontier). 4 chüan. 1807.

—— *Huang-ch'ao fan-pu yao-lüeh* 皇 朝 藩 部 要 略 (A brief account of the dependencies of our imperial dynasty). 18 chüan and 4 chüan of tables. 1884.

Chia-ch'ing ch'ung-hsiu i-t'ung-chih 嘉 慶 重 修 一 統 志 (Revised gazetteer of the Chia-ch'ing reign). 560 chüan. 1842.

CH'IEN, HSÜN 錢恂, *Chung-O chieh-yüeh chiao-chu* 中俄界約斠注 (Notes on Sino-Russian boundary treaties). 7 chüan. 1894.

CHIN, CHI-T'ANG 金吉堂, *Chung-kuo hui-chiao shih yen-chiu* 中國回教史研究 (A study of the history of Islam in China). Peiping, 1935; 224 pp.

CH'IN, HAN-TS'AI 秦翰才, *Tso-wen-hsiang-kung tsai Hsi-pei* 左文襄公在西北 (Tso Tsung-t'ang in the North-West). Shanghai, 1946; 229 pp.

Ch'in-ting Hsin-chiang shih-lüeh 欽定新疆識略 (An imperial edition of an outline of Sinkiang). 12 chüan, 1821.

Ch'in-ting Huang-yü Hsi-yü t'u-chih 欽定皇輿西域圖志 (An imperial edition of the royal atlas of the Western Region). 48 chüan. 1762.

Ch'in-ting k'uo-erh-k'a chi-lüeh 欽定廓爾喀紀略 (An imperial edition of an outline of the Qalqa). 54 chüan. 1794.

China Postal Atlas. Nanking, 1936.

Ch'ing-chi wai-chiao shih-liao 清季外交史料 (Historical materials on late Ch'ing diplomacy). Peking, 1933; chüan 1–30.

CHOU, CHIA-MEI 周家楣, *Ch'i-pu-fu-chai ch'üan-chi* 期不負齋全集 (Complete work of the Ch'i-pu-fu studio). 14 chüan. 1895.

Ch'ou-pan i-wu shih-mo 籌辦夷務始末 (The complete account of the management of the barbarian affairs). Peking, 1930; T'ung-chih period, 100 chüan.

CHU, DJANG, 'War and Diplomacy over Ili', *CSPSR* vol. xx, no. 3 (Oct. 1936), pp. 369–92.

CHU, WEN-DJANG, 'The Policy of the Manchu Government in the Suppression of the Moslem Rebellion in Shensi, Kansu, and Sinkiang from 1862 to 1878'. Ph.D. thesis, University of Washington, 1955; 439 pp.

—— 'Tso Tsung-t'ang's Role in the Recovery of Sinkiang', *Tsing Hua Journal of Chinese Studies*, New Series, vol. 1, no. 3 (Sept. 1958), pp. 136–65.

—— 'The Immediate Cause of the Moslem Rebellion in Northwest China in 1862', *Central Asiatic Journal*, vol. 3, no. 4 (1958), pp. 309–16.

Chung-kuo shih-hsüeh lun-wen so-yin 中國史學論文索引 (An index to Chinese historical articles), 2 vols. Compiled by the First and Second Institutes of Historical Research, Academia Sinica, and the history department of the University of Peking, Peking, 1957.

COATES, W. P., and K. ZELDA, *Soviets in Central Asia*. London, 1951; 288 pp.

CORDIER, HENRI, *Histoire des relations de la Chine avec les puissances occidentales*, vol. ii, Paris, 1902; 648 pp.

CSL: See *Ta-Ch'ing li-ch'ao shih-lu*.

CSPSR: *The Chinese Social and Political Science Review*.

CURTI, MERLE, and JOHN STALPER, 'The Flowery Flag Devils—The American Image in China, 1840–1900', *Proceedings of the American Philosophical Society*, vol. 96 (1952), pp. 663–90.

CURZON, GEORGE N., *Russia in Central Asia in 1889 and the Anglo-Russian Question*. London, 1889; 477 pp.

DINGLE, EDWIN J. (ed.), *The New Atlas and Commercial Gazetteer of China*. Shanghai, 1917.

DOUGLAS, ROBERT KENNAWAY, *Catalogue of Chinese Printed Books, Manuscripts, and Drawings in the Library of the British Museum*. London, 1877; 344 pp.

DUDGEON, JOHN, *Historical Sketch of the Ecclesiastical, Political, and Commercial Relations of Russia with China*. Peking, 1872; 53 pp. + appendix, 23 pp.

EFIMOV, G., *Ocherki po novoi i noveishei istorii Kitaia* (An outline of Chinese modern and contemporary history). Moscow, 1951; 575 pp.

E.H.P., 'Manchu Relations with Russia', *The China Review*, vol. 16, no. 1 (July and August, 1887), pp. 41–46.

ENGSTRAND, WARREN MAXFIELD, 'The Kuldja Affair and its Significance in Sino-Russian Relations'. M.A. thesis, University of California, Berkeley, 1933; 177 pp.

FAIRBANK, JOHN K., and MASATAKA BANNO, *Japanese Studies of Modern China*. Tokyo, 1955; 329 pp.

FAN, HSIAO 樊 嘯, 'Tui-yü A-ku-po che i-jen-wu p'ing-chia te shang-ch'üeh' 對於阿古栢這一人物評價的商榷 (An appraisal of the man Yakub Beg), *Hsin-hua yüeh-pao* (Hsinhua Monthly), no. 65 (March 1955), pp. 208–10.

FAN, WEN-LAN 范 文 瀾, *Chung-kuo chin-tai-shih* 中 國 近 代 史 (Chinese modern history), vol. i, Peking, 1949; 543 pp.

FARQUHAR, DAVID MILLER, 'The Ch'ing Administration of Mongolia up to the Nineteenth Century'. Ph.D. thesis, Harvard, 1960; 380 pp.

FORBES, ARCHIBALD, *Chinese Gordon*. New York, 1884; 171 pp.

FORSYTH, SIR T. D., *Report of a Mission to Yarkund in 1873*. Calcutta, 1875; 571 pp.

—— *Autobiography and Reminiscences*. London, 1887; 283 pp.

FOSTER, JOHN W., *Diplomatic Memoirs*. 2 vols. Boston, 1909.

FRECHTLING, LOUIS E., 'Anglo-Russian Rivalry in Eastern Turkistan, 1863–1881', *Royal Central Asian Journal*, vol. 26 (July 1939), pp. 471–89.

French diplomatic papers. Archives des Affaires étrangères (Paris): *Chine*, vol. 57 (1878–9), vol. 58 (1880), vol. 59 (1881).

FU, LO-SHU, 'Sino-Western Relations during the K'ang-hsi Period, 1661–1722'. Ph.D. thesis, University of Chicago, 1952; microfilm no. 1566.

FU, T'UNG-HSIEN 傅 統 先, *Chung-kuo hui-chiao shih* 中 國 回 教 史 (A history of Islam in China). Changsha, 1940; 240 pp.

FU-K'O (FOCKE) 福 克, 'Hsi-hsing so-lu' 西 行 瑣 錄 (Desultory notes on my Western trip), *Hsiao-fang-hu-chai yü-ti ts'ung-ch'ao* 小 方 壺 齋 輿 地 叢 鈔 (A collection of geographical writings in the Hsiao-fang-hu-chai), Series 6. Vol. 4, pp. 300–4b.

GAIMUSHŌ 外務省 (Japanese Foreign Office) (ed.), *Nihon gaikō bunsho* 日本外交文書 (The diplomatic papers of Japan), vols. 10–13 (1878–81), Tokyo, 1949–50.

GAIMUSHŌ JŌHŌ CHŌSAJO 外務省情報調査所, 'Shimmatsu no tai kaikyō seisaku' 清末の對回教政策 (The Moslem policy during the late Ch'ing period), *Kaikyō jijō* 回教事情 (Tokyo), vol. 3, no. 1 (March 1940), pp. 33–53.

—— 'Sa Sōdō no Seihoku keiei ippan' 左宗棠の西北經營一班 (A general account of Tso Tsung-t'ang's work in the North-West), *Kaikyō jijō*, vol. 3, no. 4 (Dec. 1940), pp. 86–92.

German diplomatic papers, Abth. A. Politisches Archiv d. Auswärt. Amts (Bonn): *China* No. 1 (Instructions):
  Vol. 1, Conf. vol. 2. 1 Jan. 1879–20 Aug. 1879.
  Vol. 2, Conf. vol. 3. 21 Aug. 1879–31 May 1880.
  Vol. 3, Conf. vol. 4. 1 June 1880–11 April 1881.
China No. 2 (Dispatches):
  Vol. 1, Conf. vol. 2. 9 March 1878–31 March 1880.
  Vol. 2, Conf. vol. 3. 1 April 1880–31 May 1880.
  Vol. 3, Conf. vol. 4. 1 June 1880–14 Aug. 1880.
  Vol. 4, Conf. vol. 5. 15 Aug. 1880–31 Oct. 1880.
  Vol. 5, Conf. vol. 6. 1 Nov. 1880–31 Dec. 1880.
  Vol. 6, Conf. vol. 7. 1 Jan. 1881–31 Dec. 1910.

HAN, SHU-HSIN 韓叔信, 'O-ling Hsi-t'u-erh-ch'i-ssu-t'an yü Chung-kuo tsai li-shih shang chih kuan-hsi' 俄領西土耳其斯坦與中國在歷史上之關係 (The historical relations between China and Russian Turkestan), in *Chung-kuo chin-tai-shih lun-ts'ung* 中國近代史論叢 (Collection of essays on Chinese modern history), ed. Li Ting-i, *et al.* Taipei, 1956; Series i, vol. 10, pp. 24–36.

HAYES, CARLTON J. H., *A Generation of Materialism, 1871-1900.* New York, 1941; 390 pp.

HEINS, O. K., 'Rising of the Dungens or Mussulman Population in Western China', trans. from the *Russian Military Journal* (August 1866), in *The Edinburgh Review* (Jan.–April 1868), vol. cxxvii, no. 260, pp. 357–96.

HENDERSON, GEORGE, and ALLAN O. HUME, *Lahore to Yarkand: Incidents of the Route and Natural History of the Countries Traversed by the Expedition of 1870, under T. D. Forsyth, Esq., C.B.* London, 1873; 370 pp.

HIBBERT, ELOISE T., *K'ang Hsi, Emperor of China.* London, 1940; 291 pp.

HO, CH'IU-T'AO 何秋濤, *Shuo-fang pei-sheng* 朔方備乘 (A manual of northern places). 81 chüan. 1881.

HO, HAN-WEN 何漢文, *Chung-O wai-chiao shih* 中俄外交史 (A history of Sino-Russian diplomacy). Shanghai, 1935; 490 pp.

Ho-NING 和寧, *Man-han-hoeï-kiang-tch'ouen* (Man-Han Hui-Chiang chuan) 滿漢回疆傳 (An account of Moslem Sinkiang in Manchu and Chinese). Subtitle: 'Histoire mandchou-chinoise des pays-frontières habités par des peuples musulmans, c.à.d. des pays situés à l'ouest de la Chine (La Dzongarie et le Turkestan oriental) qui ont été conquis par l'Empereur Khien-long, et dont les peuples sont mahométans'. 8 vols. 1804. British Museum: Oriental Manuscript Division. London.

Hoo, CHI-TSAI, *Les bases conventionnelles des relations modernes entre la Chine et la Russie*. Paris, 1918; 509 pp.

HOWORTH, HENRY H., *History of the Mongols*. 5 vols. London, 1876–1927.

HSIA, HSIEH 夏燮 (Chiang-shang-ch'ien-sou 江上蹇叟), *Chung-Hsi chi-shih* 中西紀事 (A record of Sino-Western events). 24 chüan. 1850 (1868).

HSIAO, I-SHAN, 蕭一山, *Ch'ing-tai t'ung-shih* 清代通史 (A general history of the Ch'ing Dynasty). 2 vols. Revised edition, Taipei, 1962.

HSÜ, CHI-YING 許壽英, 'Tseng Chi-tse yü Chung-O I-li chiao-she' 曾紀澤與中俄伊黎交涉 (Tseng Chi-tse and the Sino-Russian negotiations over Ili), *Ta-kung-pao* (Tientsin), Historical and Geographical Weekly, 26 March 1937, p. 3.

HSÜ, CHI-YÜ 徐繼畬, *Ying-huan chih-lüeh* 瀛環志略 (A brief description of the oceans round about). 10 chüan. 1848.

HSÜ, IMMANUEL C. Y., *China's Entrance into the Family of Nations: The Diplomatic Phase, 1858–1880*. Cambridge, 1960; 225 pp. + xxxvi.

HSÜEH, FU-CH'ENG 薛福成, *Yung-an ch'üan-chi* 庸庵全集 (Complete works of Hsüeh Fu-ch'eng). 21 chüan. Shanghai, 1897.

HU, CH'IU-YÜAN 胡秋原, *Ti-O ch'in-Hua shih-kang* 帝俄侵華史綱 (An outline history of Russian aggression in China). 2 vols. Taipei, 1955.

HUDSON, G. F., *Europe and China*. London, 1931; 336 pp.

Hui-hui shih-ju Chung-kuo 回回始入中國 (The Moslems first entered China). British Museum: Oriental Manuscript Division. London; 10 pp.

Hui-hui yüan-lai hsü 回回原來序 (Preface to the origin of the Moslems (in China)). British Museum: Oriental Manuscript Division. London; 1 woodblock print.

HUNG, YÜAN 洪源. 'A-ku-po cheng-ch'üan te pen-chih ho Ch'ing-ping hsi-cheng te i-i' 阿古栢政權的本質和清兵西征的意義 (The very nature of Yakub Beg's régime and the meaning of the western expedition of the Ch'ing army), *Hsin-hua yüeh-pao*, no. 65 (March 1955), pp. 206–8.

I-HSIN 奕訢 (ed.), 'Ch'in-ting p'ing-ting Shen-Kan Hsin-chiang hui-fei fang-lüeh' 欽定平定陝甘新疆回匪方略 (An imperial edition of the strategy of suppressing the Moslem rebellion in Shensi, Kansu, and Sinkiang), in *Ch'in-ting ch'i-sheng fang-lüeh* 欽定 七省方略 (An imperial edition of the strategy in the seven provinces). chüan 835–1156, preface 1896.

ILTY: 'I-li ting-yüeh Chung-O t'an-hua lu' 伊黎定約中俄談 話錄 (A record of Sino-Russian conversations on the treaty on Ili), in Ch'eng, Yin-sheng (ed.), *Chung-kuo nei-luan wai-huo li-shih ts'ung-shu* 中 國內亂外禍歷史叢書 (A historical series on China's internal disorder and external trouble). Shanghai, 1936; pp. 87–266.

IMANISHI, SHUNJŪ 今西春秋, 'Explanatory Notes on Tulisen's I-yü-lu', *Studia Serica*, vol. 9, Part i (Sept. 1950), pp. 1–17.

IMBAULT-HUART, CAMILLE, 'Deux insurrections des Mahométans du Kansou', *Journal asiatique*, huitième série, Tome xiv (Nov.–Dec. 1889), pp. 494–525.

INOUE, KAORU 井上馨, *Segai Inoue ko den* 世外井上公傳 (The biography of Prince Inoue). 3 vols. Tokyo, 1934.

IRIE, KEISHIRŌ 入江啟四郎, *Shina henkyō to Ei-Ro no kakuchiku* 支 那邊疆と英露の角逐 (The Chinese frontier and Anglo-Russian rivalry). Tokyo, 1935; 604 pp.

IWSM: See *Ch'ou-pan i-wu shih-mo*.

JACKSON, W. A. DOUGLAS, *The Russo-Chinese Borderlands*. Princeton, 1962; 126 pp.

JELAVICH, CHARLES and BARBARA (ed.), *Russia in the East, 1876–1880; the Russo-Turkish War and the Kuldja Crisis as seen through the letters of A. G. Jomini to N. K. Giers*. Leiden, 1959; 173 pp.

KADNIKOV, V. S., 'Iz istorii kul'dzhinskago voprosa (From the history of the Kuldja problem), *Istoricheskii vestnik*, vol. cxxiv (1911), pp. 893–909.

KATKOV, M. H. (ed.), *Sobranie peredovykh statei, moskovskikh vedomostei, 1878 g., 1880 g.* (Collection of leading articles in Moscow records). Moscow, 1898.

KIERNAN, E. V. G., *British Diplomacy in China, 1880 to 1885*. London, 1939; 327 pp.

KRAKOWSKI, ÉDOUARD, *Chine et Russie*. Paris, 1957; 412 pp.

KRAUSSE, ALEXIS, *Russia in Asia: A Record and a Study, 1558–1899*. New York, 1899; 411 pp.

Ku-kung O-wen shih-liao 故宮俄文史料 (Documents in Russian preserved in the National Palace Museum of Peiping), edited by Wang Chih-hsiang 王之相 and Liu Tse-jung 劉澤榮. Peiping, 1936; 312 pp.

KUNG, TZU-CHEN 龔自珍, *Ting-an wen-chi* 定盦文集 (Literary collection of Kung Tzu-chen). 3 chüan, preface 1868.

KUO, SUNG-TAO 郭嵩燾, *Yang-chih shu-wu ch'üan-chi* 養知書屋

全 集 (Complete works from the Knowledge-Cultivating Hall). 55 chüan; 1892.

KUROPATKIN, A. N., *Kashgaria*, trans. by Walter E. Gowan. Calcutta, 1882; 255 pp.

—— *The Russian Army and the Japanese War*, trans. by A. B. Lindsay, edited by E. D. Swinton, 2 vols. New York, 1909.

LANSDELL, HENRY, *Chinese Central Asia*. 2 vols. London, 1893.

LATTIMORE, OWEN, *Inner Asian Frontiers of China*. New York, 1940; 585 pp.

—— *Pivot of Asia: Sinkiang and the Inner Asian Frontiers of China and Russia*. Boston, 1950; 288 pp.

—— 'Inner Asian Frontiers: Chinese and Russian Margins of Expansion', *The Journal of Economic History*, vol. vii, no. 1 (May 1947), pp. 24–52.

LEE, DWIGHT E., 'The Origins of Pan-Islamism', *American Historical Review*, vol. xlvii, no. 2 (Jan. 1942), pp. 278–87.

LI, CHIEN-NUNG, *The Political History of China, 1840–1928*, edited and translated by S. Y. Teng and J. Ingalls. New York, 1956; 545 pp.

LI, HUAN 李 寰, *Hsin-chiang yen-chiu* 新 疆 研 究 (A study of Sinkiang). Chungking, 1944; 290 pp.

LI, HUNG-CHANG 李 鴻 章, *Li-wen-chung-kung ch'üan-chi* 李 文 忠 公 全 集 (Complete works of Li Hung-chang). 165 chüan. Shanghai, 1921.

LI, SHAO-LING 李 少 陵, *Tso Tsung-t'ang* 左 宗 棠 (Tso Tsung-t'ang) 3rd ed. Kaohsiung, 1958; 73 pp.

LI, YÜAN-TU 李 元 度, 'Lin-wen-chung-kung shih-lüeh' 林 文 忠 公 事 略 (A brief record of Lin Tse-hsü), in Tso Shun-sheng 左 舜 生, *Chung-kuo chin-pai-nien shih tzu-liao* 中 國 近 百 年 史 資 料 (Materials relating to Chinese history of the last hundred years), vol. i, pp. 1–8. Shanghai, 1928.

LIU, HSÜAN-MIN 劉 選 民, 'Chung–O tsao-ch'i mao-i k'ao' 中 俄 早 期 貿 易 攷 (A study of early Russo-Chinese commercial relations), *Yen-ching hsüeh-pao* (Yenching Journal of Chinese Studies), no. 25 (June 1939), pp. 151–212.

—— 'Russo-Chinese Relations up to the Treaty of Nerchinsk', *CSPSR*, vol. 23, no. 4 (Jan.–March 1940), pp. 391–440.

LIU, K'UN-I 劉 坤 一, *Liu K'un-i i-chi* 劉 坤 一 遺 集 (Posthumous works of Liu K'un-i). 6 vols. Peking, 1959.

LIU, PO-K'UEI 劉 伯 奎, *Hsin-chiang I-li wai-chiao wen-t'i yen-chiu* 新 疆 伊 黎 外 交 問 題 研 究 (A study of the diplomatic question of Ili in Sinkiang). Chungking, 1943; 98 pp.

LO, CHENG-CHÜN 羅 正 鈞, *Tso-wen-hsiang-kung nien-p'u* 左 文 襄 公 年 譜 (A chronological biography of Tso Tsung-t'ang). 10 chüan. 1897.

Lo, Erh-kang 羅爾綱, *Hsiang-chün hsin-chih* 湘軍新志 (A new study of the Hunan Army). Changsha, 1939; 245 pp.

Lo, Tun-yung 羅惇曧, 'Chung-O I-li chiao-she shih-mo' 中俄伊黎交涉始末 (A complete account of Sino-Russian negotiations over Ili), *Yung-yen* 庸言 ('The Justice') Tientsin, vol. i, no. 19 (Sept. 1913), pp. 1–29.

Lobanov-Rostovsky, Prince A., *Russia and Asia*. New York, 1933; 334 pp.

Ludwig, Albert Philip, 'Li Hung-chang and Chinese Foreign Policy, 1870–1885'. Ph.D. thesis, University of California, Berkeley, 1936.

Macartney, G., 'Eastern Turkestan: The Chinese as Rulers over an Alien Race', *Proceedings of the Central Asian Society* (10 March 1909), pp. 1–23.

Malozemoff, Andrew, *Russian Far Eastern Policy, 1881–1904*. Berkeley, 1958; 358 pp.

Mancall, Mark, 'China's First Missions to Russia, 1729–1731', *Papers on China*, East Asia Regional Studies Seminar, Harvard University, vol. 9 (1955).

Martens, F., *Le conflit entre la Russie et la Chine*. Brussels, 1880; 75 pp.

—— *Rossiia i Kitai* (Russia and China). St. Petersburg, 1881; 83 pp.

Martin, W. A. P., *A Cycle of Cathay*. New York, 1896; 464 pp.

—— *The Chinese: Their Education, Philosophy and Letters*. New York, 1881; 319 pp.

Meng, Ssu-ming 孟思明, 'The E-lo-ssu kuan (Russian Hostel) in Peking', *Harvard Journal of Asiatic Studies*, vol. 23 (1960–1), pp. 19–46.

Mikuniya, Hiroshi 三國谷宏, 'Ryūkyū kizoku ni kansuru Guranto no chōtei' 琉球歸屬に關するグラントの調停 (Grant's mediation of the Ryūkyū issue), *Tōhō gakuhō* (Kyoto) 東方學報, vol. 10, Part 3 (Oct. 1939), pp. 29–64.

Miliutin, D. A., *Dnevnik* (Diary). 4 vols. Moscow, 1947–50.

Morse, H. B., *The International Relations of the Chinese Empire*, vol. 2, *The Period of Submission, 1861–1893*. Shanghai, 1918; 479 pp.

Nakada, Yoshinobu 中田吉信, 'Dōchi nenkan no Senran no kairan ni tsuite' 同治年間の陝甘の囘亂について (The Moslem rebellion in Shensi and Kansu during the T'ung-chih period), *Kindai Chūgoku kenkyū* 近代中國研究, vol. 3, pp. 71–158 (1959).

—— 'Shindai kaikyōto no ichisokumen' 清代囘教徒の一側面 (An aspect of Moslem life in the Ch'ing period), *The Tōyō gakuhō* 東洋學報, vol. 36, no. 1 (June 1953), pp. 66–86.

Nishida, Tamotsu 西田保, *Sa Sōdō to Shinkyō mondai* 左宗棠と新疆問題 (Tso Tsung-t'ang and the Sinkiang question). Tokyo, 1942; 302 pp.

NOBEL, JOHANNES, *Central Asia: The Connecting Link between East and West.* Nagpur, 1952; 160 pp.

NŌHARA, SHIRŌ 野 原 四 郎, 'Yakubu·begu no Dōngan tōbatsu' ヤ ク ブ ・ ベ グ の ド ウ ン ガ ン 討 伐 (Yakub Beg's war with the Dungans), *Kaikyōken* 囘 敎 圈 ('Le Monde islamique'), Tokyo, vol. i, no. 4 (Oct. 1938), pp. 36–42.

NORINS, MARTIN R., *Gateway to Asia: Sinkiang.* New York, 1944; 200 pp.

PAI, SHOU-I 白 壽 彝, *Hui-hui min-tsu ti hsin-sheng* 囘 囘 民 族 底 新 生 (The new birth of the Moslem people). Shanghai, 1951; 116 pp.

PAO ERH-HAN 包 爾 漢, 'Lun A-ku-po cheng-ch'üan' 論 阿 古 栢 政 權 (On the régime of Yakub Beg), *Li-shih yen-chiu* 歷 史 研 究 (Historical Research), no. 3 (1958) pp. 1–7. A translation from Burhan Shakhidi, 'O vlasti Iakub-beka'.

PARES, BERNARD, *Russia and Reform.* London, 1907; 576 pp.

PARRY, ALBERT, 'Russian (Greek Orthodox) Missionaries in China, 1689–1917, Their Cultural, Political and Economic Role'. Ph.D. thesis, University of Chicago, 1938; microfilm no. 3572.

PASZKIEWICZ, HENRYK, *The Origin of Russia.* New York, 1954; 556 pp.

PAVLOVSKY, MICHEL N., *Chinese–Russian Relations.* New York, 1949; 194 pp.

—— 'La Chine et la Russie en Asie centrale', *Bulletin de l'Université l'Aurore*, no. 36 (Oct. 1948), pp. 311–25.

PELCOVITS, NATHAN A., *Old China Hands and the Foreign Office.* New York, 1948; 349 pp.

PELLIOT, PAUL, *La Haute Asie.* 37 pp.

PIASSETSKY, P., *Russian Travellers in Mongolia and China.* 2 vols. London, 1884.

PIERCE, RICHARD A., *Russian Central Asia, 1867–1917.* Berkeley, 1960; 359 pp.

PREJEVALSKY, COL. N., *From Kulja across the Tian Shan to Lob-Nor*, trans. by E. D. Morgan. London, 1879; 251 pp.

RAWLINSON, SIR HENRY, *England and Russia in the East.* London, 1875; 412 pp.

RICHTHOFEN, BARON F. VON, *Letters, 1870–1872.* Shanghai, 1903; 149 pp.

ROSEN, BARON R. R., *Forty Years of Diplomacy*, vol. i. New York, 1922; 315 pp.

SADIQ, MUHAMMAD, KASHGHARI, *Tazkira-i-khwājagān* (Memoirs of Khoja Muhammad Sadiq of Kashgaria), summarized by Robert B. Shaw under the title *The History of the Khojas of Eastern Turkestan*, edited by N. Elias, published as supplement to the *Journal of the Asiatic Society of Bengal*, vol. lxvi, Part i, 1897; 67 pp.

SAGUCHI, TŌRU 佐 口 透, 'Shinkyō Uiguru jin no hanran 新 疆 ウ イ グ ル 人 の 反 亂 (The rebellion of the Uighur in Sinkiang), *Hokuri shigaku* 北 陸 史 學, no. 8 (Nov. 1959), pp. 1–18.

—— 'Kōkando kankoku no Tōhō hatten' コ ー カ ン ト 汗 國 の 東 方 發 展 (The eastward expansion of the Khokand khanate),

The Tōyō gakuhō 東洋學報, vol. 36, no. 2 (Sept. 1953), pp. 61–96.

—— *Jūhachi-jūkyū seiki Higashi Torukisutan shakaishi kenkyū* 十 八 一 十 九 世 紀 東 ト ル キ ス タ ン 社 會 史 研 究 (The social history of Eastern Turkestan in the 18th–19th centuries). Tokyo, 1963; 755 pp.

SCHUYLER, EUGENE, *Turkistan*, vol. ii. New York, 1876; 463 pp.

SEBES, JOSEPH, S.J., *The Jesuits and the Sino-Russian Treaty of Nerchinsk (1869)*. Rome, 1961; 341 pp.

SHAW, ROBERT B., *Visits to High Tartary, Yarkand, and Kashghar*. London, 1871; 486 pp.

Sheng-chia ch'in-cheng Ko-erh-tan fang-lüeh 聖 駕 親 征 噶 爾 旦 方 略 (A brief account of His Imperial Highness's personal expedition against Galdan). 1 chüan. 1696.

SHIMODA, REISUKE 下 田 禮 佐, 'Ro-Shin kankei no kenkyū' 露 清 關 係 の 研 究 (A study of Russian-Ch'ing relations), in *Ogawa hakushi kanreki kinen shigaku chirigaku ronsō* 小 川 博 士 還 暦 紀 念 史 學 地 理 學 論 叢 (Collected writings in history and geography to commemorate the 60th birthday of Dr. Ogawa). Tokyo, 1930; pp. 403–52.

SKACHKOV, P. E., *Bibliografiia Kitaia* (Bibliography on China). Moscow, 1960; 690 pp.

SKALKOVSKY, C., *Les ministres des finances de la Russie (1802–1890)*, translated from the Russian by P. de Nevsky. Paris, 1891; 325 pp.

SKRINE, C. P., *Chinese Central Asia*. Boston, 1926; 306 pp.

SKRINE, FRANCIS H., and EDWARD D. ROSS, *The Heart of Asia: A History of Russian Turkestan and the Central Asian Khanates from the Earliest Times*. London, 1899; 444 pp.

STOECKER, HELMUTH, *Deutschland und China im 19. Jahrhundert: Das Eindringen des deutschen Kapitalismus*. Berlin, 1958; 307 pp.

SUMNER, B. H., *Russia and the Balkans, 1870–1880*. Oxford, 1937; 724 pp.

SUNG-YÜN 松 筠, *Hsi-ch'ui tsung-t'ung shih-lüeh* 西 陲 總 統 事 略 (A brief account of the administration of the Western frontier). 12 chüan. 1809.

—— *I-li tsung-t'ung shih-lüeh* 伊 黎 總 統 事 略 (A brief account of the administration of Ili). 12 chüan. 1809.

Ta-Ch'ing li-ch'ao shih-lu 大 清 歷 朝 實 錄 (Veritable records of successive reigns of the Ch'ing dynasty). Tokyo, 1937–8.

TERENT'EV, M. A., *Istoriia zavoevaniia Srednei Azii* (A history of the conquest of Central Asia). 3 vols. St. Petersburg, 1906.

TERENTYEF, M. A., (Terent'ev), *Russia and England in Central Asia*. St. Petersburg, 1875. Trans. from Russian by F. C. Daukes. 2 vols. Calcutta, 1876.

THIERSANT, P. DABRY DE, *Le Mahométisme en Chine et dans le Turkestan oriental.* 2 vols. Paris, 1878.

TING, PAO-CHEN 丁 寶 楨, *Ting-wen-ch'eng-kung tsou-kao* 丁 文 誠 公 奏 稿 (Memorials of Ting Pao-chen). 26 chüan. 1896.

Tōyōshi kenkyū bunken ruimoku 東 洋 史 研 究 文 獻 類 目 (A catalogue of research articles on Far Eastern history), edited by Kyoto Daigaku Jinbunkagaku Kenkyūsho 京 都 大 學 人 文 科 學 研 究 所, 12 vols. 1936–58.

Treaties, Conventions, &c., between China and Foreign States. 2 vols. Shanghai, 1917.

TROTTER, SIR HENRY, 'The Amir Yakoub Khan and Eastern Turkistan in Mid-Nineteenth Century', *Journal of Central Asian Society*, vol. 4, no. 4 (1917), pp. 95–112.

TSENG, CHI-TSE 曾 紀 澤, *Tseng-hui-min-kung i-chi* 曾 惠 敏 公 遺 集 (Posthumous works of Tseng Chi-tse). 17 chüan. 1893.

TSENG, WEN-WU 曾 問 吾, *Chung-kuo ching-ying Hsi-yü shih* 中 國 經 營 西 域 史 (A history of China's management of the Western Region). Shanghai, 1936; 713 pp.

TSO, TSUNG-T'ANG 左 宗 棠, *Tso-wen-hsiang-kung ch'üan-chi* 左 文 襄 公 全 集 (Complete works of Tso Tsung-t'ang). 98 chüan. 1890.

TULISEN 圖 理 琛, 'I-yü lu' 異 域 錄 (Description of a foreign land), in Ho Ch'iu-t'ao, *Shuo-fang pei-sheng*, chüan 43–44.

'*T'u-erh-hu-t'e ch'üan-pu kuei-shun chi*' 土 爾 扈 特 全 部 歸 順 記 (The submission and return of the entire tribe of Torγud), *Yü-chih-wen* 御 製 文 (Imperial writings), Series ii, chüan 11, pp. 6b–10b.

TUNG, KAO 董 誥, *et al.*, (comp.), *Huang-Ch'ing chih-kung t'u* 皇 清 職 貢 圖 (Illustrations of the regular tributaries of the imperial Ch'ing). 9 chüan, 1761.

UEDA, TOSHIO 植 田 捷 雄, 'Ryūkyū no kizoku o meguru Nisshin kōshō' 琉 球 の 歸 屬 を 繞 る 日 清 交 渉 (Sino-Japanese negotiations over the sovereignty of Ryūkyū), *Tōyō bunka kenkyūjo kiyō* 東 洋 文 化 研 究 所 紀 要, vol. ii (Sept. 1951), pp. 151–201.

United States diplomatic papers, National Archives, Washington, D.C.:
China: Instructions. Vol. 2, 13 Sept. 1867–27 Dec. 1878, vol. 3, 1 Jan. 1879–28 Feb. 1885.
China: Dispatches. Vols. 48, 52–57 (1878–81).
China: Consular Reports, Shanghai. Vol. 30, 3 Feb. 1880–30 Sept. 1880.
Russia: Dispatches. Vols. 34–35 (1880–1).

VAKAR, NICHOLAS, 'The Annexation of Chinese Turkestan', *The Slavonic Review*, vol. 14, no. 40 (July 1935), pp. 118–23.

VALIKHANOF, CAPT. M. VENIUKOF, *The Russians in Central Asia*, trans. from Russian by John and Robert Michell. London, 1865; 552 pp.

VLADIMIR (VOLPICELLI, ZENONE), *Russia on the Pacific and the Siberian Railway*. London, 1899; 373 pp.

WANG, HSI-CH'I 王 錫 祺, *Hsiao-fang-hu-chai yü-ti ts'ung-ch'ao* 小 方 壺 齋 輿 地 叢 鈔 (A collection of geographical writings in the Hsiao-fang-hu studio). 64 chüan. 1877.

WANG, YÜN-SHENG 王 芸 生, *Liu-shih nien lai Chung-kuo yü Jih-pen* 六 十 年 來 中 國 與 日 本 (China and Japan in the last sixty years). 7 vols. Tientsin, 1932.

WCSL: See *Ch'ing-chi wai-chiao shih-liao*.

WEI, KUANG-TAO 魏 光 燾, *K'an-ting Hsin-chiang chi* 戡 定 新 疆 記 (An account of the pacification of Sinkiang). 8 chüan. 1899.

WEI, YÜAN 魏 源, *Sheng-wu chi* 聖 武 記 (A record of imperial military exploits). 14 chüan. 1842.

—— *Hai-kuo t'u-chih* 海 國 圖 志 (An illustrated gazetteer of the maritime countries). 100 chüan. 1876.

WEIGH, KEN-SHEN, *Russo-Chinese Diplomacy*. Shanghai, 1928; 382 pp.

WEN, KUNG-CHIH 文 公 直, *Chung-O wen-t'i chih ch'üan-pu yen-chiu* 中 俄 問 題 之 全 部 研 究 (A complete study of Sino-Russian problems). Shanghai, 1929; 222 pp.

WENG, T'UNG-HO 翁 同 龢, *Weng-wen-kung-kung jih-chi* 翁 文 恭 公 日 記 (Diary of Weng T'ung-ho). Shanghai, 1925; 40 ts'e.

WU, AITCHEN K., *China and the Soviet Union*. London, 1950; 434 pp.

WU, CH'I-YÜ, *China, Russia, and Central Asia*. Ph.D. thesis, Princeton University, 1933.

—— 吳 其 玉, 'Ch'ing-chi shou-hui I-li chiao-she shih-mo' 清 季 收 囘 伊 黎 交 涉 始 末 (A complete account of the negotiations about the return of Ili in the late Ch'ing period), *Kuo-wen chou-pao* (Kuo-wen Weekly), vol. 11, no. 19 (14 May 1934), pp. 1–8.

—— 'Ch'ing-chi Hui-Chiang tu-li chih shih-mo chi ch'i wai-chiao' 清 季 囘 疆 獨 立 之 始 末 及 其 外 交 (The Moslem independence in Sinkiang and its diplomacy during the late Ch'ing period), *Kuo-wen chou-pao*, vol. 11, no. 11 (19 March 1934), pp. 1–12.

WU, HSIANG-HSIANG 吳 相 湘, *Ti-O ch'in-lüeh Chung-kuo shih* 帝 俄 侵 略 中 國 史 (A history of Russian imperialism in China). Taipei, 1957; 672 pp.

WU, JU-LUN 吳 汝 綸, *T'ung-ch'eng Wu-hsien-sheng jih-chi* 桐 城 吳 先 生 日 記 (Diary of Mr. Wu of T'ung-ch'eng). 16 chüan. 1928.

YAKHONTOFF, VICTOR A., *Russia and the Soviet Union in the Far East*. New York, 1931; 454 pp.

YAO, HSIN-AN 姚 欣 安, 'Ch'ing-mo Hsin-chiang cheng-ts'e ti shih-te fa-chan' 清 末 新 疆 政 策 底 史 的 發 展 (The historical development of the Sinkiang policy at the end of the Ch'ing dynasty), *Hsi-pei yen-chiu* 西 北 研 究, no. 3 (Jan. 1932), pp. 19–34.

YOUNG, GEORGE, 'Pan-Islamism', *Encyclopaedia of the Social Sciences*, pp. 542–4. New York, 1937.

YÜ, SHIH-YÜ 于 式 玉, and LIU HSÜAN-MIN 劉 選 民 (ed.), *I-pai ch'i-shih-wu chung Jih-pen ch'i-k'an chung tung-fang-hsüeh lun-wen p'ien-mu fu yin-te* 一 百 七 十 五 種 日 本 期 刊 中 東 方 學 論 文 篇 目 附 引 得 (A catalogue and index to articles on Far Eastern studies in 175 Japanese journals). Peiping, 1940.

YUAN, TSING, 'Yakub Beg (1820-1877) and the Moslem rebellion in Chinese Turkestan', *Central Asiatic Journal*, vol. vi, no. 2 (June 1961), pp. 134–67.

Glossary

A-kuei	阿桂
Abderrahman	阿布都拉門
Aksu	阿克蘇
Albazin (Yacsa)	雅克薩
Alim Kul	阿來姆爾若
Amur River	黑龍江
An-ting	安定
Andijan	安集延
Anhsi	安西
Ayüki	阿玉奇
Barkul	巴里坤
beg	伯克
Book of Changes	易經
Bukhara	布哈爾
Burhan-al-Din	布拉尼敦(大和卓)
Büzürg	布素魯克
Cewang Arabdan	策妄阿拉布坦
Chaghadai (Čaɣadai)	察哈台
ch'an-t'ou-hui	纏頭回
Chang Chao-tung	張兆東
Chang Ch'ien	張騫
Chang Chih-tung	張之洞
Chang Liang-chi	張亮基
Chang P'ei-lun	張佩綸
Chang Yao	張曜
Chang-chia-ch'uan	張家川
Ch'ang-an	長安
Ch'ang-ch'ing	常清
Chefoo	烟台
Chekiang	浙江
Ch'en Lan-pin	陳蘭彬
Ch'eng-lu	成祿
ch'i-ts'ai	奇才
Ch'i-ying	耆英
Chia-yü-kuan	嘉峪關
Chihli	直隸
chin	斤
Chin-chi-pao	金積堡
chin-shih	進士
Chin-shun	金順
Chin-ting-ssu	金頂寺
Ch'in	秦
Ch'in-ting huang-yü Hsi-yü t'u-chih	欽定皇輿西域圖志
Ching-lien	景廉
Chinggis Khan (Činggis Qan)	成吉思汗
Ch'ing	清
ch'ing-i	清議
chü-jen	舉人

Chu-ko Liang	諸葛亮	Ho-ma-liu-hu	賀麻六乎
Chuguchak (Tar-bagatai)	塔城(塔爾巴哈台)	Hsi-lin	熙麟
		Hsi-lun	錫綸
Ch'ün, Prince	醇親王	Hsi-ning	西寧
Chun-chi-ch'u	軍機處	Hsi-yü	西域
Chung P'ei-hsien	鍾佩賢	Hsiang	湘
Ch'ung-hou	崇厚	Hsiang-hsiang	湘鄉
		Hsiang-yin	湘蔭
Dahur	達呼爾	*hsiao-i-t'ung*	小一統
Dairen	大連	*hsien-chan hou-tsou*	先斬後奏
Djungaria (Dzungaria)	準噶爾(準部)	Hsiung-nu	匈奴
		Hsü Chan-piao	徐占彪
En-lin	恩麟	Hsü Ch'ien-shen	許鈴身
		Hu Lin-i	胡林翼之
Fan Tseng-hsiang	樊增祥	Hu P'ing-chih	胡聘州
Fengt'ien	奉天	Huachow	華州
		Huai army	淮軍
Galdan	噶爾丹	*Huang-Ch'ing-chih-kung-t'u*	皇清職貢圖
Galdan Cereng	噶爾丹策零	Huang T'i-fang	黃體芳
		Hui-ning	惠寧
Gordon, Charles	戈登	*Hui-t'ung kuan*	會同舘
		Hui-yüan	惠遠
Hai-kuo t'u-chih	海國圖志	Hunan	湖南
Hakim Beg (Ak'im Beg)	阿齊木伯密		
Hami	哈密	*i-i chih-i*	以夷制夷
Han	漢	I-li	伊黎
Han-lin Academy	翰林院	*I-t'ung-chih*	一統志
Hankow	漢口	*I-yü lu*	異域錄
Hart	赫德	Ishikagha Beg	伊什伯克
Haz Beg	哈孜伯克		
Heilungkiang	黑龍江		
Ho Ch'iu-t'ao	何秋濤	Jau Modo	昭莫多

Jihangir (Jǎngγar)	張格爾
Kalgan	張家口
Kan Ying	甘英
K'ang-hsi	康熙
Kansu	甘肅
Kashgar	喀什噶爾
Kashgaria	喀什噶爾部 (回部)
Kaufman	高福曼
Kharashar (Karashar)	喀喇沙爾
Khazanachi Beg	噶雜納齊克伯克
Khoja (Khwāja)	和卓
Khoji Khan	霍集占 (小和卓)
Khokand	浩罕
Khoten	和闐
Kiakhta	恰克圖
Kirin	吉林
Kobdo	科布多
kowtow	叩頭
Ku-ch'eng	古城
Kuang-feng	廣鳳
Kuché	庫車
Kueichow	貴州
Kueihua	歸化
Kung, Prince	恭親王
Kung Tzu-chen	龔自珍
Kuo Sung-tao	郭嵩壽
Kuo-tzu-chien	國子監
Lan Ta-shun	藍大順

Lanchow	蘭州
li	里
li	黎
Li, Prince	禮親王
Li Han-chang	李瀚章
Li Hung-chang	李鴻章
Li Kuang-li	李廣利
Li Tan-yai	李丹崖
Li Yün-lin	李雲麟
Liangchow	凉州
likin	厘金
Lin Tse-hsü	林則徐
Lin-t'ung	臨潼
Liu Chin-t'ang	劉錦棠
Liu Hsi-hung	劉錫鴻
Liu Jung	劉蓉
Liu K'un-i	劉坤一
Liu Ming-ch'uan	劉銘傳
Liu Sung-shan	劉松山
Liu Tien	劉典
Lo-ch'a-miao	羅刹廟
Lo-yang	洛陽
Ma Chan-ao	馬占鰲
Ma Chao-kuei	馬兆元
Ma Chao-yüan	馬兆元
Ma Hua-lung	馬化龍
Ma Liang-kuei	馬良貴
Ma Ming-hsin	馬明心
Ma Wan-kang	馬萬岡
Ma Wen-lu	馬文祿
Macartney, Halliday	馬臣

Manas	瑪納斯		Se-erh-ho-o-lu-le (Zharbolak?)	色爾魯冷	賀勒格 鄂
Mazam Khan	邁孜木雜特		Selenginsk	色商	伯友 克濂
Ming	明		Shang Beg		
Ming-hsü	明緒		Shao Yu-lien	邵	友桂 芬
Mirab Beg	密喇布克伯		Shen Kuei-fen	沈	葆保 楨
Mu-t'u-shan	穆圖善		Shen Pao-chen	沈	
Mufti Habitulla	馬福迪		Sheng-pao	勝	
			Shensi	陝	西冶
Nan-lu	南路		Shun-chih	順	
Nerchinsk	尼布楚		*Shuo-fang pei-sheng*	朔方	備 乘
Newchwang	牛莊		Sian	西安	
Nien	捻		Sibo	錫伯	
			Solon	索倫	
O-lo-ssu	俄羅斯特		Su-ssu-shih-san	蘇四	十 三
Ölöd (Kalmuk)	厄魯特		Suchow	肅州	
			Sung	宋	
Pai Yen-hu	白彥虎		Sung-yün	松筠	
Pan Ch'ao	班超		Sungari River	松花	江
Pao-t'ing	寶廷頭				
Paot'ou	包頭		Ta-Ch'in	大秦	
Pei-lu	北路		*Ta-Ch'ing hui-tien shih-li*	大清會事例	典
Pei-yang	北洋		*ta-i-t'ung*	大一統	麟
P'eng Yü-lin	彭玉麟		T'an Chung-lin	大一鍾 譚	
p'ien-an	偏安		T'ang	唐	
Potuna	伯都訥		Tashkent	塔什干斯	河
Rasheddin *Khoja*	黃和卓		Tekes River	帙克山	
Russian Hostel	俄羅斯舘		Tien-shan (T'ien-shan)	天山	
Sadiq Beg	金相印		Ting Jih-ch'ang	丁日昌	
Samarkand	撒馬爾罕		Ting Pao-chen	丁寶楨阿	
Sarim Sak (Sarimsaq)	薩木薩克		To-lung-a	多隆	

T'o-ming	明時	妥
T'o-shih	爾紀	托
Toryūd	屌澤 特	土
Tseng Chi-tse	國荃	曾
Tseng Kuo-ch'üan	國藩	曾
Tseng Kuo-fan	宗棠	曾
Tso Tsung-t'ang	理衙 門	左
Tsungli Yamen	興阿	總
Tu-hsing-a	理琛	都
Tulisen (T'u-li-ch'en)		圖
Tun, Prince	親 王	惇
t'ung	獐	
T'ung-chih	治	同
Tungan (Dungan)	干	東
Tunhuang	煌	敦
Turfan	魯安 番	吐
Tz'u-an	禧	慈
Tz'u-hsi		慈
Uighur	吾 族	維
Ulan Butung	蘭布 通	烏
Uliasutai	里雅 蘇	烏
	台	
Urumchi	魯 木 齊	烏
Wali Khan	里 汗	倭
Wang Hsien-ch'ien	先 謙	王

Wang Jen-k'an	仁 堪	王
Wang K'ai-t'ai	凱 泰	王
Wang Wen-shao	文 韶	王
Wei Yüan	魏 源	
Wen-hsiang	祥	文
Wen-pin	彬	文
Wu Ju-lun	汝 綸	吳
Wu Yüan-ping	元 炳	吳
Wu-sun	孫	烏
Wu-ti	帝	武
Yakub Beg	古 柏	阿
Yang Ch'ang-chün	昌 濬	楊
Yang Shih-ch'üan	石 泉	楊
Yang Yüeh-pin	岳 斌 沙	楊
Yangihissar	英 吉	
yao	猺	
Yarkand	葉 爾 羌	
Ying-ch'i	瑛	
Ying-han	翰	英
Yingk'ou (New-chwang)	營 口	
Yü-lu	裕 祿	
Yü-men	玉 門 氏	
Yüeh-chih	月 氏	
Yung-ch'üan	榮 全 正	
Yung-cheng	雍	
Yunnan	雲 南	

Index

Abaza, 185.
Abderrahman, 27, 28.
Abul Oghlan, 30.
Admiralty, 110, 123.
Āfāq, 27.
Afghanistan, 11, 154.
Akmasjid, 28.
Akmolinsk, 4.
Aksu, 27, 28, 39, 44, 96, 194.
A-kuei, 19.
Alabama case, 147.
Albazin (Ya-k'e-sa), 7, 73, 189, 190.
Alcock Convention, 1, 60.
Alexander II (1855–81), his Balkan policy, 154; his domestic reforms, 155–6.
Alim Kul, 27.
Alim-tu, 30.
Allen, Clement, 137.
Amoy, 116.
Amur River, 2, 158.
Andijan, 6.
Anglo-Russian rivalry, 10–12, 102, 141, 153–4.
Anhsi, 194, 195.
An-Hsi protectorate, 5.
Annam, 191.
anti-Jewish riots in Russia, 157.
An-ting, 23.
Arrow War, 189.
Ayüki, 199.

Bakunin, 156.
Bales, W. L., 197.
Balitskii, Major, 30.
Baring Brothers, 58.
Barkul, 19, 27, 43, 145, 162, 194.
beg, 20; six major kinds of *begs*, 20–21; 194, 195.
Beg Kuli Beg, 43, 44.
Bekovich-Cherkasskii, Prince, 4.
Bessarabia, 154.
Bismarck, Prince, 119, 120, 154, 199.
Black Flag Army, 200.
Black Sea, 162.
Board of Civil Offices, 79, 195.
Boguslavskii, Colonel, 32; negotiated with Yung-ch'üan, 33; came to Peking, 33.
Bombay, 125.
Borokhudzir, 30.
Bosnia, 154.
Bosphorus, 11, 153.
Bourée, A., 88; viewed Ili from European politics, 115; asked Paris to support Marquis Tseng's peace mission in St. Petersburg, 115; reported expression of Brandt, 118; 165.
Boxer Rebellion, 193.
Brandt, Max von, 85, 89; estimated Chinese strength, 99; 109; tried to convince Wade of harmless Russian intentions, 112–13; had no respect for China and Japan, 117; stimulated war sentiment, 117–18; took strange stand, 118; his view not supported by Berlin, 119; pursued a personal policy, 119; reputedly urged Li Hung-chang to rebel, 121, 127; as a peacemaker, 132; spoke of 'extreme fatalism' in Gordon, 133; his alleged plot, 200.
British northward movement from India, 10.
British trade in China, 14, 109, 111.
Buchanan, Sir Andrew, 31–32.
Bu-erh-fan, 73.
Bukhara, 4, 6, 10, 11.
Bulgaria, 154.
Burlingame, 45.
Butzow (Biutsov), Eugene K., 44, 45, 53, 55, 67, 82, 159; sent to Peking to open negotiations, 163; left for China without instructions, 167; recalled to St. Petersburg, 170; temporized with Tseng, 172, 174.
Büzürg, 27, 28.

Cambridge, Duke of, 125.
Campbell, J. D., 122; his tactful explanation about Gordon, 125; 126, 133.
Caspian Sea, 5.
Central Asian Trading Company, 35.
Ceylon, 126.
Chaghadai Khan, 5.
Chakhar, 19.
Chang-chia-ch'uan, 24.
Chang Ch'ien, 5.
Chang Chih-tung, 9; urged rejection of the Treaty of Livadia, 70–71; his recommendations, 71–74; argued that Russian should be grateful to China because of past favours, 73; meteoric rise to fame, 74; an explanation of his success, 74–75; offered plans to pardon Ch'ung-hou, 91–92; attacked Li Hung-chang and Liu K'un-i, 92; suggestion followed by the court, 92–93; 98; Chang and

ch'ing-i, 104, 191; 141; urged collective planning for the strategy in reopening negotiations with Russia, 145; tried to console the court, 166.
Ch'ang-ch'ing, 26, 27.
Chang Liang-chi, 198.
Chang P'ei-lun, 49; protested against Ch'ung-hou's vast discretionary powers, 49–50; 80, 191.
Chang Yao, 43, 65, 96.
ch'an-t'ou hui, 20.
Chefoo, 95, 119, 126.
Ch'en Lan-pin, 82.
Cherniaev, M. G., 4, 11.
Chia-yü-kuan, 57, 62, 145, 162, 185.
Ch'ien-lung, 6, 7, 16; his policy in Sinkiang, 21; 36, 37, 74, 84.
Chin-chi-pao, 24, 36.
Ch'in Kuei, 191.
Chinese missions abroad, 45.
Chinese war preparations, 99.
Chinggis Khan, 5.
ch'ing-i (*literati* opinion), 104, 107, 147, 190, 191, 192.
Chin-shun, 54, 60, 70, 96.
Ch'i-ying, 49, 79, 86.
Chou, Duke of, 143.
Chuguchak (Targabatai), 18, 26, 32, 34, 65, 68, 194.
Chu-ko Liang, 198.
Ch'un, Prince, 69, 91, 130, 165, 192.
Chung, P'ei-hsien, 91.
Ch'ung-hou, 1, 2; origin of his mission to Russia, 45; recommended by Shen, 47; his career, 47; his appointment and audience, 48; lack of preparations, 50; received flattering reception from the Russians, 52; reported early progress in negotiations, 53; anxious to leave Russia, 56; negotiated Treaty of Livadia, 57; ignored the Yamen's order, 57; signed treaty, 58; returned home, 58; explained his mission to Li, 65; defence of the treaty, 67–68; dismissed from office, 78; tried by a special council, 79; sentenced to death, 80; reasons for his failure, 80–81; misunderstood his function, 82–84; foreign sympathy for him, 84–85; foreign intercession for his life, 86–87; Queen Victoria's appeal for his life, 87–88; given reprieve, 92; given pardon, 93–94; case misunderstood by foreigners, 113; 114, 140, 141, 142, 144, 159, 160, 161, 163, 164, 167, 169, 174.
Church of the Assumption, 8.
Church of the Purification of the Virgin, 9.

Church of St. Nicolas, 8.
Chu Wen-djang, 197.
Confucius, 143.
Congress of Berlin, 11, 53, 55, 97, 149, 150, 154, 155.
'Consolidation School', 12, 15.
Convent of Candlemas, 8–9.
Cordier, Henri, 123.
Court of Colonial Affairs, 9.
Court of Sacrificial Worship, 140, 141, 161.
Crimean War, 153.
Cyprus, 150, 154.

Dahur, 19.
Dairen, 95.
Dardanelles, 153.
Denny, O. N., 123; interviewed Gordon, 126.
Derby, Lord, 13, 41; sent note of mediation to Kuo, 42.
Detring, 124; reputedly urged Li to 'strike a blow', 127; 132.
Dilke, Sir Charles, 125, 135.
Disraeli, 12, 13, 41, 123.
Djungaria, 16, 41.
Dufferin, Lord, 100, 153; gave Tseng advice, 159; learnt of Tseng's first meeting with Giers, 160; praised Tseng, 188.

Elgin, Lord, 47, 49.
Empress Dowager, *see* Tz'u-hsi.
En-lin, 35.
Evarts, William M., 85.

Fan Tseng-hsiang, 79; demanded Ch'ung-hou's death, 79; 143.
Fengt'ien, 95.
Focke, 97.
Foochow, 99.
Foochow Dockyard, 98, 153, 166, 192, 198.
Foreign warships in China, 100.
Formosa crisis, 36.
Forsyth, T. Douglas, led missions to Yakub Beg, 13; 29, 30, 34, 41.
'Forward School', 12, 13, 15, 110.
Foster, John W., 152; remark on Russian finances, 156–7; report on Russian economic conditions, 158; approached by Tseng for mediation, 183, 184; talked with Giers about the Chinese case, 184.
Fraser, Hugh, 43.
Fukang, 41.

Galdan, Cereng, 200.
Giers, N. K., 15, 52, 53; opposed large Chinese indemnity, 54; 58, 67, 82,

157, 159; allowed Tseng to present credentials to the Tsar, 160; specified Peking as the place for negotiations, 161; 163; agreed to open negotiations in St. Petersburg, 170; explained Russian goal, 181; his view on Chinese payment, 183; agreed on final terms with Tseng, 185; praised Tseng, 188.

Giguel, Prosper, 153.

Gladstone, 12, 14.

Gorchakov, Prince A. M., 53.

Gordon, Charles, 1, 109, 121; leader of the 'Ever-Victorious Army', 122; position in India, 122; received telegram from Hart, 122; left for China, 122; who invited him? 123; relations with London, 125; his trip to China approved by London, 126; interviewed by American consul-general in Shanghai, 126; offered his service to Li Hung-chang, 127; offered to renounce his citizenship, 129; his state of mind, 130; his blunt conduct before Chinese high council, 130–1; his advice to move Chinese court to the interior, 130–1; usefulness in China doubted by Wade, 132; his exit from Peking, 132; statement on Li's relations with Peking, 134–5; his twenty recommendations, 135–7; some of his suggestions impracticable, 137; accepted 1,000 taels from Li, 137; returned home without losing his citizenship or commission, 138; the result of his visit to China, 138; advice to China, 157; report of his activities in China arrived in Russia, 179; his alleged role in the German minister's plot, 200.

Grand Council, 192.

Grand Secretariat, 192, 199.

Grand Unification, 6, 9, 39, 74, 193, 196.

Grant, General, 109, 125, 127.

Granville, Lord, 12, 93, 114, 128, 129, 152, 165, 168, 187.

Greig, Admiral S. A., 52; opposed large Chinese indemnity, 54.

Gros, Baron, 47, 49.

Hagan, 50.

Hak Kuli Beg, 43.

Hamburg, 179.

Hami, 27, 43, 57, 61, 62, 66, 70, 96, 145, 162, 185, 194.

Han, 5, 193.

Han-chung, 57, 166, 185.

Hankow, 57, 68, 146, 185.

Hannecken, von, 127.

Hart, Robert, 2; authorized to engage foreign officers for China, 109; possessed information on Japanese striking force, 116; hoped to engage 100 British officers for China, 123; asked Gordon to by-pass Tientsin, 126; belittled by Li, 129; considered Gordon's mind unsound, 133; remitted funds to Tseng, 144; 200.

Heilungkiang, 103.

Herzegovina, 154.

Heyden (Geiden), Count F. L., 51.

Hindu Kush, 10.

Hochow, 24, 36.

Hsiang-hsiang, 139.

Hsiang-yin, 198.

Hsi-lin, 35.

Hsi-lun, 54, 70, 145.

Hsi-ning, 23.

Hsiung-nu (Huns), 5.

Hsi-yü (Western Region), 4, 6; renamed Sinkiang in 1768, 6; 7, 150; made a province, 193; 196, 198.

Hsü Chan-piao, 43.

Hsü Ch'ien-shen, 82.

Hu Kuang-yung, 99.

Hu Lin-i, 198.

Hu P'ing-chih, 91.

Huachow, 24, 25, 197, 198.

Huai Army, 95, 96; its relations with the Hunan Army, 96; budget reduced by 40 per cent., 101; 105, 107.

Huang T'i-fang, 78; demanding punishment of Ch'ung-hou, 78; 90.

Hui-ning (Bayandai), 19, 26.

Hui-t'ung kuan, 8.

Hui-yüan, 19.

Hu-ma-liu-hu, 23.

Hunan, 95, 198.

Hung Hsiu-ch'üan, 200.

Hunter, William, 93.

Ides mission, 8.

I-fan (Ivan), 73.

i-i chih-i, 109, 138.

Ili River, 4, 16, 19.

Ili Valley, 1, 2, 4, 5; possible invasion by Yakub Beg, 14; general description of, 16; population in, 16, 197; trade with Russia, 16; strategic importance, 18; Moslem rebellion in, 26-27; Russian advance to, 18; Russian occupation of, 4, 29–34; Russian strength at, 99; fortress of Sinkiang, 150.

Imperial Academy (*Kuo-tzu chien*), 9.

Inoue, Kaoru, 116, 117.

I-yü lu, 199.

Jihangir, 22.
Jomini, A. G., 15, 53, 58, 82, 157, 158, 159; elated by good news, 166; favoured St. Petersburg as a place of negotiations, 168, 169–70; asked Giers some pointed questions, 172–3; postponed the deadline for the exchange of ratifications of treaty, 173; critical of Russian position, 176–8; knew Russian weakness, 179; extension of deadline again, 180; pressed for Chinese financial compensation as a penalty, 182; settled the sum of military compensation, 186.

Kalat, 10.
Kalgan, 19, 57, 65, 108.
Kalmuk, 197.
Kan Ying, 5.
K'ang-hsi, 6, 7, 73, 84.
Kansu, 22, 194, 195.
Kao-tsung (T'ang), 5.
Kashgar, 18, 23, 26, 57, 100, 194.
Kashgaria, 16, 18, 22, 28, 42, 43, 51, 55, 65, 68, 118, 146, 154, 162, 185.
Kashmir, 10.
Kaufman, K. P. von, appointed governor-general of Turkestan in 1867, 4; detached Samarkand from Bukhara, 11; attempted invasion of India, 11; ordered invasion of Ili, 14, 30; 45; wanted to avoid war with China, 51; made recommendation of returning Ili to China for 120 million roubles, 52; second recommendation, 54; 56, 57; moved headquarters to Vernyi, 99; his strategy of war, 99–100; 163; recommended the return of Tekes Valley for 100 million roubles, 172; his recommendation rejected, 173.
Kaulbars, Baron, 30; signed treaty with Yakub Beg, 34; 197.
Kazakh khanates, 4.
Kennedy, John G., 117.
Kharashar, 26.
Khiva, 4, 10, 11.
khojas (khwāja), 22; the 'Holy War' of, 22; rebellions, 22.
Khokand, 4, 11, 22, 27, 57.
Khoten, 6, 27.
Kiakhta, 189.
Kirghiz, 30.
Kirin, 103.
Kobdo, 26, 32, 57, 145, 162, 185.
Koiander, 89, 161, 166, 167, 184.
Kolpakovskii, G. A., 14; occupied Ili, 14, 30–31; declared Ili annexed 'in perpetuity', 31; 32, 51.

Koran, 24.
Korla, 43.
Krupp, 99, 118.
Kuang-feng, 26.
Kuché, Moslem rebellion at, 26.
Ku-ch'eng, 19, 26, 41, 57, 145, 162, 185.
Kuei-liang, 49.
Kuldja, 16, 31, 58.
Kung, Prince, 29, 33, 47, 85, 87, 88, 113, 139, 192.
Kung Tzu-chen, 193.
Kuo Sung-tao, 42; advocated acceptance of British mediation, 42; met Ch'ung-hou in Paris, 50; proposed postponement of the restitution of Ili, 67; predicted Ch'ung-hou's failure, 80; 82; urged commutation of Ch'ung-hou's sentence, 89; criticized war advocates, 105; 140, 141.
Kuropatkin, Col. A. N., 51; submitted proposal, 51; 52, 54.

Lake Issyk-Kul, 18.
Lake Manuto, 199.
Lake Zaisan, 18.
Lan Ta-shun, 25.
Lanchow, 23, 41.
Law Officers, 112; not in favour of prosecuting Gordon, 128.
Lazareff, 117.
Lesovskii, S. S., 2; dispatched to China with 23 ships, 97; 164, 165, 166, 168, 178, 179.
Li, Prince, 76; suggested a second mission to Russia, 76–77; 80, 92, 140, 142.
Li Hung-chang, his advocacy of maritime defence, 36–37; argued for acceptance of British mediation, 42; 60; his comments on the Treaty of Livadia, 63–65; sympathetic to Ch'ung-hou's position, 65; warned the Tsungli Yamen of the danger of rejecting the treaty, 65–66; feud with Tso, 66; recommended partial rejection of the treaty, 68–69; 87; approached by Wade to intercede for Ch'ung-hou's life, 87; reprimanded by court, 93; ordered to guard North China, 95; urged peace settlement with Russia, 100–1; estimate of Chinese defence and international situation, 101–2; chided war advocates, 103; attacked Tso, 103–4; attached ch'ing-i, 104; an interpretation of his position, 106–8; offered resignation, 107; feared possible Russian–Japanese collusion, 116; reputedly urged by the German

minister to rebel, 121; asked to assess Gordon's fitness to serve China, 124; moved by Gordon's devotion, 129; his delicate position, 133–4; moved by Gordon's recommendations, 137; view on Tseng's appointment, 141–2; encouraged Tseng, 143; view on Tseng's instructions, 147; urged a flexible course, 166; his policy did not help Chinese diplomacy, 190; attacked by the *ch'ing-i* group, 191–2.
Li Tan-yai, 141.
Liangusov, 8.
Liaotung, 101.
Liberal government, 125.
Lin Tse-hsü, 198.
Ling-t'ung, 24.
Liu Chin-t'ang, 36; his swift army movement, 31; 43; made a baron, 44; 61, 66, 96, 194; made governor of Sinkiang, 195.
Liu-ch'iu, 64, 102, 116, 117, 118.
Liu Hsi-hung, 82.
Liu K'un-i, 88, 90; reprimanded by court, 93; 95, 116.
Liu Ming-ch'uan, 104.
Liu Sung-shan, 36.
Lo-ch'a miao, 8.

Ma Chan-ao, 36.
Ma Hua-lung, 24, 36.
Ma Jen-te, 41.
Ma Ming-hsin, 23; regarded as the saintly founder of the New Sect, 24.
Ma Wen-lu, 36.
Macartney, Halliday, 153, 160.
Macedonia, 154.
MacGahan, James, 11.
Manas, 26, 33, 41, 44.
Manchuria, 89, 95, 98, 100, 101, 102, 105, 158.
Marseilles, 50, 167.
Martin, W. A. P., 89, 139.
Mayo, Viceroy of India, 12–13, 29, 34.
Mel'nikov, A. A., 180.
'Midlothian elections' of 1880, 13.
Miliutin, Count D. A., opposed return of Ili, 51; believed Britain prompted China against Russia, 155; dreaded war with China, 158; urged negotiations with China be short, 161; high conference at his office, 163–4; conferred with Giers, 178; received information on China war preparations, 180; rejoiced at the peace settlement, 187.
Ming-hsü, 26, 27.
Ming-i, 55, 62, 185.
Minor Unification, 6, 193.
Mirza Shadi, 28.

Moslem league, 12; British encouragement of, 12.
Moslem rebellion (*see* Tungan), 189, 197, 198.
Mufti Habitulla, 27, 28.
Muzam Khan (Mai-tzu-tsa-t'e), 26.
Muzart Pass, 18, 30, 59, 70, 163, 166, 173.

Nagasaki, 97, 117.
Napoleon's 'Grand Project', 10.
narodnichestvo, 156.
Nerchinsk, 73, 162, 189.
New Sect (*Hsin-chiao*), 23–24; its centres, 24; rebellion by the, 24; 197.
Newchwang, 95, 100.
Nicholas I (1825–54), 4, 155.
Nien, 98, 105, 189.
Ning-yüan (I-ning), 16.
Northbrook, Viceroy of India, 12–13, 34.

Obruchev, 52, 54.
Okinawa, 102.
Old Sect, 23; its centre, 24.
Ölöd, 19, 199, 200.
Opium War, 189.
Order in Council, 128.
Orenburg, 10, 18.
Oxus region, 11.

Pai Yen-hu, 35, 41; escaped to Russia, 44; not extradited, 48; 53, 74, 175.
Palmerston, 11; statement on Russian advance to India, 11.
Pamirs, 10.
Pan Ch'ao, 5.
Pan-Islamism, 12.
Pan-Slavism, 154.
Pao Ch'ao, 95.
Paoting, 65.
Pao-t'ing, 104, 108, 142.
Pao-yün, 69.
Partial Security, 7.
Patterson, Admiral, 87.
Paul I (1796–1801), 10.
Pauncefote, Sir Julian, 110; argued against Russian blockade of treaty ports in China, 112; wrote secret memorandum on Chinese situation, 114; not in favour of prosecuting Gordon, 128; dropped the issue of punishing Gordon, 129; 165.
P'eng Yü-lin, 95, 98.
Perovskii, V. A., 4.
Persian Gulf, 5.
Peter the Great (1682–1725), 4, 10.
Piassetsky, 199.
Piskent, 28.
Plunkett, F. R., 52; ordered not to advise the Chinese to ratify the

treaty, 114; placed in close contact with the Chinese mission, 153; saw Macartney, 160; suggested ratification of the treaty by China, 168; reprimanded by London for suggestion, 168; questioned Russian demand for an indemnity from China, 181; urged Jomini not to press China too hard, 182; his good offices requested by the Chinese, 184.
Poggio, de, 50.
Port Arthur, 193.
Pottinger, Sir Henry, 49.
Potuna, 56, 58, 68, 69, 146.
Precarious Security, 7, 193.
Punjab, 10.
Pusan, 117.

Quai d'Orsay, 115.

Rasheddin, 27, 28.
raznochintsy, 156.
Rice, Captain Ernest, 100.
Ripon, Lord, 122, 125.
Russell, Odo, 119, 120.
Russian caravans to China, 8.
Russian domestic problems, 155–7.
Russian economic difficulties, 156–7.
Russian expansion into Central Asia, 10–11.
Russian General Staff, 30, 51, 157, 158.
Russian Hostel, 8, 73.
Russian international position, 153–5.
Russian land acquisitions in China, 2–4.
Russian language school in Peking, 9.
Russian military position, 157.
Russian priests in China, 8.
Russian prisoners of war in China, 7–8.
Russian ships in the Pacific, 100.
Russian students in China, 9.
Russo-Turkish war, 11, 51, 71, 98, 115, 156, 157.

Sabir Akhun, 43.
Sadiq Beg, 27, 28.
Saguchi, Tōru, 23.
Sa'id Yakub, 34; sent to London, 41.
Salar areas, 23.
Sa-ling-a, 26.
Salisbury, Lord, 12, 13, 41, 110; believed Britain should have a greater hold on Chinese maritime power than on that of any other nation, 110–11.
Samarkand, 6, 99.
San Francisco, 98.
Savatiev, 8.
Schuyler, E., 197.
Se-erh-ho-o-lu-le, 33.
Semipalatinsk, 4.

Semirechie, 30.
Seng-ko-lin-ch'in, 47.
Seward, George, 75, 85, 87.
Shao Yu-lien, 141, 164.
Shaw, Robert, 28, 30.
Sheik Nizamuddin, 28.
Shen Kuei-fen, 47, 79.
Shen Pao-chen, 66; opposed Treaty of Livadia, 66–67.
Sheng-pao, 25, 35.
Shensi, 22.
Shufelt, Commodore, 97, 100.
Sian, 25, 57, 166, 185.
Siberia, 158.
Siberian railway, 51, 52, 157.
Sibo, 16, 197.
Sind, 10.
Sinkiang, 1, 2, 4; strategic position, 7; general description of, 16; Ch'ing administration in, 18–22; high officials in, 20; corruption in, 21; 59, 101, 102, 104, 105, 106, 149, 150; re-establishment of imperial authority in, 44, 189; made a province, 193, 195; Communist control of, 195–6.
Sino-French War, 191.
Sino-Russian secret alliance, 193.
Solon, 19, 89.
Struve, K. V., 176.
Suchow, 36, 41, 185, 187.
Sufism, 23.
Sui-ting, 25, 30.
Summer Palace, 192.
Sung, 192.
Sungari River, 56, 58, 70, 146, 166, 173, 181, 185.
Su-ssu-shih-san, 23.
Syr-Daria, 4.

t'ai chi, 195.
Taiping, invasion of Shensi in 1862, 25; 27, 95, 98, 105, 122, 124, 197.
T'ai-tsung (T'ang), 5.
Taku, 103, 130.
Talki Pass, 59.
Taranchi, 16, 197.
Tarbagatai (*see* Chuguchak), 4, 145, 162, 185, 199.
Tarim Basin, 5, 16.
Tashkent, 4, 28, 99.
Tekes Valley, 58, 59, 61, 70, 96, 163, 166, 169, 172, 173, 175, 177, 178, 181, 185.
Terent'ev, M. A., 197.
Thiers, 47.
Three Kingdom Period, 198.
Tien-shan, 16, 19, 41, 57, 62, 63, 64.
Tientsin, 57, 95, 96, 103, 123, 126, 127, 130, 132, 165, 185.

Tientsin Massacre, 1, 47.
Ting Jih-ch'ang, 37, 143.
Ting Pao-chen, 38, 69; volunteered to be envoy to Russia, 70; 81, 103.
Toksun, 43.
To-lung-a, 25, 35.
T'o-ming, 27, 28.
Tongking, 115, 191.
T'o-shih, 45, 189, 200.
Trans-Siberian Railway, 187.
Treaty of Aigun, 2, 68.
Treaty of Ili, 18.
Treaty of Kiakhta, 2, 8, 9.
Treaty of Livadia, 51, 57, 76, 77, 78, 111, 140, 143, 146, 147, 160, 161, 163, 171, 173, 175, 177, 178, 180, 182, 183, 185, 186, 187.
Treaty of Nanking, 49.
Treaty of Nerchinsk, 2.
Treaty of Paris, 153.
Treaty of Peking, 2, 18.
Treaty of San Stefano, 154.
Treaty of St. Petersburg, 9, 191, 193, 195.
Treaty of Tarbagatai, 18.
Treaty of Tientsin, 49.
Tsar, 51, 52, 53, 56, 57, 58, 65, 68, 71, 154, 155, 160, 161, 169, 171, 172, 174, 180, 183, 187.
Tsarskoe Selo, 161.
Tseng Chi-tse, Marquis, 47, 73; appointed envoy to Russia, 77; 79, 81, 87, 88; pleaded for complete pardon of Ch'ung-hou, 93; 96; criticized Tso's over-confidence, 104–5; his early life, 139; studied English, 139; appointed minister to England, 140; appointed minister to Russia, 141; his reluctance to go to Russia, 142; the difficulty of his mission, 143; his pro-Western views, 143–4; admonition from court, 144; suggested arbitration as a way out, 147; his strategy, 148–51; displeased the court, 151; asked for help from Granville and Foster, 152; left for Russia, 153; received advice from Dufferin, 159; first encounter with Giers, 159; presented the Emperor's letter to the Tsar, 161–2; presented statement to Giers, 162; received a stern warning from court, 164; received an urgent order from Peking, 168; pleaded with Jomini to keep negotiations in St. Petersburg, 169; argued with Butzow, 175; his tactics, 176; showed no desire to end negotiations, 178; pressed for Russian reply, 180; received the reply, 181; sharp exchanges with Jomini, 182; praised by

Giers and Dufferin, 188; returned home, 188; warned countrymen against pride, 190–1.
Tseng Kuo-ch'üan, 80, 95.
Tseng Kuo-fan, 47, 139, 143.
Tso Tsung-t'ang, 2, 13; victory over Yakub Beg, 15; attack on Moslem rebels, 35–36; argued for frontier defence, 38–39; appointed imperial commissioner in Sinkiang, 39; his preparations for the Sinkiang campaign, 41; pacification of Djungaria, 41; argued against acceptance of British mediation, 42–43; pacified Sinkiang, 44; made a marquis, 44; views on Ili, 44–45; views on Ch'ung-hou's appointment, 49; ordered by court to be merciful towards Moslems, 54; views on Ch'ung-hou's negotiations with the Russians, 56; criticized Ch'ung-hou's performance, 61; attacked the treaty, 61–62; suggested a dual policy, 62–63; satirized Li, 66; put in charge of defence of north-west, 95; moved headquarters to Hami, 97; believed Russia would not start war with China, 97; confident of defeating Russian army, 98; an interpretation of his stand, 106; recalled to Peking, 108; view on Tseng's appointment, 141; urged court to stand firm, 166; report of his recall to Peking reached Russia, 184; urged to make Sinkiang a province, 193, 194; his biography, 198–9; Marxist view on his reconquest of Sinkiang, 199.
Tsungli Yamen, 27, 33, 47, 49, 53; its attitude toward relaxation of trade ban, 55; alarmed by Russian demands, 55–56; shocked by the Treaty of Livadia, 57; asked Ch'ung-hou to renegotiate the treaty, 57; found the treaty unacceptable, 59–60; its plight, 60; warned by Li Hung-chang to avoid war with Russia, 65–66; commented on Ch'ung-hou's defence, 68; 71; forced by public opinion to take a stronger stand than it wanted, 75; remiss in duty in not providing Ch'ung-hou with proper instructions, 83; pleaded for Ch'ung-hou's pardon, 89–90; prepared a circular on Ch'ung-hou's case, 113–14; relieved by Japanese attitude, 117; received letter from Li Hung-chang about Gordon's devotion to China, 129; informed of Gordon's coming to Peking, 130; 143; formulated seven guiding principles for Tseng, 145–6;

its difficult position, 147; confidential telegram to Tseng, 148; 151.
Tulisen, 45, 189, 199.
Tun, Prince, 165.
Tungan, 16; in Shensi and Kansu, 22; their habits, 22–23; discriminated against by Chinese and Manchus, 23; 52, 175, 181, 185; rebellion, 24–25, 197.
T'ung-chih, Emperor, 47.
Tungchow, 57, 136.
Tungwen College, 50, 89, 139.
Tun-huang, 195.
Tunis, 154.
Turfan, 43, 44, 185, 187.
Turyūd, 197, 199.
Turkey, 154, 174.
Turks, Eastern, 5.
Turks, Western, 5.
Tz'u-an, 76.
Tz'u-hsi, 1, 48, 69, 71, 76, 78.

Uch Turfan, 96.
Uighur, 20.
Uliasutai, 57, 185.
Ural, 4.
Urumchi, 19, 26, 27, 33, 39, 41, 43, 44, 57, 70, 194, 195.
Ussuri River, 2, 173, 178.

Valley of Black Irtysh, 30.
Vernyi (Alma-Ata), 4, 18, 30.
Victoria, Queen, 87, 88, 92, 154.
Villiers, George, 100.
Vlangaly, General G., 32, 33, 34, 67.
Volga, 199.

Wade, Thomas, 13, 29; unaware of Russian occupation of Ili, 32; attempted mediation between China and Yakub Beg, 41–42; view of Ch'ung-hou, 48; 58; did not think Ch'ung-hou was bribed, 81; believed Ch'ung-hou terrified by the Russians, 82; 85; made a plea for Ch'ung-hou's life in the name of the Queen, 87–88; suggested British help to China, 109–10; doubted Chinese ability to recover Sinkiang, 111; view on the secret role of the Customs Inspectorate, 113; offered advice to Tsungli Yamen, 113; convinced China had a 'case', 114; suspicious of Brandt's activities, 118; analysed Brandt's policy, 119–20; warned Gordon, 128; ordered by

London not to prosecute Gordon, 128; doubted Gordon's usefulness in China, 132; believed Gordon's mind was off balance, 133; urged China to ratify the treaty, 165; his stand not approved by London, 165–6; instructed by London to urge the Chinese to accept the Treaty of St. Petersburg, 187.
Wāli, 22, 28.
Wang Hsien-ch'ien, 91.
Wang Jen-k'an, 91.
Wang K'ai-t'ai, 37.
Wang Wen-shao, 37; argued for frontier defence, 38.
Wan-nien-ch'ing, 99.
War Office, 110, 111, 123, 124, 125, 132.
Warring States Period, 149.
Wen-hsiang, 39, 67, 139.
Wen-pin, 37.
Wen-yung, 26.
Western Region, see *Hsi-yü*.
Woosung, 136.
Wu Ju-lun, 105.
Wu-sun, 5.
Wu-ti, 5.
Wu Yüan-ping, 93.

Yakub Beg, 12; Forsyth mission to, 13; granted recognition by Britain, 13; resisted the Russians at Ak Musjid and Tashkent, 14; perpetuated by Russia and Britain, 15; early life, 28; rise to power, 28; given title of 'Atalik Ghazi', 28; known as 'Badaulet', 28; posed problem for Russia, 29; signed treaties with Russia and England, 24; 36, 41; sought British mediation, 41–42; death of, 43; 51, 118, 154, 187; views of Marxist historians on, 199.
Yang Shih-ch'üan, 61.
Yangihissa, 26.
Yangtze River Valley, 6.
Yarkand, 4, 26, 27.
Yellow River Valley, 6.
Yüeh-chih tribe, 5.
Yung-cheng, 6, 7, 73, 200.
Yung-ch'üan, 32, 33.

Zanzibar, 122, 138.
zemstvo, 156.
Zhukovsky, 155.

PRINTED IN GREAT BRITAIN
AT THE UNIVERSITY PRESS, OXFORD
BY VIVIAN RIDLER
PRINTER TO THE UNIVERSITY

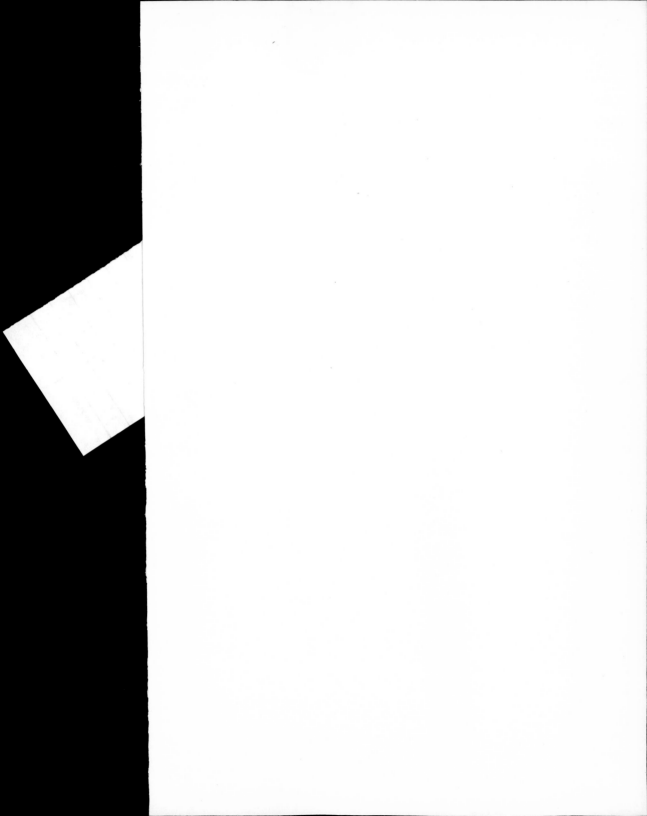

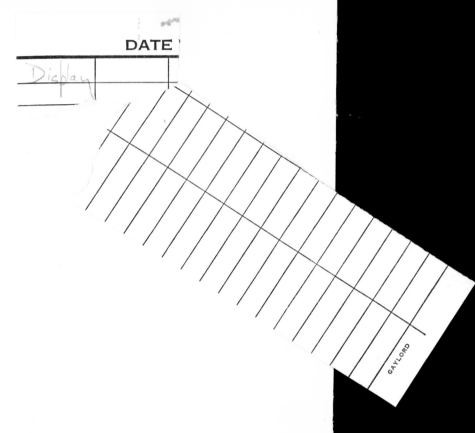